The Economics of Australian Labour Markets

The Economics of Australian Labour Markets

Third edition

Keith Norris

Professor of Economics
Murdoch University

I am very grateful for the help given to me by my colleagues at Murdoch University, particularly Sarah Clancy, Paul Flatau, Peter Kenyon, Sue Lambert, Robert Leeson and Phillip Lewis. Paul Miller and Charles Mulvey of the University of Western Australia were also helpful. None of them are, of course, responsible for any errors or deficiencies. I am also very appreciative of the excellent support of Meg Jadlowkier who produced most of the manuscript and of Sheila Anderson who did the rest. Finally, I thank those who provided me with questions from their labour economics examination papers, a selection of which appear at the end of each of the main chapters.

Longman Cheshire Pty Limited
Longman House
Kings Gardens
95 Coventry Street
Melbourne 3205 Australia

Offices in Sydney, Brisbane, Adelaide and Perth. Associated companies, branches and representatives throughout the world.

First published 1983
Second edition 1989
Third edition 1993

Edited by Maja Ingrassia
Designed by Lauren Statham, Alice Graphics
Set in 10.5/12.5 Sabon
Produced by Longman Cheshire Pty Ltd
Printed in Australia by McPherson's Printing Group

National Library of Australia
Cataloguing-in-Publication data

Norris, Keith, 1940–
The economics of Australian labour markets

3rd ed.
Includes bibliographical references and index.
ISBN 0 582 87108 5.

1. Labour market – Australia. 2. Labor supply – Australia. I. Title.

331.10994

Contents

CHAPTER 1

Labour markets: an overview

1.1 Introduction

Labour economics is the study of labour markets, where buyers and sellers of labour interact to determine the wage and the quantity of labour bought and sold. Labour markets have several characteristics that distinguish them from other markets. These are described in more detail in the next section where it will be explained that, for example, the existence of long lasting employment relationships, or the need to motivate workers means that some care has to be taken in applying standard tools of economic analysis to labour markets.

For a long time this caution was exercised to excess and the study of labour economics tended to be rather descriptive with some emphasis being placed on institutional features. Thus, up until the 1960s it was often suggested that labour economics was one of the backwaters of economics, suited perhaps to those who found the rigours of economic theory a little too demanding.

In the last thirty years or so, however, labour economics has been transformed into an area where exciting, important, and central developments, both theoretical and empirical, have taken place. Many factors have contributed to this change, but four major influences may be identified. First, the development around 1960 of the theory of human capital in which people through undertaking education and training can add to their 'human' capital in a way analogous to a firm adding to its stock of physical capital through net investment. This notion, formally developed, has given great insights into a range of labour market behaviour.

Second, the formalisation and extension, around 1970, of the analysis of internal labour markets. Institutional labour economists had, in the 1940s, suggested that most employing units can be seen as operating their own labour market. Such markets are known as internal labour markets and, in our view, it is impossible to understand how labour markets, in the broadest sense, function without a clear understanding of the operation of these internal labour markets.

A third major influence has been the stimulus given to both theoretical and empirical analysis of labour markets by the desire to strengthen the microeconomic foundations of macroeconomics. Particularly important in this context has been the search for explanations of wage rigidity and consequently of involuntary unemployment.

Finally, the empirical analysis of labour economics has been enormously advanced by the appearance of unit record data. Such data provide information on the characteristics, such as earnings, education, union membership, of large numbers of individuals. One important use to which such data have been put is to estimate earnings functions which seek to statistically explain people's earnings by their education, experience and other personal characteristics. We shall make reference to earnings functions at various stages of this book.

The purpose of this book is to present up-to-date labour market theory in the context of the Australian labour market. The plan of the rest of this chapter is as follows. In Section 2, we describe in a little more detail the distinguishing features of labour markets in general, while the subsequent sections are concerned with the Australian labour market in particular. In Section 3 we describe the Australian system of wage determination and in Section 4 we provide a statistical description of the Australian labour market. The final section provides an overview of the contents of the book.

1.2 The distinguishing features of labour markets

Outside of slave societies, it is not the labourer who is bought and sold but labour services, and labour services cannot be separated from the labourer. In this sense, labour is a unique input into the productive process, as it is the only input which cannot be separated from the owner. If a firm buys a machine the previous owner of the machine does not have to be present when it is being used. A worker, however, has obviously to be present and actively engaged in the delivery of his or her labour service. There has to be, therefore, some personal relationship between employer and worker.

There is an important implication of this worker non-separability. The worker retains control over the quality of the delivery, whether he or she works hard or not, co-operatively, or non-co-operatively, shows initiative or not and so on. A machine, on the other hand, if properly maintained can be operated as the user wishes. In some cases this apparent lack of control over the efficiency of labour services is of no concern to the employer. If workers are employed at an unskilled task on a piece rate basis, that is, they are remunerated on the basis of what they actually produce, then low quality work will be paid accordingly. Normally, however, this is not the case and firms have to resort to a variety of methods to induce workers to work close to their potential. The use of supervisors and inspectors is one such method. Another is to develop corporate spirit so that workers identify themselves with the firm. A third alternative is to provide what are termed job ladders by which workers can progress in pay and status as a reward for efficient work. Many methods can only be used if the worker remains with the same employer for a considerable time, which leads us to another feature of labour markets.

Transactions in markets for goods and services typically take place on a one-off basis with no expectations on either side of a continuing relation. Many purchases by consumers of goods and services are of this sort. Similarly many sales and purchases by firms are not repeated, although large firms may attempt to build-up long-term links with some suppliers and large customers. In the case of labour services, however, the great bulk of transactions take place on a continuing basis. Normally if a worker is hired by an employer there is some expectation that if the worker performs to some minimum level of competence he or she will be employed as long as they wish to remain with that employer. There are exceptions to this. Some people are employed on a short-term, casual basis to perform some clearly defined task but often such workers, such as students working part-time, do not seek long lasting employment.

So most people have an attachment to their job, they speak of 'my job'. Most readers will probably not be in full-time employment and will probably be young so, to relate to this idea, think of your parents' work. Presumably they start each week confident that their job will be there when they turn up at work; they have probably worked for the same employer for some time and expect to continue to do so. Equally, their employer would be disappointed if they did not turn up for work each day. Obviously this cannot always be true; for some industries decline and jobs are lost, but as long as a particular job exists, its occupant will feel that it belongs to him or her.

The facts support this proposition that employment relations are long lasting. If we consider those who are currently employed we know that their jobs will last, from when they started in the past to when they will end in the future, that is, an average of fifteen years—which is a very long time. There is every reason to believe that labour markets will behave in a different way from most other markets. Labour services are inseparable from labour and participants in the market often have long lasting relations.

Labour economists have formalised the notion that both firms and workers view jobs as belonging to the worker, and that most people are not exposed to competition from outsiders for their jobs, in terms of 'internal labour markets'. Each firm can be seen as operating its own labour market, normally using some set of administrative rules to allocate tasks and determine pay. Firms are not acting altruistically in this respect. As we have seen they will gain if, as a result, people work efficiently. Further, as we shall see, many job skills are acquired partly through training and partly through experience within the firm. Such skills are referred to as firm specific. If the worker leaves he or she takes these skills. The firm cannot replace such workers directly as newcomers have to acquire firm-specific skills from scratch. This involves the firm in costs and hence it is in their interest to induce people to stay with them.

At the same time as there exists a majority of people working in fairly long lasting jobs there is, paradoxically, considerable movement in the labour market as a whole. This partly arises because there are some workers, mainly the young who shop around, who do seek to change jobs. It mainly arises, however, because large numbers of people enter, and leave, the labour market in any period of time. Some of those entering the labour market, those just completing study, for example, are doing so for the first time. Others are re-entering the labour market, married females who have devoted time to childraising, for example. Thus, the labour market exhibits stability and movement simultaneously.

Although the labour market may operate differently from other markets it has the same role as other markets. On the supply side, individuals bring forward a diverse range of skills and other characteristics and have differing preferences between work and leisure, and hence supply different number of hours of work.

On the demand side, employers differ in the types of labour they seek. It is the (ideal) task of labour markets to allocate labour to its most productive uses to maximise the output of goods and services and the collective utility of workers. The set of relative wages may play an important role in this allocation. As we shall see, however, there are constraints on the ability of wages to adjust fully as circumstances change. Where this is the case, adjustment has to take other forms such as changes in quality. For example, an employer who, for reasons we shall see, is unable to, or does not wish to, raise the wage to attract more of a certain type of labour may nonetheless succeed in obtaining more labour at the same wage if they reduce their hiring standards.

No market can be analysed without reference to its main institutional features and labour markets in advanced economics all contain one key set of institutions—trade unions. In Australia about two in five workers belong to unions although as we shall see the influence of unions is probably greater than that proportion implies. A further key institution in the Australian labour market is the Industrial Relations Commission, which we shall describing shortly.

The labour market has a number of distinguishing features and institutions. What sort of analysis can we apply to labour markets? It does not follow that because labour is different from other inputs, that we cannot apply standard economic analysis. We just have to be judicious in our approach, being sensitive to the special features of labour and of labour markets. Thus the tools that we shall apply are those of mainstream economic theory and we shall assume that the reader is equipped with these tools in the sense that he or she has completed an introductory course in economics.

1.3 The Australian system of wage determination

The Australian system of wage determination, known as compulsory arbitration, is unique. (Until 1984 wages were set in a similar way in New Zealand, but in that year compulsory arbitration was abolished.) The unique feature of compulsory arbitration is that the majority of workers have their minimum, or award, rates of pay set by one of a range of arbitration and conciliation tribunals. The dominant institution in this context is the Industrial Relations Commission and its awards are largely followed by the various state tribunals which, in terms of workers covered, are quantitatively more important. In 1990, 80.0 per cent of all employees (83.5 per cent of females and 77.3 per cent of males) were covered by awards. Award coverage is much more extensive (97.8 per cent) in the public than in the private sector (72.4 per cent). Award coverage is declining; in 1985, 85 per cent of workers were covered. In the vast majority of western countries, pay is determined by bargaining between employers and their employees. In many bargains workers act in concert in trade unions; such bargains are known as collective bargains.

Compulsory arbitration originated in the final years of the nineteenth century and the dominant position of the Commission (or the Commonwealth Court of Conciliation and Arbitration as it was then called) really dates from 1907. In that year, in what has become known as the Harvester Judgement, the Court established a basic wage for all workers coming within its jurisdiction. Originally, the basic wage was determined by a needs criterion, being the wage necessary for a married man to live in 'a civilised community', but from the 1920s onwards the capacity of the economy to pay became the dominant influence as workers' real wages tended to increase in line with the growth of productivity. Most workers received in addition to the basic wage a margin for skill, these margins being fixed on an industry-to-industry basis. Changes to the various skill margins were made on a piecemeal basis up to 1954 although there was a tendency for most margins to change more or less in line with those operating in the metal trades. From 1954 onwards, however, there was a series of national margins decisions. In 1967, this decomposition of award rates of pay into two elements, the basic wage and a margin for skill, was abandoned and since then a total wage has been awarded. Changes in the total wage for all workers have subsequently been made in a series of national wage decisions.

The decisions of the Industrial Relations Commissions in National Wage Cases affect the rates of pay of all workers covered by awards. If the increases are awarded in percentage terms, they leave relative award pay unaltered. If the increases are flat rate, that is if all awards are increased by the same dollar amount, then relativities between high and low paid workers become smaller. This latter effect occurs because it is conventional to discuss wage differences in proportionate rather than absolute terms. Thus say unskilled workers earn $350 a week and skilled workers $500 a week; the pay of both groups is increased by $40 a week. Although the difference in pay between the two groups has remained the same in absolute terms, it has decreased in proportionate terms. For while initially unskilled workers earned 70 per cent as much as skilled workers, after the increase they earn 72 per cent.

The award rate of pay of an individual worker will also change if there is an increase in the award under which he or she is covered, while other awards remain unaltered. Some awards are on an industry basis, others cover occupational groups. Changes to individual awards obviously have the potential to change relative pay. Thus, one bench may be hearing a submission for a wage increase for (say) professional engineers and concurrently another an increase for (say) print workers. According to the arguments presented, changes to the award may be made in each case but these need not necessarily be the same. In general, however, the Commission has been reluctant to depart substantially from established relativities. Further, when one group has won an above-average award there has been a tendency for this to flow on to other groups, normally on the basis of 'comparative wage justice', and hence any substantial changes are fairly quickly reversed.

Since 1983, there have been very few wage claims heard on an industrial or occupational basis. In this period the government and the

Australian Council of Trade Unions (ACTU) have had an agreed, although evolving, set of policies on wage determination and other issues known as the Accord. This is discussed in detail in Chapter 11. Here we should note that, by and large, the Commission has accepted the submissions made by the government and the ACTU and has thus been the instrument through which the Accord has operated. Virtually the only changes that have been made to award wages since 1983 have been through National Wage Cases and thus most awards have been equally affected. We write 'most' awards because in some decisions in the latter period of the Accord the Commission allowed awards to be increased by (say) 4 per cent in return for changes to working practices but the actual increase had to be negotiated within each award. In some cases this did not occur and some groups of workers missed out on wage increases. However, the main point remains: with a very few exceptions the only changes to awards have been those brought about by National Wage Cases.

Although minimum rates of pay for most workers are set within the system of compulsory arbitration there is for many workers a gap between the award pay for a standard week and weekly earnings, the rest being overtime, payment by results, and over-award pay. Overtime rates of pay are set by the Commission but the latter elements are determined outside the system. Over-award pay refers to the payment of wage rates in excess of those set by the Commission; its incidence is uneven, with large numbers of employees receiving none. It arises largely at the level of the plant or of the enterprise, and the extent to which it reflects union bargaining or the independent response of individual employers to shortages of particular types of labour is not clear. For the average male worker in 1991 award pay comprised 87.5 per cent of weekly earnings, while for females the proportion was 96 per cent.

To summarise, consider how the weekly earnings of an individual worker may increase in the Australian system of wage determination, assuming the individual is one of the majority covered by an award. Increases in his or her average weekly earnings will arise first, from National Wage Case decisions, second from decisions made to the industrial or occupational award by which he or she is covered, and third through changes to over-award pay, increases in overtime working, or bonuses received or any other change in his or her circumstances, such as promotion to a higher pay scale.

As commented at the outset, the Australian system is unique, although the differences between compulsory arbitration and collective bargaining are not as sharp as might first appear. Collective bargaining does occur in Australia and many awards are the formal ratification of collective bargains. Further, the outcomes of the Australian system do not, in general, appear to be markedly different from those of other methods of wage determination. At the time of writing there is a trend towards the encouragement of enterprise bargaining although the precise form this will take is not clear. Enterprise bargaining is discussed in Chapter 9.

1.4 A statistical summary of the Australian labour market

For purposes of labour market analysis, the population aged fifteen and over can be placed in three categories. First, those who are in employment; second, those who are not working but who are actively seeking work, the unemployed; and third those who are not part of the labour force. The proportion in each category are shown in Table 1.1.

Table 1.1 Percentage distribution of the population aged fifteen years and over, 1992

	Males	*Females*	*Persons*
Employed	66.2	46.8	56.3
Unemployed	8.1	5.2	6.7
Not in the labour force	25.7	48.0	37.0

Source: *The Labour Force*, (ABS, cat. no. 6203.0).

It can be seen that over two people in three are part of the labour force, that is they are working or looking for work. This simple fact highlights the importance of the subject matter of labour economics. As we would expect, a smaller proportion of females are in the labour force, as more women than men are engaged in unpaid work in the home. Nonetheless, over one half of all women over fifteen years are in the labour force.

Although the dividing line between the labour force and the rest of the population is rather blurred we shall, of course, be concerned with the former. Let us first look at the unemployed. It is conventional and convenient to talk in terms of unemployment rates; the unemployment rate is the number of unemployed expressed as a percentage of the labour force (the employed plus the unemployed). In 1992, 11 per cent of males, 10.1 per cent of females and 10.6 per cent of persons were unemployed. As is well known, unemployment rates fluctuate cyclically and the levels of unemployment in 1992 occurred in the depths of a recession, and were among the highest experienced since the post-war period. Over this long period of time, however, a significant change has occurred in the average level of unemployment. In the 1950s and 1960s unemployment rates averaged between 1 and 2 per cent whereas in the 1980s the average unemployment rate was over 7 per cent.

The vast majority (90.1 per cent) of employed males are employed on a full-time basis. Part-time work is more prevalent among females: 58.1 per cent work part-time and 41.9 per cent work full-time. In fact, 75.4 per cent of part-time workers are female. One of the major trends that have occurred in the Australian labour market in recent decades has been a marked increase in the proportion of employees that work on a part-time basis. As most part-timers are female it follows that this trend is inextricably bound up with an increase in female employment. The differential rates of growth of various forms of employment over the last two decades is presented in Table 1.2.

Table 1.2 Percentage growth in employment, 1972–92

Full-time males	10.1
Part-time males	264.4
All males	18.7
Full-time females	37.5
Part-time females	176.8
All females	74.8
All full-time employees	17.6
All part-time employees	194.5
All employees	37.2

Source: *The Labour Force*, (ABS, cat. no. 6203.0).

The growth rates show some very marked differences. Employment of full-time males only grew by 10.1 per cent over a twenty-year period and of all males by only 18.7 per cent. (The very high rate of growth of male part-time employment was from a very low base and hence has only a modest arithmetic affect on the growth of total male employment.) The growth of female employment, particularly of part-time employment, has been relatively very high. Reflecting these differences, part-time employment has nearly doubled while full-time employment has increased by less than 40 per cent.

The substantial growth of female employment has led to large increases in the proportion of married women who work. In 1971, 32.8 per cent of married females were in the labour force and by 1991 this proportion had reached 52.8 per cent.

At the same time significant changes were taking place in the industrial composition of employment, as shown in Table 1.3. While little change has occurred in the share of employment of agriculture, mining or transport the share of manufacturing has nearly halved while there has been a substantial growth in finance, property and community services.

Thus the composition of both the supply and the demand for labour has changed in recent years. Within this broad statement other significant

Table 1.3 Percentage shares of employment: industries

	1966	*1991*
Agriculture, forestry and fishing	8.8	8.4
Mining	1.1	1.2
Manufacturing	26.2	14.4
Electricity, gas, water	1.9	1.4
Construction	9.7	6.7
Wholesale and retail trade	19.8	20.7
Transport, storage and communication	7.6	6.9
Finance property and business services	6.6	11.7
Public administration and defence	3.4	4.7
Community services	9.8	19.1
Recreation, personal and other services	5.0	7.9

Sources: *The Labour Force*, (ABS, cat. no. 6203.0) and *The Labour Force, Australia, Historical Summary, 1966-84* (ABS, cat. no. 6204.0).

changes have occurred in the labour market and these will be described and explained at various stages of the book.

Throughout the book are a number of other statistical tables, which are designed to give the reader an idea of trends and of the magnitudes involved. These are largely drawn from the publications of the Australian Bureau of Statistics (ABS). Each table is referenced and the reader is encouraged to keep the information up-to-date from ABS publications which are usually readily accessible at university libraries.

1.5 Overview

In this section we set out the broad plan of the book and indicate some of the questions addressed in each chapter. Chapter 2 is concerned with the supply of labour to the market. We begin with the individual's decision as to how many hours of work to supply. We develop a framework which enables us to analyse how workers will change their supply of hours if there is a change in the wage rate or if they are offered overtime at penalty rates of pay. We also look at moonlighting and at labour absence. We then use the framework to analyse the question of how individuals decide whether to offer any labour at all, to participate in the labour force or not. This enables us to understand why people of different ages and gender make their decisions about participation and in particular to understand one of the major trends in the Australian labour market in recent decades, the increasing participation in the labour market of married females.

Chapter 3, on the demand for labour, will probably and understandably strike the reader as rather dry. It is also, fortunately, relatively brief. However, we have to understand how employing units decide how much labour to hire at any given wage as these demands determine, in part, labour market outcomes. The chapter is largely theoretical and subsequent chapters will qualify and enrich its conclusion.

In Chapter 4 we consider some qualitative aspects of labour supply. Some workers are unskilled, others bring to the labour market considerable amounts of expertise acquired through formal education and through training received in the work place. How do individuals decide whether to incur the costs, largely in the form of lost earnings, of education and training? The basic argument, which we formalise, is that they weigh these costs against the returns to education and training which in turn take the form of higher earnings through their working life. Is it a good investment to study for a degree? We also ask who bears the costs of industrial training and what should be the role of government in this process?

Armed with a knowledge of labour supply and demand we then come to a series of chapters of how these interact in labour markets. Chapter 5 begins by sketching how a competitive labour market, analogous to a market for a good or service, might operate and, building upon the material in Section 2 of this introductory chapter, suggests how this might have to be qualified. Most of the remainder of Chapter 5 is concerned with the operation of internal labour markets which were introduced earlier in this chapter. Most workers are employed in enterprises which insulate themselves, to a greater or lesser extent, from the competitive forces of the market. They tend, on average, to work for their employers for long periods of time. Why? How do internal labour markets adjust to changes in the general labour market?

Forty two per cent of Australian workers are members of a trade union, and Chapter 6 is devoted to unions. What is it that trade unions are seeking to achieve? We shall see that they have many goals, some of which—most obviously to increase the relative wages of their members and their employment—are contradictory, as the analysis of Chapter 3 would suggest. How do they trade off one objective against the other? Are there circumstances in which they can achieve both? Do union members earn more than non-union members, and, if so how much more? Chapter 6 ends with a discussion of a question which readers may not have considered—do unions increase productivity?

Chapter 7 is concerned with discrimination. We distinguish between discrimination which occurs before the labour market, the lesser amounts of education received, on average, by Aborigines for example and discrimination which occurs within the labour market. The latter occurs if some racial and gender groups are rewarded, in a lesser way in the labour market, for their characteristics such as their human capital. We look at estimates that have been made of the extent of discrimination against females in the labour market.

As we explained in the introduction, there have been several theoretical developments in labour economics in recent decades and some of these have been concerned with explaining the downward rigidity of money wages. Two such theories, implicit contract theory and efficiency wage theory, are outlined in Chapter 8. We will see that efficiency wage theory also appears capable of explaining quite a few other observed features of labour markets. Chapter 8 also contains a discussion of the dual labour market hypothesis which has proved influential in the discussion of low pay and poverty and which also provides an explanation of involuntary unemployment.

It will be apparent that much of labour economics is concerned with the determinants of what people get paid, an issue of some importance to most of us. Chapter 9 brings together various pieces of analysis to summarise the determinants of pay relativities between occupations and industries. We also come across a surprising trend. When we look at the pay of individual workers we find that the number of people occupying low and high paid jobs has increased leaving fewer people in the middle of the earnings distribution. The middle has shrunk.

The final two chapters are devoted to the macroeconomics of the labour market, that is with the issues of unemployment and wage inflation. We have already noted that there has been a marked increase in the average level of unemployment. The major objective of this chapter is to understand what determines the level of unemployment. We also discuss the composition of unemployment. Some people experience repeated spells of unemployment but do not remain unemployed for very long, others experience very long unemployment durations, while to the majority of employed people unemployment is a remote possibility. Thus we address the question of why unemployment is distributed so unevenly. Finally, in Chapter 11 we look at what determines the rate at which money wages grow each year and whether trade unions cause wage inflation. We end by looking at one of the longest running wages policies that has occurred in the world—the Accord. It has survived (up until the time of writing) despite causing reductions in real wages and being accompanied by adverse changes in the distribution of earnings. What advantages has it brought to set alongside these costs?

CHAPTER 2

The supply of labour

2.1 Introduction

This chapter analyses several aspects of labour supply. The total supply of labour is determined by the number of persons who supply labour and by the number of hours each person supplies. The number of persons who supply labour is, in turn, determined by the number of people of working age and the proportion of this group who wish to work. This proportion is known as the participation rate.

The plan of the chapter is as follows. We begin by looking at hours of work, and develop, in Section 2.2, two frameworks which analyse the individual decision how many hours of labour to supply per unit of time. In Section 2.3 the basic analysis is extended to include the effects of taxation, penalty rates of pay for overtime, and moonlighting. In Section 2.4 we analyse the determinants of participation rates. We pay particular attention to the participation rates of married females as the marked increase in these has been one of the most dramatic changes to have occurred in the Australian labour market in the last forty years. In the final section we look at some quantitative aspects of immigration which has had a major impact on the total supply of labour in the economy. Elsewhere in the book, we will discuss more generally the labour market experience of migrants.

For the purposes of this chapter we shall ignore an important qualitative dimension of labour supply which is that different types of workers, lawyers versus carpenters for example, supply different sorts of labour. These issues will be discussed in Chapter 4 which analyses the economics of education and training.

2.2 The supply of hours of work

Actual hours of work

This section analyses what determines how many hours of work people supply per week. Let us begin by looking at how many hours a week people actually work in Australia. These figures do not reflect supply perfectly, that is, how many hours people would like to work, but show the interaction of the supply of and demand for hours of labour. Thus some people we observe working (say) twenty hours a week would like to work (say) forty hours. Nonetheless, this actual pattern, shown in Table 2.1, will give us some broad indication of supply.

Table 2.1 Distribution of hours of work, 1992

	Percentage of employees	
Weekly hours worked	*Males*	*Females*
0–15	10.6	24.8
16–29	6.0	17.8
30–34	5.6	8.2
35–39	17.0	18.2
40	20.8	15.2
41–44	5.4	3.8
45–48	9.6	4.4
49 and over	25.0	7.6

Source: *The Labour Force, Australia* (ABS, cat. no. 6203.0).

The Australian Bureau of Statistics classifies those who work less than thirty-five hours a week as part-time workers. In 1992, 22.2 per cent of males and 50.8 per cent of females worked part-time. More generally, it is clear from the table that, as we would expect given current family arrangements, males work longer hours than females. Some work very long hours, nearly a quarter working more than forty-nine hours a week. However, the main purpose of the table is to indicate the great diversity in hours of work of different employees.

There are two approaches to the analysis of the number of hours of work that individuals supply: the neoclassical theory and the allocation of time theory.

The neoclassical theory

This is a straightforward application to labour supply of the neoclassical theory of consumer demand.

To simplify matters, at least initially, we will assume that the individual has made his or her decision to participate, has no unearned income, pays no taxes, that the wage rate is invariant with the number of hours worked, and that there is a free choice in the hours of work. We will look at the effect of relaxing these assumptions as we proceed. For convenience we will take the price of goods as given, hence a change in money wage rates represents a similar change in real wage rates.

In neoclassical theory individuals are seen as choosing between two things which give utility: leisure and goods. As goods can only be acquired through work and as, in this analysis, time not spent as leisure is spent at work, it is clear that by analysing individuals' choices we will discover how many hours of work they wish to supply.

We can represent an individual's preferences between goods and leisure with a set of indifference curves as shown in Figure 2.1.

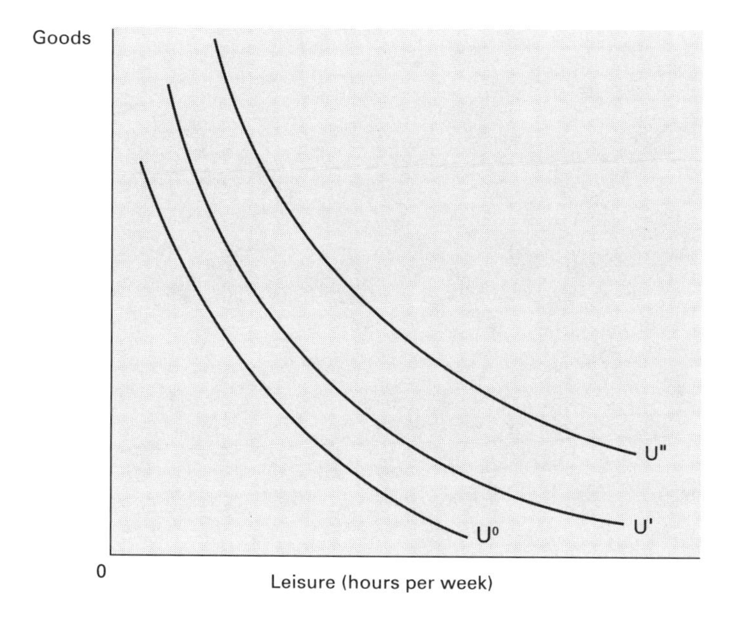

Figure 2.1 The preference map

These curves have the same characteristics as the indifference curves used in the analysis of consumer behaviour. First, each curve represents combinations of goods and leisure between which the individual is indifferent, and second there are an infinite number of curves of which we have represented just three on the diagram. As the curve labelled U' lies to the northeast of curve U°, it represents larger combinations of goods and leisure. It is thus preferred and we imagine the individual striving to reach the highest feasible indifference curve.

Second, they are downward sloping. As the individual is indifferent about the various combinations of goods and leisure traced out by any curve and as goods and leisure are things that he or she derives utility from, it follows that as the individual gives up some units of goods, additional units of leisure will be needed to compensate.

Third, the curves are convex to the origin. To understand the significance of this let us first see what the slope of one of these curves represents. It tells us the precise quantity of goods necessary to compensate for the loss of one (small) unit of leisure. We call this the marginal rate of substitution between leisure and goods. The convexity of the curves means that the slope gets steeper as we move from right to left. In economic terms, as less leisure is enjoyed increasing amount of goods are needed to compensate for the loss of unit of leisure.

The individual is constrained in his or her choice by the fact that there are only 168 hours in a week and that the wage rate offered is outside his or her control. We show the constraint as the line AB in Figure 2.2.

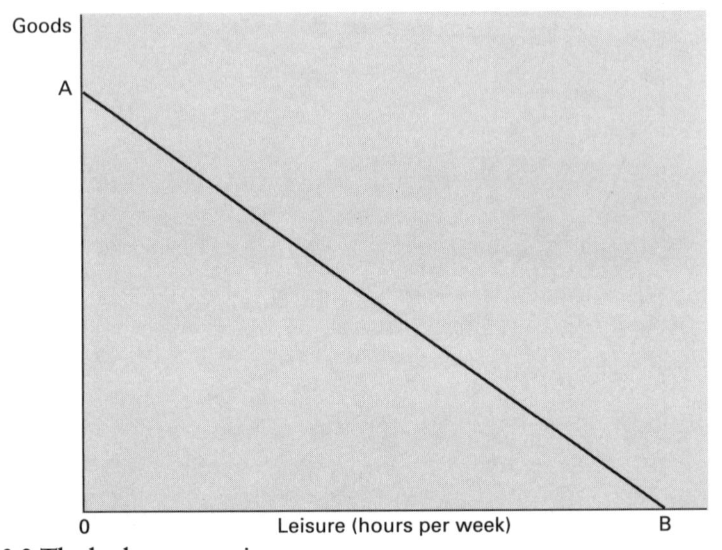

Figure 2.2 The budget constraint

The position of the constraint, AB, is fixed in the following way. On the horizontal axis the maximum number of hours of leisure that is available is 168 hours a week. Alternatively, if all hours are devoted to work, the maximum goods that can be consumed (or income earned) is 168 times the hourly wage rate. The slope of the budget constraint is thus, where W is the hourly wage rate,

$$= -\frac{OA}{OB}$$

$$= -\frac{168W}{168}$$

$$= -W$$

We can now bring together in Figure 2.3 the individual's preference map and the budget constraint he or she faces.

To maximise utility, the individual wishes to attain the highest possible indifference curve. The line AB is the outer boundary of the area that is possible to reach. The highest curve that can be reached is the one tangential to the budget constraint, and thus the optimum position is represented by the point D in Figure 2.3.

At D we read off from the horizontal axis that the individual enjoys OE hours of leisure. Thus the rest of the 168 hours in the week, that is EB, are spent working. The payment for EB hours of work enables OF goods to be bought.

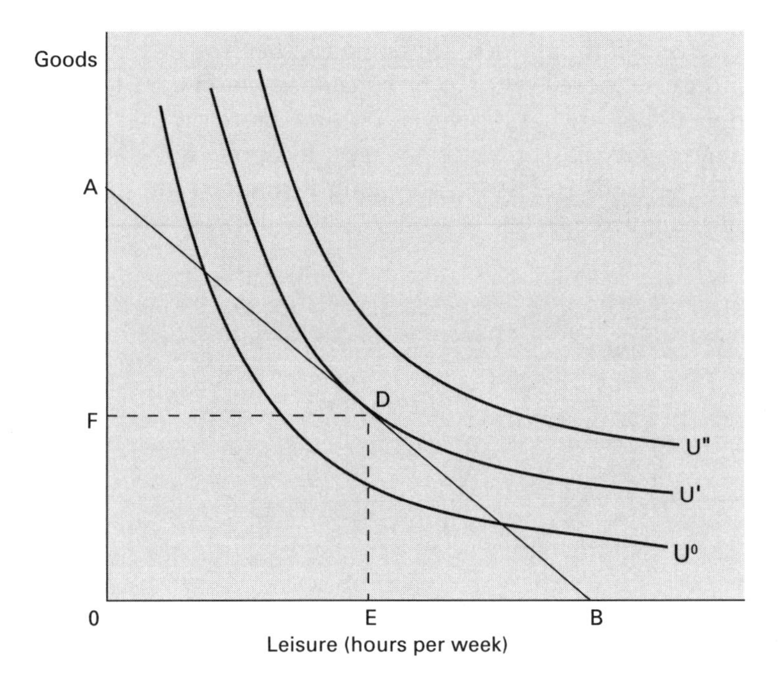

Figure 2.3 Equilibrium hours of work and goods consumed

At the equilibrium point, D, the slope of the indifference curve is equal to the slope of the budget constraint. Remember that the slope of the indifference curve is the marginal rate of substitution between leisure and goods and that of the budget constraint is the (negative of the) wage rate.

Thus the basic result of neoclassical theory is that individuals will supply hours of labour up to the point where their marginal rates of substitution between leisure and goods are equal to (the negative of) their wage rate.

Workers of a certain type will face the same wage rate and we thus explain differences in hours worked within a group of workers through differences in their preferences for work and leisure. The preferences of any individual are taken as given for the purposes of this analysis but are likely to be influenced by age and family circumstances.

To investigate how the individual may react to a change in the wage rate let us take the case where there is an increase in the wage rate. In terms of the diagram, the effect is to change the slope of the budget constraint for, although the total number of hours available remains the same, the number of goods that can be consumed for any given number of hours of work increases. Thus in Figure 2.4 the budget constraint becomes GB rather than AB (for the moment ignore the line KM). The increase in the wage rate has both an income and a substitution effect on the individual's demand for leisure. If leisure is assumed to be a normal good, that is to have a positive income elasticity of demand, then the income effect on its own would cause more leisure to be consumed, and hence fewer hours of work supplied. Leisure has, however, become more expensive in the sense that its opportunity cost, foregone wages, has gone up. The substitution effect therefore leads to less leisure being demanded and more hours of work being supplied.

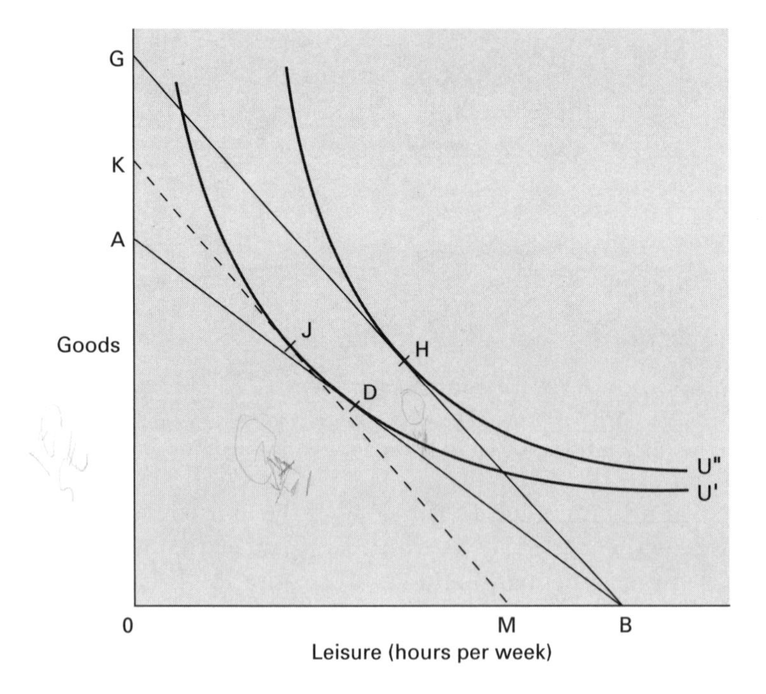

Figure 2.4 The effect of an increase in the wage rate

The income and substitution effects of a wage-rate change always pull in opposite directions and unfortunately it is not possible, a priori, to say which will be stronger. Therefore, we can say nothing about the effect on hours of work of a change in the wage rate. In Figure 2.4 the individual facing the budget constraint AB was originally at point D; when the wage rate increases and the constraint becomes GB the new point of utility maximisation is H. As we have drawn the worker's preferences, H is to the right of D and more leisure is consumed and fewer hours of work supplied. We could just as easily have drawn a set of preferences such that the new equilibrium was to the left of D.

We can use the diagram to decompose the move from D to H into the income and pure (or compensated) substitution effects, using the dotted construction line KM, which has two properties. First, it is parallel to GB and hence represents the new wage rate. Second, it is tangential, at J, to the indifference curve (U') upon which D lies.

The move from D to H can be seen as the outcome of two separate moves, from D to J and from J to H. Take first the move from D to J. As J lies on the same indifference curve as D it represents the same level of utility; this move is thus made solely in response to the change in the wage rate (remember the slope of KM is the new wage rate). The move to J is thus the pure substitution effect. As the indifference curves are convex to the origin, J always lies to the left of D. We have demonstrated Slutzky's theorem that the pure substitution effect of an increase in the price of leisure is to lower the individual's consumption of it.

The move from J to H represents the income effect as GB is parallel to but to the right of KM. The income effect leads to more leisure being consumed and, as we have drawn it, is stronger than the substitution effect. To repeat, however, the net effect of the wage change on hours of leisure, and thus of work, is not deducible a priori from this analysis, and with a different preference map drawn in Figure 2.4 H could lie to the left of D.

The matter has to be settled by reference to the empirical evidence. Before turning to this and to some extensions of the analysis we turn to an alternative approach to individual labour supply.

The allocation of time theory

The choice between work and leisure can be seen as one part of a more general theory of the allocation of time that has been developed by Becker.[1] This theory has subsequently been applied to a great range of human activity, and it has led to economic theories of marriage, childrearing, church attendance, and so on (which has sometimes appeared to be taking economics too far).

Becker's theory holds an advantage over the neoclassical analysis not because it yields clearer results but because, in three main ways, it starts from a more realistic base. First, in the above analysis goods and leisure were seen as substitutes, but they are also complements. Most goods require some time to consume, obvious examples being food, going to the theatre, or watching a cricket match, and many leisure activities require an input of goods, for example participating in most sports requires sports goods. Following on from this, the distinction between work and leisure that we drew earlier was too sharp. Many activities, such as travelling to work, are neither work nor leisure. Finally, in neoclassical analysis the work decision and decisions about what goods to purchase are entirely separate. In Becker's analysis the two sets of decisions are integrated and are made simultaneously.

Here we shall present a rather simplified version of the theory but one which nonetheless brings out its main features. (We shall retain the assumptions made earlier.) The goods of traditional theory are replaced by commodities which combine time on the one hand and market goods on the other. Each commodity has a goods element and a time element, and correspondingly the price of each commodity is made up of the cost of the time and the cost of the good. The time used up in consuming commodities is valued at its opportunity cost which is of course the wage. For example, if your wage rate is \$6 an hour, and admission to a cinema costs \$10, then the price of watching a two-hour film is \$22. This concept of the price of a commodity, including the cost of time, Becker calls its 'full price'.

In general the full price of Z_i, a unit of any commodity, is derived in the following way:

Let t_i be the input of time per unit of any commodity Z_i, and W be the wage rate. Then, the time element of the full price is:

$$t_i W Z_i$$

Similarly, if B_i is the input of market goods per unit of commodity Z_i, and P_i is the price of the good, then the goods element of the full price is:

$$B_i P_i Z_i$$

Thus the full price, π_i, of a unit of commodity Z_i is given by:

$$\begin{aligned}\pi_i &= t_i W Z_i + B_i P_i Z_i \\ &= (t_i W + B_i P_i) Z_i\end{aligned}$$

These, then, are the full prices of the commodities, and if we can derive the total resources of the individual (or household) we will be able to write the budget constraint. Total resources are total number of hours available per week, T, times the wage rate, W; total resources are thus TW. In case this seems implausible because people cannot work both day and night, remember that the individual devotes some resources to consumption. In so doing, the person is foregoing earnings and hence 'spending' some resources.

The individual derives utility from the consumption of the commodities and therefore is seen to formally maximise his or her utility function, $U = U(Z_i)$, subject to the resource constraint, which can be written: $\sum \pi Z_i = TW$, $i = 1, ..., n$. That is, expenditure on commodities must equal total resources. It can be shown that individuals will maximise their utilities if they consume any pair of commodities up to the point where the marginal rate of substitution between them is equal to the ratio of their full prices. This is, of course, similar to the basic result of orthodox consumer demand theory except that here we refer to commodities rather than goods and to full prices rather than conventional market prices.

At this point the reader may be forgiven for wondering what this has to do with labour economics in general and hours of work in particular. The point is that in deciding which commodities to consume, and in which quantities, individuals simultaneously settle their hours of work. It is easiest to show this through a numerical example. To keep things simple we divide all commodities into two groups, time intensive and goods intensive. In effect we have a two-commodity world. The data we will use are:

- wage rate = $5 an hour;
- hours in a week = 168.

time-intensive commodities require, per unit:

- 1 two hours consumption time;
- 2 input of goods costing $2.

goods-intensive commodities require, per unit:

- 1 twelve minutes, or hour, consumption time;
- 2 input of goods costing $5.

Thus total resources are given by:

$$TW = \$5 \times 168 = \$840$$

The full price, π, of a unit of the time-intensive commodity:

$$\begin{aligned}\pi &= \text{cost of consumption time} + \text{cost of market goods}\\ &= (2 \times \$5) + \$2 = \$12\end{aligned}$$

Similarly the full price of a unit of the goods-intensive commodity

$$= (\frac{1}{5} \times \$5) + \$5 = \$6$$

We can now plot the budget constraint, as on Figure 2.5. If the individual devoted all resources ($840) to time-intensive commodities with a full price of $12, seventy units could be bought. Alternatively, with all resources devoted to goods-intensive commodities costing $6, the worker could buy 140 units. As the market price of goods and the wage rate can be assumed constant, we have the linear budget constraint AB. We can represent the utility function by a set of indifference curves (only one of which is shown) and, by the usual tangency rules, the optimum point is C, where sixty units of time-intensive commodities and twenty units of goods-intensive commodities are consumed. At C the marginal rate of substitution between the pair of commodities (the slope of the indifference curve) is equal to the ratio of their full prices (the slope of the budget constraint).

We can check that this is a feasible allocation, and hence derive the individual's hours of work:

$$\text{time spent on consumption} = (60 \times 2) + (20 \times \frac{1}{5})$$
$$= 124 \text{ hours}$$

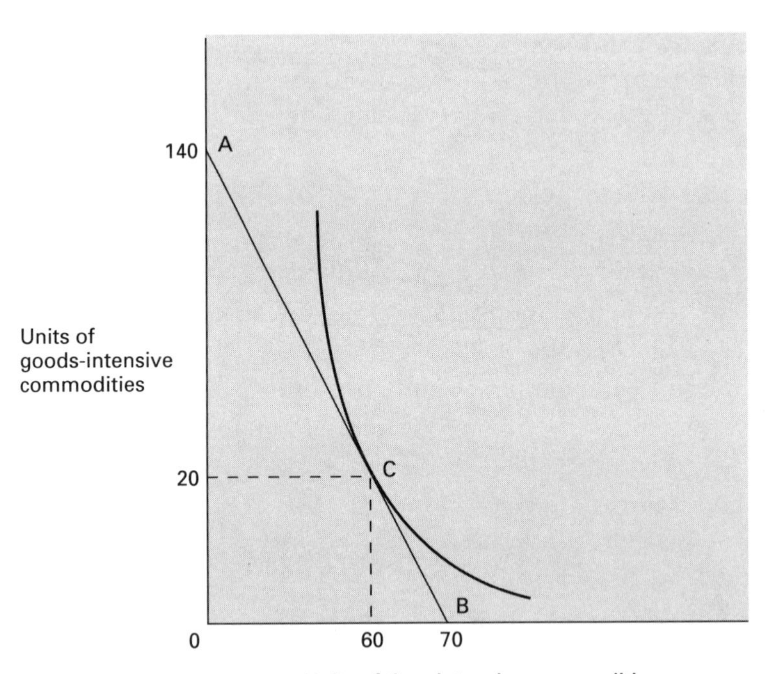

Figure 2.5 The allocation of time approach: the basic model

Thus the remaining forty-four hours are devoted to work, bringing a weekly wage of \$220. This money income is fully used in purchasing the commodities the total market price of which is:

$$(60 \times \$2) + (20 \times \$5) = \$220$$

We see that the worker has the time and the income for this consumption pattern and that we have at the same time derived the individual's hours of work.

Finally, we look at the effect of a change in the wage rate. Say it rises to \$6 per hour. This increases the full price of each commodity, but not proportionately:

full price of the time-intensive commodity $= (2 \times \$6) + \$2 = \$14$

full price of the goods-intensive commodity $= (\frac{1}{5} \times \$6) + 5 = \$6.20$

Thus the full price of time-intensive commodities increases relative to that of the goods-intensive. At the same time total resources are increased by the change in the wage rate and become \$1008, that is 168 × \$6. The corresponding change in the budget constraint is shown in Figure 2.6. The individual is now able to reach a higher indifference curve, but because the wage change has an income and a substitution effect, it is not possible to predict the new consumption pattern. Because of the convexity of the indifference curves, the pure substitution effect of an increase in the wage rate leads to the consumption of more goods-intensive commodities, as their relative price has fallen, and of fewer time-intensive commodities. As this leads to less time being spent in consumption, it follows that the substitution effect on its own leads to more hours devoted to work. The net outcome of the pure substitution effect and the income effect is, however, unknown.

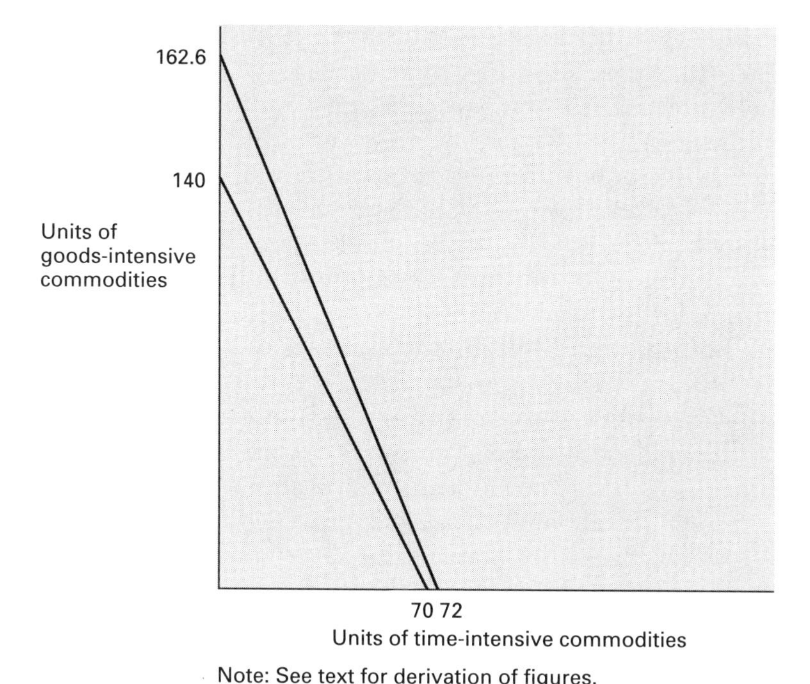

Figure 2.6 The effect of an increase in the wage rate on the budget constraint

We therefore arrive at precisely the same conclusion that we reached from neoclassical analysis. The allocation of time approach is a richer analysis and the neoclassical analysis can in fact be seen as a special case of this more general theory in which the only cost of leisure is foregone earnings and the only cost of other commodities is the cost of the goods element.

2.3 Extensions to the analysis of hours of work

In this section we first extend the basic model of individual choice, using the framework of the neoclassical theory, and second, we survey the evidence on hours of work.

One of the assumptions made in the previous section was that people have the freedom to choose their hours. As standard working weeks have been established in most industries and occupations it would appear that this is not the case. The standard working week is defined as the hours to be worked per week, at standard rates of pay, by full-time workers. Standard working weeks vary by industry and occupation and the weighted average duration is currently around thirty-eight hours per week. The standard working week has declined during this century, from around forty-nine hours in 1914, although little change has occurred since 1948.[2] We should note that the decline in the standard working year has been rather greater than this due to an increase in leave entitlements. Thus between 1948 and 1982 the standard working week for males declined by 1.7 per cent, whereas the standard working year fell by 6.5 per cent.

Full-time workers have to work at least the standard week in their occupation or industry. There is thus the possibility that some full-time workers would prefer to work fewer hours, but are unable to do so because of the existence of the standard working week which sets minimum hours for full-time workers.

Others, both part and full-time workers, may wish to work more hours than are offered by their employer. There is thus a danger, if significant numbers of workers are constrained in their choice, that when we look at the evidence on hours of work we are merely identifying employers' demands for labour in a given institutional framework rather than learning anything about the actual supply of labour.

The Australian Bureau of Statistics (ABS) from time-to-time undertakes a survey (cat. no. 6341.0) which sheds some light on this question. In the latest survey of 1986, 30 per cent of males stated that they would have preferred to work more hours and 5 per cent would have preferred fewer hours. Rather surprisingly 18 per cent of those males who were working in excess of forty-nine hours a week stated that they would have liked to work longer. In the case of females 19 per cent would have preferred longer hours and 9 per cent shorter hours of work.

Thus the evidence suggests that while most workers are content with their hours of work there are significant numbers who are constrained in their choice. Generally, preferences are for longer hours.

We now turn to a discussion of how, in the presence of institutional constraints, people can vary their hours of work. People who work on their own account are of course able to choose how long to work each week. In the case of employees there are five main sources of flexibility in hours of work. These are overtime working, multiple job holding, part-time employment, absenteeism and job selection. We look at each in turn.

Overtime working

We have seen that in most industries and occupations there is a standard working week. Work undertaken in excess of the standard week is remunerated at what are termed penalty rates of pay.

The penalty differs between awards but, in general, the first three hours overtime on any weekday is paid at a penalty of 50 per cent while subsequent weekday hours and overtime worked on Sundays attract higher penalties, typically 100 per cent. Overtime hours are the outcome of employer and employee preferences. Employers may prefer to pay for extra hours at a penalty rate rather than hire more workers at standard rates because of the existence of fixed costs of employment. In Chapter 5 we shall analyse these fixed costs closely as they enable us to understand many facets of labour market behaviour. Suffice to say here that when a new workers is recruited the employer incurs some costs, notably recruitment and training costs, which are invariant with the duration of employment. The decision of how much extra labour to demand in the form of extra hours rather than of additional employees is influenced by the extent of these fixed costs and the size of the overtime penalties.

How much overtime is supplied by employees depends on their preferences and on the wage rate. In Figure 2.7 the wage rate for the standard week, which we will assume to be forty hours, is given by the slope of the constraint EF (ignore the line FG). We will initially, and conveniently, assume that the worker chooses to work forty hours, represented by the distance AF, at that rate and that there is an indifference curve, labelled U^o, tangential to EF at a point C. Now the individual is offered overtime, at penalty rates, for hours worked in excess of forty hours per week. Thus to the left of C, the budget constraint is steeper, with a slope of CT, reflecting the higher wage paid for overtime hours; the budget constraint therefore has a kink in it at point C. If the indifference curves are convex to the origin there must be a higher curve that can be reached now that the constraint is TCF. In the diagram the curve labelled

U' can be attained at point D, and hence the individual supplies an additional AB hours of work a week. The move from point C to point D is made in response to a pure substitution effect, the income effect being zero, or negligible, as the higher wage is only paid on the hours worked in excess of the standard working week.

There are, however, many workers who decline opportunities to work overtime. Some of these may be workers who are unwillingly working the standard week. In terms of Figure 2.7 their preferences are such that their utility-maximising point lies to the right of C, that is they would like to work fewer than AF hours per week. Yet they have to work AF hours, or not at all. Alternatively there may be workers whose preferences are not truly convex in the sense that their indifference curves are vertical above C.

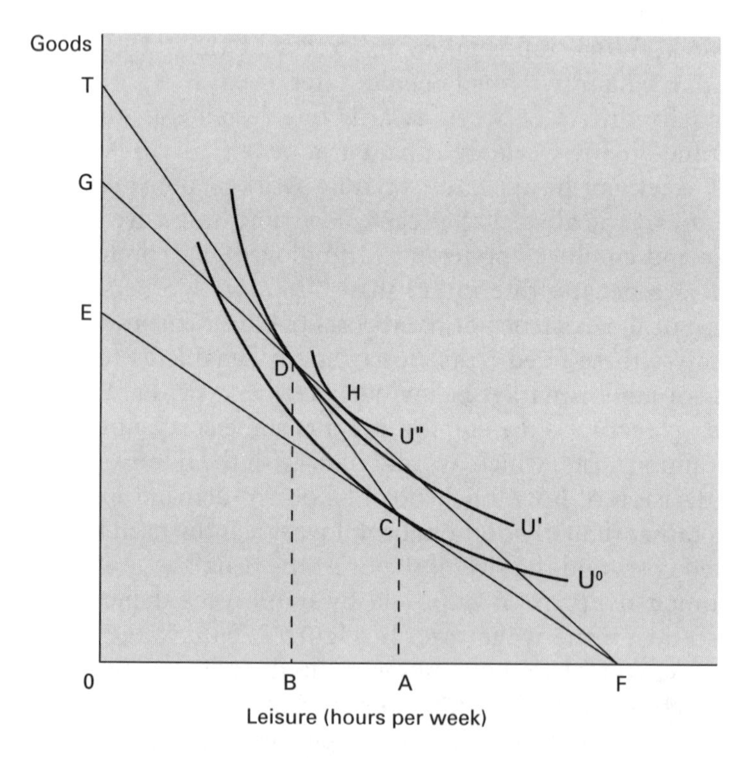

Figure 2.7 The effect of penalty rates for overtime work on hours of work supplied

We can use Figure 2.7 to demonstrate one further proposition, that had the worker been offered the weekly earnings level corresponding to point D in the form of a higher flat wage for all hours of work, then that person would have worked fewer hours than under the two-tiered wage-rate structure brought about by penalty rates. To show this we plot a line passing from F, through D, and on to G. As it passes through D this line represents the same average wage (over all hours) as is given by AF hours at standard rates, and AB hours at overtime rates. Faced with this constraint there is a higher indifference curve, U* (only a segment of which is shown), that can be reached by moving to H. At H fewer hours are worked than at D. Thus employers, at the same cost to themselves, induce more hours through offering one rate of pay for the standard week and a higher rate for overtime than they would by offering higher flat rates for all hours worked.

Overtime working thus gives the individual some additional flexibility, in the presence of standard working weeks, in his or her hours of work. Some respondents to offers of overtime are those whose preferences are such that they would prefer, in any event, to work more than the standard week. It is probable, therefore, that overtime penalties are higher than is strictly necessary to bring forth the extra hours of labour. This view is supported by the tendency for overtime, where available, to be rationed, workers with seniority rights being given preference.

Table 2.2 provides information on the extent of overtime working in 1992.

Table 2.2 Overtime working: all employees, 1992

Industry	*Average overtime per employee (hours per week)*	*Employees working overtime (%)*	*Average overtime per employee working overtime (hours per week)*
Mining	4.2	40.8	10.3
Manufacturing	2.5	31.5	7.8
Electricity, gas and water	1.9	23.6	8.1
Construction	2.2	24.2	9.2
Wholesale trade	1.3	18.6	6.7
Retail trade	0.5	12.3	4.4
Transport	2.1	26.1	8.0
Public administration	0.7	14.4	5.0
Community services	0.4	7.0	5.7
Other industries	0.4	7.4	5.4
All industries	1.1	15.9	7.0

Source: *Job Vacancies and Overtime* (ABS, cat. no. 6354.0).

The overall incidence of overtime is not great. The average hours of overtime per employee was 1.1 hours per week, although those who did work overtime averaged seven hours per week. The extent of overtime is influenced by the level of economic activity as it provides firms with some flexibility in increasing output when demand for their product is relatively high and thus varies procyclically. It is a mistake, however, to believe that overtime working is a phenomenon confined to periods of high economic activity. The figures in Table 2.2 confirm this as they relate to a period when the economy was in recession and when the unemployment rate was around 10.5 per cent.

Further it always tends to be the same industries which work above (or below) average hours of overtime whatever the level of economic activity. Thus the ranking of industries by overtime working was virtually the same in 1991 as it was in 1980. The evidence also suggests that the pattern of overtime working across firms within industries is fairly stable.

The amount of overtime worked by individuals varies with age and family commitments with male workers typically working most overtime between the age of twenty-five and forty. Thus people's preferences between income and leisure seem to change with age and overtime provides one means of fulfilling these preferences.

Multiple job holding

The second source of flexibility in hours of work is through multiple job holding or moonlighting. From time-to-time, the ABS carries out a survey of multiple job holding (cat. no. 6216.0). In the most recent, that for 1991, 3.7 per cent of male employees and 5.3 per cent of female employees, that is a total of 331 600 persons, were found to have more than one job (these proportions have been increasing in the last ten years). The survey enables us to provide the following facts about multiple job holders. Most moonlighters are married (66 per cent), and are aged between twenty-five and forty-four years (61 per cent). There is a marked tendency for moonlighters to be employed in the recreation and personal service group of industries, where second jobs account for 12.5 per cent of all jobs. There were about 15 000 people who worked over forty hours a week in their main job and over twenty hours a week or over in their second job.

On the basis of wider evidence it has been suggested that while males tend to have a full-time job and work a few hours in a second job, females (particularly those with dependent children) often have several part-time jobs to give them the ability to cope with the demands of work in the household.[3] Both tend to take second jobs when debt obligations are highest—we saw above that nearly two-thirds of moonlighters are aged between twenty-five and forty-four years. Most male moonlighters tend to have short working weeks in their main job and have few opportunities to work overtime.

Part-time employment

Part-time work provides an obvious source of flexibility in hours of work for those who wish to work less than the standard week as well as enabling the existence of multiple job holding. A worker is held to be part-time if he or she works less than thirty-five hours a week. About one-quarter of part-time workers are employed on a permanent basis enjoying (proportionate to their hours of work) the same rights as full-time workers. The majority, however, are employed on a casual basis.

In 1992, part-time workers accounted for 23.4 per cent of total employees. Part-time working is concentrated among females. Of females, 41.9 per cent work part-time, whereas for males the proportion is only 9.9 per cent. There are significant differences between the age distribution of part-time workers of males and females. Most male part-timers are either young or old whereas most female part-time workers are aged between twenty-five and forty-four years. This latter tendency is most pronounced among married females and provides an excellent example of how part-time working enables people to exercise their preferences about hours of work, and how there are, for most people, inter-temporal changes in preferences.

In the last two decades, part-time employment has grown far more rapidly than full-time employment and is hence accounting for an increasing proportion of total employment. This trend has occurred throughout most of the industrialised world. In Australia part-time employment, as a percentage of total employment, has risen from 11.9 per cent in 1978 to 19.2 per cent in 1986 and 23.4 per cent in 1992. The great majority of part-time workers are casual workers.

Absenteeism

If an employed person is in a sub-optimal position in that they are required to work more hours per period of time than they prefer, an obvious solution is to be absent from work. Labour absence has not been researched extensively which is surprising given its magnitude. In Australia in recent years the number of working days lost per year through labour absence were about fifteen times greater than the number lost through industrial disputes.

Kenyon and Dawkins have developed a utility maximising model of labour absence.[4] This predicts that, other things being held constant, labour absence will be positively influenced by standard hours of work and by non-labour income, and negatively influenced by the penalties that employees may impose on workers who do not turn up for work. These penalties will tend to take the form of a reduction in promotion possibilities and an increased probability of suspension or dismissal. The model also predicts that the wage rate and the amount of overtime worked will determine levels of labour absence, but the direction of the effect is not clear as both income and substitution effects are at work (see Section 2.2).

Their model was then tested on data covering the period between 1966–84. The main results were that increases in the wage rate lead to declines in labour absence and that absence is positively related to changes in employment. The latter result may arise because when employment is growing the perceived penalties associated with absence may become less severe. As predicted, absence is positively related to the length of the standard working week. Overall, the utility maximising model seems to explain variations in labour absence quite well.

Kenyon and Dawkins also found that tradespersons and production employees who tend to work in unattractive and relatively dangerous conditions have relatively high labour absence rates. Labour absence tends to be high prior to periods of time with a high level of industrial disputation, indicating that it tends to be associated with discontent.

Wooden has found that labour absence rates are significantly above average in industries where public sector employment is important and that it is not possible to explain this difference by demographic or other variables.[5] He suggests that the explanation lies in various characteristics of public sector employment such as job security and ineffective control mechanisms (both of which reduce the perceived penalties of absence), generous sick leave entitlement and low job satisfaction.

In conclusion, it seems that economic and industrial relations variables are important determinants of variations in labour absence.

Job selection

Different jobs possess different characteristics. They come with different wages, different rates at which earnings increase with age, they vary in working conditions, they vary in the stability or instability of employment and so on. They also vary, of course, in the length of the standard working week, and in the availability of part-time employment and of overtime working. Thus, those wishing to work relatively long hours are able, other things being equal, to choose to work in occupations or industries where long hours of work are typical.

The flexibility is limited over time because of the costs of movement and, as we shall see in Chapter 4, because of the way in which internal labour markets operate. However, for younger workers and, perhaps, for unskilled workers, these constraints on flexibility may be weaker.

The labour supply curve

We concluded in Section 2.2 that it was not possible to predict from either of the two models of labour supply how the hours of work supplied by an individual would change if there was a change in the real wage rate. In this section we look at empirical work that has been undertaken on this matter.

The section is headed 'the labour supply curve' because when we answer the question posed above we will be able to determine the slope of the curve relating to the supply of hours of work to the wage rate.

In empirical work we have to recognise that, in diagrammatic terms, the shape of the budget constraint is not as simple as shown in Figure 2.2. We have already seen that the existence of penalty rates of pay is one reason for this and here we show the effect of introducing non-labour income and income taxes.

If the individual derives some unearned income then clearly, if he or she does not work, there is still an income and, in terms of the diagrammatic representation we have been using, the budget constraint does not reach the horizontal axis. If taxes are paid on earned income then the wage rate net of tax becomes the appropriate variable for the rational utility maximiser, and the imposition of an income tax has the same effect as a reduction in the wage rate. In many tax systems the marginal tax rate varies with income and hence the budget constraint becomes non-linear. The way in which taxes and unearned income can be included in the diagrammatic representation of the basic model is shown in Figure 2.8.

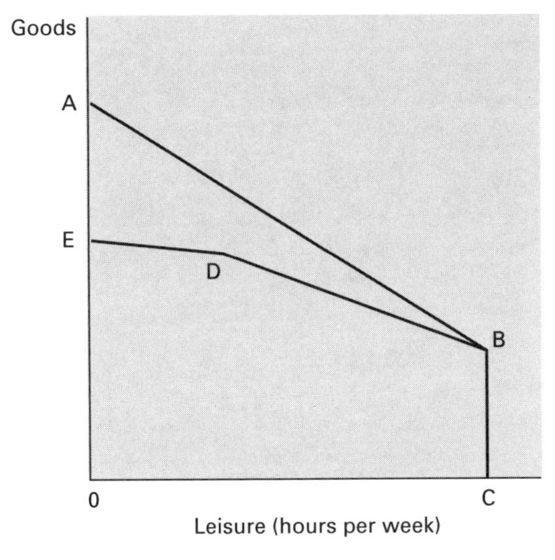

Figure 2.8 The effect on the budget constraint of introducing unearned income and taxes on earnings

The individual's unearned income net of tax is BC, and the wage rate if given by the slope of the constraint AB. Now taxes are imposed on earned income. Say the tax system is of the form that tax is payable at a constant marginal rate until a certain income represented by point D is earned; subsequent income attracts a higher marginal rate of tax. Thus the net of tax budget constraint has a kink in it at D where the higher tax threshold is passed. The constraint facing the individual is thus EDBC.

The specific issue in which we are interested is whether the supply curve which relates hours of work to the wage rate is upward or downward sloping. Most of the results are presented in terms of elasticities—the percentage change in hours of work that will result from a percentage change in the real after tax wage rate—and thus we wish to know whether these elasticities are positive or negative.

Evidence on this matter has accumulated from analyses using three main sources of data. First, time series where the observation on hours of work and real wage rates comes from different periods of time; second, cross-section data on hours and wages in different industries and occupations; and finally unit record data. Unit record data give us, in this instance, information on the hours worked by and the wages of individual people. They also give us information on other characteristics which affect hours of work, such as age and marital status and this enables us to control for these other variables. Unit record data have only become available even in the United States in the last twenty years or so and have enabled more sophisticated analysis of many aspects of labour market behaviour than

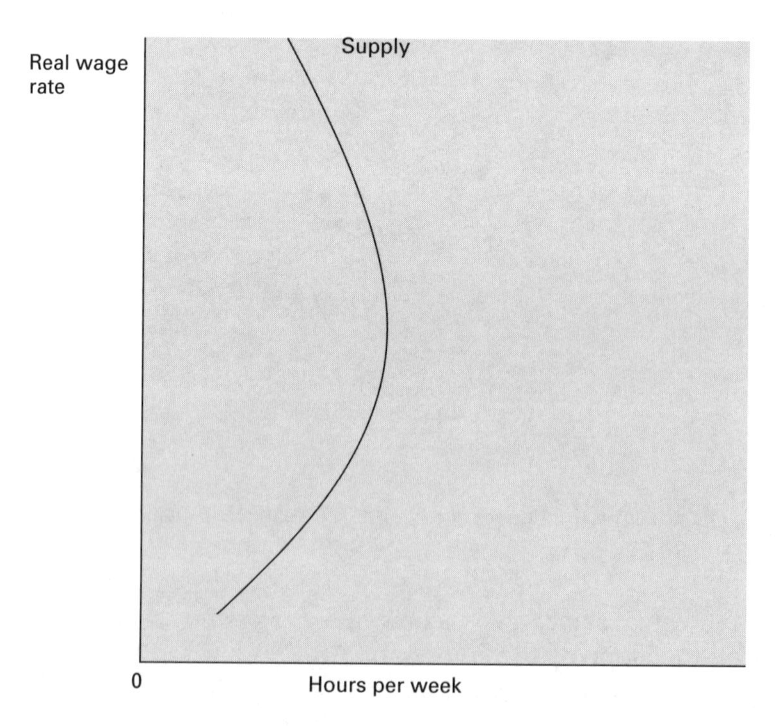

Figure 2.9 The supply curve of hours of work for males

was previously possible. In this case, however, more recent analysis has broadly supported the results obtained from previous work.

In analysing unit record data researchers have to overcome the difficulty posed by kinked budget constraints. That is because of overtime penalties, different marginal rates of tax and multiple job holding the individual's after tax wage rate is not the same for all hours. A number of ingenious methods have been developed to cope with this problem.

The results that have been obtained in Australia and Britain and the United States can be summarised as follows. First, for men the elasticities are found to be small, sometimes positive, sometimes negative. Second, again for males, there is a tendency for the elasticities to be positive when actual hours of work are relatively low and to become negative at relatively high hours of work. Thus, at the risk of oversimplification, the empirical work suggests that the supply curve of hours of work of males is as shown in Figure 2.9.

At low wage rates an increase in wage rates leads to an increase in hours supplied, that is the substitution effect outweighs the income effect. At some point, however, the income effect of an increase in the wage rate outweighs the substitution effect, more leisure is demanded and the supply of hours declines.

For females the empirical results normally find that the elasticities are positive and that the supply curve of hours of work is upward sloping throughout. The responsiveness of the female supply of hours of work to changes in hours is not large, however, the elasticity being of the order of 0.4–0.5. If, for illustrative purposes we take the value to be 0.4, this would imply that the average female working (say) twenty hours a week would, in response to a 10 per cent increase in her real wage rate wish to increase her hours of work by 4 per cent or forty-eight minutes a week.

2.4 Labour force participation

In the analysis of the previous two sections we assumed that the individual had decided to participate in the labour force and we were concerned with how many hours of work he or she would supply. Here we go back a step and ask how decisions are made about whether to supply any labour at all, that is whether to participate in the labour force or not. We use the neoclassical theory of labour supply and the same diagrammatic treatment as was adopted in the previous sections.

In Figure 2.10 the individual has a non-labour income of BC and the wage rate is represented by the slope of AB. Thus the budget constraint is ABC, where C is positioned at 168 hours a week. The individual's preferences between goods and leisure are represented by a set of indifference curves and he or she attempts to maximise utility and attain the highest possible indifference curve. There is no indifference curve that is tangential to the budget constraint and the highest curve that can be reached is U' at point B. Instead of a tangency solution we have what is termed a corner solution. Point B represents 168 hours of leisure and hence the individual supplies no work and does not participate in the labour force.

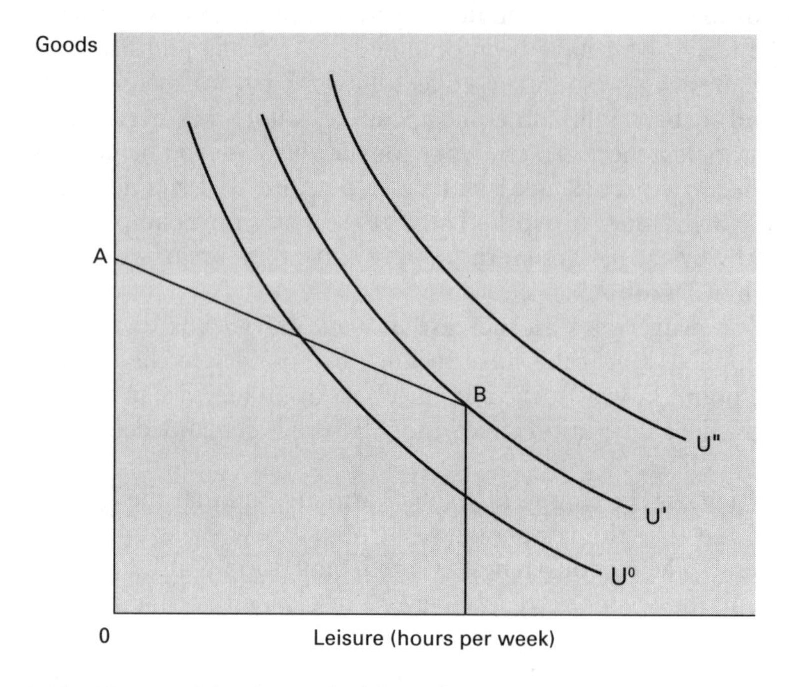

Figure 2.10 Non-participation in the labour force

The intuitive explanation for non-participation is that the wage rate offered is not adequate to compensate for the utility lost by the one hour of leisure (which would have to be given up if one hour a week were worked). Let us now ask what wage would be necessary to induce this individual to participate.

To do this let us first ask what is the effect of an increase in the wage rate. At the present wage, given by the slope of AB, the individual does not participate. Say the wage rate increased such that the budget constraint became EB. There would now be a higher indifference curve, labelled U" that could be reached and the utility maximising position is at F, and the individual now supplies DC hours of work a week.

Now ask what wage would be necessary to induce the individual to supply the smallest possible unit of labour, say one hour. This wage will be given by the slope of the indifference curve (U') at the corner point B. Why is this? Because, recall, the slope of the indifference curve is the

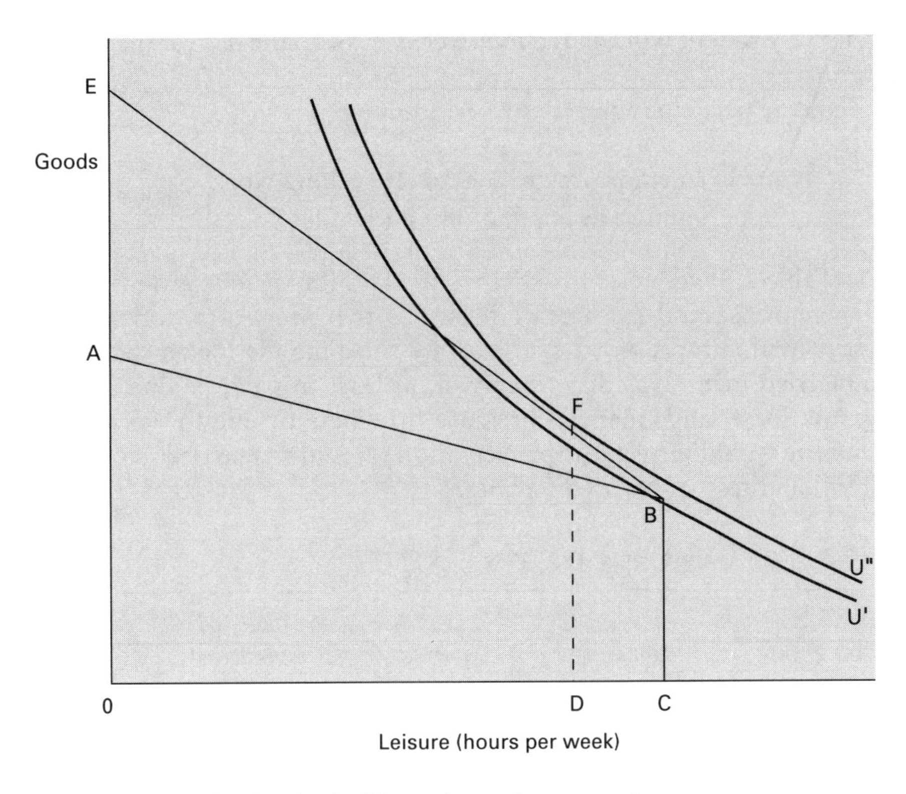

Figure 2.11 Participation in the labour force: the reservation wage

marginal rate of substitution between leisure and goods. That is, it shows how many goods (what wage) would be necessary to induce the individual to give up one (small) unit of leisure. This wage is known as the reservation wage. It is the wage necessary to induce the individual to participate in the labour force.

Some individuals who are not participating will have reservation wages close to the current wage and may tend to move in and out of the labour force as their real wage changes. Others will have reservation wages a long way above the going wage and will not participate unless their preferences (or circumstances) change.

Participation rates in Australia

We measure the extent to which people participate in the labour force by participation rates. To be counted as participating in the labour force a person must either be in employment or must be actively seeking work. Information on participation comes from a monthly survey of households and the interviewer provides a list of things, like responding to a job advertisement for example, that count as 'actively seeking work'. Formally, to be counted as part of the labour force a person not in employment must have actively sought work in the four weeks prior to the date of the Labour Force Survey.

Thus the participation rate of any group is:

$$\frac{\text{Number in employment or actively seeking work}}{\text{Number in population as a whole}} \times 100$$

In Table 2.3 we present participation rates for various groups.

There are several features of Table 2.3 that are worth noting. First, the participation rates of married men are substantially higher than those of unmarried men. This difference will, at least in part, be due to there being less social and financial pressure for single people to work. Note that, as one would expect, the participation rates of unmarried females are greater than those of married females.

Table 2.3 Participation rates, 1991 (%)

	Males		*Females*	
Age group	*Unmarried*	*Married*	*Unmarried*	*Married*
15–19	56.1	90.7	54.8	55.0
20–24	87.6	94.1	82.6	77.6
25–34	91.0	97.1	77.9	67.1
35–44	88.5	96.0	74.9	72.0
45–54	78.9	91.9	65.1	63.3
55–59	57.4	77.9	42.2	35.8
60–64	37.9	51.7	17.3	16.1
Total: 15–64	76.6	89.8	66.3	59.7

Source: *The Labour Force, Australia,* (ABS, cat. no. 6203.0). Separate figures for unmarried and married males available only on microfiche.

Second, for all groups participation rates at first rise with age and then fall. Relatively low participation rates for young people are due, of course, to their enrolment in schools, universities and in technical training. The lower participation rates for older workers reflect an increased desire for leisure. In terms of the analysis earlier in this section this causes reservation wages to increase. Non-participation of older workers are forms of intertemporal flexibility in hours of work. Faced with a rise in real wage rates at earlier ages, individual workers may, instead of working fewer hours then, decide to retire earlier than they would otherwise have done. Thus the income effect of a rise in wage rates (see Section 2.2), which leads to more leisure being taken, is postponed. This will be particularly relevant where standard working weeks constrain the choice of hours. Participation rates of older persons in Australia have declined quite sharply in recent decades.

Third, the participation rates of unmarried females are less than those of unmarried males. In the age range between twenty-five and fifty-four the difference is of the order of 13–14 percentage points. The reasons for such a substantial difference are not clear. Part of the explanation lies in the fact that large numbers of sole parents do not participate in the labour force and the overwhelming majority of sole parents are female. Another factor is that couples in de facto relationships, appearing as unmarried in the statistics, probably make their labour force participation decisions in the same way as married couples.

Fourth, and following directly, we can see from Table 2.3 that the participation rates of married males are, over all age ranges, substantially higher than that of married females. This difference arises from traditional Australian (and western) views about the division of labour within households, particularly those containing children. Thus husbands work in the labour market while the burden of work in the home tends to fall on wives. One of the striking changes in the Australian labour market in the last forty years has been a dramatic increase in the participation rates of married females and we now turn to discuss the participation decision of married females in detail.

The participation rates of married females

In discussing labour supply so far we have based our analysis on the individual. The neoclassical approach used in Section 2.2 was firmly based on the utility maximising individual and we chose to discuss Becker's theory in terms of the individual. We have to recognise, however, that in married households participation decisions are taken within the family.

In our earlier analysis the individual chose between work (goods) and leisure. In a household we should more realistically talk in terms of a three-way choice, between leisure, work in the market and work in the home—childrearing, house cleaning, cooking and so on. This three-way choice is, in fact, faced by husbands and wives and by working-age children who, just to complicate things, have a further choice which is to participate in education. To simplify things let us concentrate on the husband and wife. As we argued above, traditionally the role of the husband is to provide a source of income for the family. There is no reason to suppose this will always be the case but it is true in a great majority of households at present. So now consider the wife's participation decision.

From our previous analysis, we would expect that the quantity of labour supplied by a married woman would depend upon her wage rate, the income of her husband and a set of other variables such as her age, the number and age of her children, and so on.

Consider the effect of an increase in her wage rate. An increase in the wage rate increases the opportunity cost of both leisure and of home work.

Recall from Section 2.2 that an increase in the wage rate has a substitution and an income effect. The substitution effect would be expected to lead to less of both leisure and home work being undertaken and to more labour being supplied. How much more is supplied (either in the sense of participating rather than not participating, or of working more hours) will depend upon preferences and upon how easy or difficult it is to substitute market work for home work.

This latter will depend upon what is termed the elasticity of substitution in home production between the wife's effort and other production inputs. Say this elasticity were zero. This would mean that certain tasks like washing, preparing food, caring for children would be undertaken by the wife and there was no possibility of substituting other inputs. In practice this is not the case, of course. Washing machines or laundry facilities can be used, pre-cooked meals can be purchased and fast food outlets used, children can be placed in child-care centres and so on. The greater the elasticity of substitution the more likely it is that the substitution effect of the wage increases will lead to less home work being undertaken and hence that labour supply will increase. The wage change also has an income effect, and so, once again the net effect is not known a priori. However, empirical work has shown conclusively, that the substitution effect is the stronger and that an increase in wage rates leads to an increase in the number of married females working and to a tendency for those in the labour force to work longer hours.

Now consider the influence of a husband's income on the labour supplied by the wife. An increase in income is assumed to have a positive effect on the demand for leisure and a negative effect on work supplied. In the context of the contemporary family this negative effect will tend to fall on the work supplied by the wife. But the wife supplies both market work and home work. How much of the reduction falls on each will depend, again, on the elasticity of substitution in home production. The greater this is, the greater the reduction in home production and the smaller the increase in leisure. Empirical work supports the prediction that the higher a husband's income the less labour will tend to be supplied by the wife.

Finally, there are other variables other than the wage rate and husband's income which might be expected to influence married female participation. Cross-sectional empirical work suggests that age and number of children, place of birth, and years of education received by the wife also influence participation.[6] The former of these influences is obvious enough but the latter two require some explanation. The participation rate of women born overseas is significantly higher than that of Australian-born women. There are several possible reasons for this, such as different attitudes in the country of origin, but whatever the cause, the longer immigrant wives stay in Australia the more similar to Australian born women their participation behaviour becomes. The main reasons for expecting an association between education and labour force participation are, first, that additional years of schooling increase earnings and the wife is thus encouraged to substitute market for home work. Second, additional education may change preferences towards market rather than home work.

Trends in married female participation rates

The participation rates of married females over a long period of time are shown in Table 2.4.

Table 2.4 Labour force participation rates of married females, 1921–91 (%)

1921	*1947*	*1954*	*1961*	*1971*	*1981*	*1991*
4.2	8.0	12.6	17.3	32.8	44.3	52.3

Sources: P. Volker,[7] and *The Labour Force, Australia*, (ABS, cat. no. 6203.0).

For several reasons the figures for various years are not strictly comparable but the trend is unmistakable. The participation rate increased slowly up until 1954 but has since increased rapidly. Thus in rough terms it took twenty-six years for the rate to double from its 1921 level of 4.2 per cent, fourteen years for it to double again and since 1961 the participation rate has tripled. This increase has had profound social and economic implications. How can it be explained?

The analytical framework we have just developed suggests a number of explanations. First, the real wage rates of women have increased substantially both absolutely and relative to those of men. We shall discuss this latter change in some detail in Chapter 7. Here, by way of example, we can note that between 1969 and 1980 average female wage rates as a proportion of average male wage rates increased from 72 per cent to 93 per cent.

Second, we saw that at any point in time participation is higher the lower the number of children in a family. A marked decline in childbearing has occurred in recent decades. One way of showing this is to examine trends in the total fertility rate. The total fertility rate for any year is the number of children the average woman would bear during her lifetime if she experienced the birth rate of that year. In the period 1956–60 the total fertility rate was 3.4, but by 1989 this had declined to 1.9. This marked tendency for women to have fewer children has been accompanied, as we would expect, by a trend for women to have their last child at an earlier age. Thus, freed earlier from the duties of childrearing, they are more able to work in the labour market.

There is no doubt of an effect running in the opposite direction. That is, that other influences, for example the increase in the real wage, have led women to wish to participate to a greater extent in the labour force and as a result they wish to have fewer children. Raising children is a very expensive business. There are many direct costs, such as clothes, food, school expenses, which parents incur over a long period of time but there are also the earnings that women forego through raising children. The loss of earnings comes about in three ways. First, and most obviously, raising children involves a period of time during which women do not participate at all in the labour force. Second, raising children often causes women to work part-time rather than full-time. Third, while women are out of the labour force their work skills may decay and this leads to their earnings after the return to the labour force to be lower than they would otherwise be.

Beggs and Chapman have made estimates of the magnitude of the foregone earnings from childrearing in 1986.[8] The losses occur over a woman's life and have to be discounted into present value terms. (The technique of discounting is described on p.74.) Beggs and Chapman suggested in 1986 that the value of the earnings losses due to raising one child was on average about $300 000. The cost of second and third children was much lower $50 000 and $35 000 respectively. They concluded that 'it is obvious that the big decision in terms of foregone earnings is whether or not to have a first child. Second and subsequent children matter, but the consequences are relatively slight.'

Returning to our main theme, the third explanation of the increase in participation rates of married women is that the average number of years of education received has increased. We saw that at any point in time the higher the educational attainment of a married woman the more likely it is that she will participate in the labour force. In recent decades there has been a substantial increase in the years of education undertaken by females, again both in absolute terms and relative to men (see Chapter 4), which will have led to an increase in labour force participation.

Thus the increase in female wage rates and in the amount of education received and the decline in fertility will all have led to an increasing wish to participate in the labour force. At the same time there has undoubtedly been an increase in the elasticity of substitution in home production. The increase in the range and sophistication of labour saving domestic appliances and of convenience foods and the increasing availability of child-care facilities have enabled married women to participate in the labour force. Thus this constitutes a fourth explanation for the increase in participation, although there are some simultaneous influences at work. For example, the increase in the number of places in child-care centres would not have occurred if the demand for them had not increased.

We should note that our analysis suggests that the increase in male wage rates should have had a negative influence on participation. This influence, however, has probably weakened over time. We saw that an increase in husband's income leads to a decrease in the amount of market and home work combined that is undertaken by the wife. The increase in the elasticity of substitution in home production will have led to an increasing proportion of the decline in total work falling on home work.

Fifth there has been an immense change in social attitudes to married women working. It is not much of an exaggeration to write that in half a century we have moved from a situation where it was thought unusual for a married woman to work to one where it is thought unusual for a married woman without young children not to work.

Thus far we have described influences on the supply side but it is likely that the increase in the demand for female labour has also influenced participation. For it is possible that the female wage has been set above the market clearing wage so that supply is highly elastic and hence demand becomes a major influence on female employment.

The main point here is that women (and here we are talking of both married and single women) tend to be concentrated in certain occupations and industries. In 1991, for example, two-thirds of all female employees worked in just three industries—the retail and wholesale trade; finance, property and business services; and recreation, personal and other services. Thus women are over-represented in the tertiary sector. Yet, it has been this sector which has grown more rapidly than any other in employment terms in the post-war period. Some manufacturing industries, for example, textiles and clothing and footwear, which employ relatively large numbers of women, have declined. On balance, however, the sorts of industries in which women are over-represented have expanded their share of total employment. Changes in the employment of women will be discussed in more detail in the final section of Chapter 7.

We saw too, in the previous section, that there has been a significant increase in part-time employment. Over three-quarters of all part-time workers are females. For obvious reasons many married women, particularly those with young children, prefer part-time employment and indeed may be unable to work full-time. Thus, this change in the composition of employment will also have acted to increase participation.

There have been five main factors leading to an increase in participation rates of married females and, at the same time, changes in the composition of employment have led to the demand for female labour increasing relatively rapidly.

Cyclical variations in participation rates

The long run secular trend in the participation rates of married females is clearly upwards but around this trend there have been cyclical variations. There are two effects that changes in the level of unemployment may have on the participation rates of married women (or of any group of worker).

The first is known as the 'additional worker effect'. This is that if the traditional main wage earner in a family becomes unemployed, or faces an increased probability of becoming unemployed, then there is an additional incentive for the wife to work or to seek work in order to maintain family income. As male unemployment rises the additional worker effect therefore leads to an increase in the participation of married women.

Alternatively, as male unemployment rises married women, faced with increasingly poor job prospects, may become discouraged from seeking work and temporarily withdraw from the labour force. Participation rates therefore fall in cyclical downswings. This is known as the 'discouraged worker effect'.

In any recession both effects are operative, some married women being discouraged and others being drawn into the labour force. The point at issue is: Which effect predominates? As far as married women are concerned, the evidence from Australian studies is inconclusive with some finding the discouraged worker effect to dominate, some finding a net additional worker effect and others not identifying any discernible net effect. We shall return to this issue in the context of the whole labour force in Chapter 10.

2.5 Immigration

A major determinant, in both the long and the short run, of the rate of growth of the population and of the labour force has been the rate of net immigration. By net immigration we mean the excess of the numbers of people entering Australia from abroad who state that they intend to settle here permanently over the numbers of Australian residents who leave intending to settle permanently abroad. Over the whole of the post-war period net immigration has accounted for about 40 per cent of the increase in the total population. To give another impression of the importance of immigration, in the post-war period migrants and their children have accounted for 60 per cent of the growth of the labour force.

Figures for net immigration since 1960 are shown in Table 2.5. It is evident that there has been considerable variation in the annual level of net migration. This has been caused by variations in the number of migrants allowed to enter the country because for virtually the whole period covered by the table the number of people wishing to migrate to Australia exceeded the quota set by the Department of Immigration.

Let us begin by asking what the objectives of the immigration policy are. We confine our attention to the post-war period. In the early part of this period defence and political considerations were important. The war had seemed to demonstrate that the population was too small to defend

Table 2.5 Net immigration, 1960–90

	Number ('000s)	*Percentage of population*
1960-64 (av.)	93.2	0.87
1965-69 (av.)	124.6	1.11
1970-74 (av.)	93.0	0.72
1975-79 (av.)	44.2	0.31
1980-84 (av.)	71.7	0.48
1985-89 (av.)	80.5	0.53
1990	91.2	0.53

Note: Net immigration is the difference between permanent arrivals and permanent departures.

Sources: *Overseas Arrivals and Departures, Australia,* (ABS cat. no. 3404.0); and *Australian Demographic Statistics*, (ABS, cat. no. 3101.0).

itself and the proximity of some over populated areas in South-East Asia also had some influence. This defence argument, however, is no longer heard.

For most of the period the main argument in favour of immigration was that it raised the rate of economic growth, that is the rate of growth of Gross Domestic Product (GDP) per head. There are various ways in which this might occur. One is that an increase in population would lead to an increase in the scale of production and enable economies of large scale production to be gained. Another possibility is that migrants may bring new ideas and increase the rate of technological advance. Whether immigration has in fact led to an increase in the rate of economic growth is extremely difficult to answer using econometric techniques. While the balance of the evidence seems to suggest that immigration has had a favourable effect on growth the impact is probably small.[9] Whether or not immigration has led to an increase in GDP per head there is no doubt that it has increased the growth of GDP and for this reason is generally favoured by the business lobby. It is easier for firms to expand their own output when total demand is rising.

A third argument advanced in favour of immigration is more directly concerned with the labour market. Here the case rests upon the use of immigration to alleviate labour shortages. In the first twenty or so years after the war there was, in most years, an overall excess demand for labour and this was, at least in part, met by a large inflow if predominantly European migrants. More recently, even in years of relatively high unemployment, there have existed shortages of certain types of skilled labour and immigration policy has attempted to address these. Firms can recruit skilled labour overseas and can then nominate (or sponsor) them for immigration. The immigration authorities have, also, in recent years operated the Occupational Shares System which allows potential migrants to qualify for a permanent resident visa if they are in an occupational group deemed to be in shortage in Australia. Applicants attempting to enter under some other immigration categories have greater chances of success the more educational qualifications they possess. Fourth, there is a case for immigration based on humanitarian grounds and a significant number of refugees, notably from Vietnam, have settled in Australia in recent decades.

Early in the post-war period a '1 per cent' policy was developed. This set the annual target for immigration at a level equivalent to 1 per cent of the population and in many years this was achieved and in some exceeded. From Table 2.5 we can see, for example, that the average annual net immigration in the period 1965-69 was equivalent to 1.11 per cent of the population. More recently, the levels of immigration have tended to be lower and the targets (or quotas) are set more pragmatically.

The marked decline in immigration targets in the late 1970s was largely due to the increase in unemployment rates in Australia. The reason for varying the target rate of immigration inversely with the unemployment rate is a fear that when unemployment is relatively high, immigration simply adds to it. Immigrants do, of course, add to the supply of labour but they also add to domestic expenditure and hence to the demand for labour. Thus, immigration need not cause unemployment. It is clear from the available evidence that there has been no causal link running from immigration to unemployment and thus that widely expressed fears about the economic impact of immigration are unfounded, at least at the levels of net immigration that have been experienced in the recent past. One factor contributing to this result has been the tendency we described above for immigration policies to be targeted at groups for which labour market shortages exist.

An enormous amount of research has been undertaken in Australia into the economics of immigration. Some of this has been concerned with issues such as the effect of immigration on the rate of economic growth that we discussed earlier. Other work has investigated the labour market experience of migrants and we shall refer to the results of this research at various stages of this book.

Concepts for review

- Participation rate
- Marginal rate of substitution between goods and leisure
- Income effect of a change in wage rate
- Substitution effect of a change in wage rates
- Full price of a commodity
- Reservation wage
- Elasticity of substitution in home production
- Additional worker effect
- Discouraged worker effect

Questions

1. Compare the two main approaches to the analysis of how the individual decides on the number of hours of work to supply (Macquarie University).
2. Provide a definition of labour supply and describe the main changes in female labour supply in Australia since 1945. What explanations can you provide for these changes? (University of Melbourne).
3. Using the income–leisure model of labour supply explain why labour absence occurs. How is labour absence affected in this framework by:
   a) an increase in the wage rate?
   b) a weekly bonus for 100 per cent attendance?
   c) sick leave entitlements (Curtin University)?
4. What impact would a significant cut in personal income tax rates be expected to have on the level and composition of labour supply? (University of Adelaide).
5. Describe the main trends in labour force participation in Australia in the post-war period and explain why they have occurred (University of Western Australia).

References

1. G.S. Becker, 'A theory of the allocation of time', *Economic Journal*, vol. 75, no. 299, 1965, pp. 493-517.
2. J. Steinke, 'The long term decline in the standard working year', *Journal of Industrial Relations*, vol. 25, no. 4, 1983, pp. 415-30.
3. A. Harris and A. Preston, 'Multiple job holding: trends in labour market flexibility in Australia during the 1980s', *Labour Economics and Productivity*, vol. 2, no. 1, 1990, pp. 71-6.
4. P. Kenyon and P. Dawkins, 'A time series analysis of labour absence in Australia', *Review of Economics and Statistics*, vol. LXXI, no. 2, 1989, pp. 232-9.
5. M. Wooden, 'The "sickie": a public sector phenomenon', *Journal of Industrial Relations*, vol. 32, no. 4, 1990, pp. 560-76.
6. P.W. Miller and P. Volker, 'Married women and the labour force: aspects of supply analysis', and R.T. Ross, 'Disaggregate labour supply functions: some evidence, from the 1980 survey of married women in Sydney', in *Labour Force Participation in Australia*, Bureau of Labour Market Research Monograph Series, no. 1, 1984.
7. P. Volker, 'Female labour supply: an overview of research in Australia' in *Women in the Labour Force*, Bureau of Labour Market Research Monograph Series, no. 4, 1984.
8. J.J. Beggs and B.J. Chapman, 'The foregone earnings from child rearing in Australia', *Centre for Economic Policy Research Discussion Paper*, no. 190, 1988.
9. M. Wooden, et al., *Australian Immigration: a Survey of the Issues*, AGPS, Canberra, 1990, Chapter 3.

CHAPTER 3

The demand for labour

3.1 Introduction

The demand for labour is derived from the value of the goods and services it produces. We would expect an employer who is aiming to maximise profits to employ labour as long as the value of the goods produced by additional units of labour is greater than, or at the margin equal to, the cost of labour. This is the basis of the marginal productivity explanation of the demand for labour, and it is our task in this chapter to investigate formally the relationships between employment and marginal productivity under various conditions.

In this chapter our analysis is microeconomic and of a partial equilibrium nature. That is to say, the focus is on the firm, and on the industry holding the aggregate level of output, prices, and employment constant. In Chapter 10 we shall see the extent to which the analysis can be extended to the macroeconomic level.

The plan of the chapter is as follows. We first analyse the demand for labour of a perfectly competitive firm. This is the longest section, not because we believe that such firms are typical (they clearly are not) but because it is easiest to derive the basic principles in this case and subsequently to modify the argument when other conditions hold. We go on to discuss the demand for labour or competitive industries and then of firms which are monopolistic. Although the marginal productivity theory holds the ring, it has come in for sustained attack over the years and in the final section of the chapter we shall look at the main thrust of opposing arguments and attempt an assessment.

In setting out both the theory and the criticism of it we state the main points without drawing the implications for various parts of labour economics. In virtually every chapter that follows we shall have cause to return to the issues discussed here. Thus this chapter should be seen as a building block, rather than as a complete construction, and consequently is relatively short.

3.2 The demand for labour of the competitive firm

By 'competitive' we mean that the firm both sells its product and hires its labour (and other inputs) in perfectly competitive markets. Thus it is a price taker. We shall assume that its objective is to maximise its profits. To keep things simple, but leaving the argument unaltered, we shall assume that only one type of labour is hired and that there is only one other factor input, capital. We now proceed to analyse the firm's demand for labour first in the short run and then in the long run.

The short-run demand for labour

By the 'short' run we mean that period of time in which the stock of capital of the firm is constant. The calendar length of the short run will vary from industry to industry. In hairdressing, for example, it may be a matter of days, just the time necessary to purchase a chair and some equipment. In petrochemicals it may take several years to design and construct a new plant. Either way, the essential point is that in the short run, in our simple model with two inputs, labour is the only variable factor. As the firm hires additional units of labour under these conditions then output increases. The most plausible relation between output and employment is that output increases more than proportionately with employment at first, but at some point the increase becomes less than proportionate. The relationship is thus as in part A of Figure 3.1, which plots the total physical product of labour (TPPL), the adjective 'physical' telling us that we are measuring output in physical (for example, tonnes of steel) rather than value terms. The tendency for the successive additions to output made by additional units of labour, holding capital constant, to diminish after some point is of course the law of diminishing marginal returns. This law is based on empirical observation. A commonsense explanation of the tendency is that as more units of labour are added to a constant stock of capital the amount of capital available to each worker obviously gets less and less. At some level of employment this causes the amount produced by each successive unit of labour to decline.

A Total physical product of labour

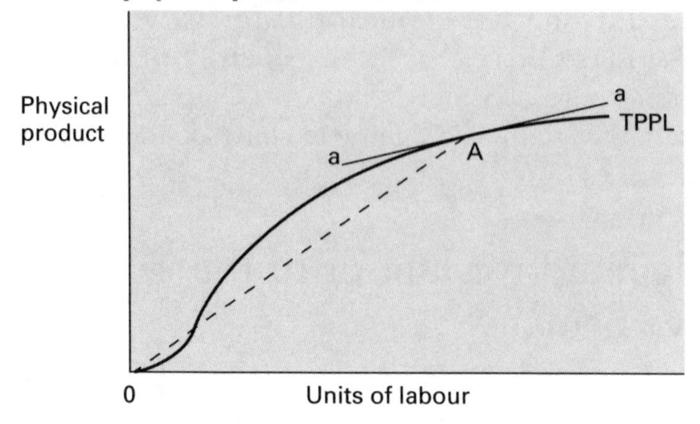

B Marginal and average physical product of labour

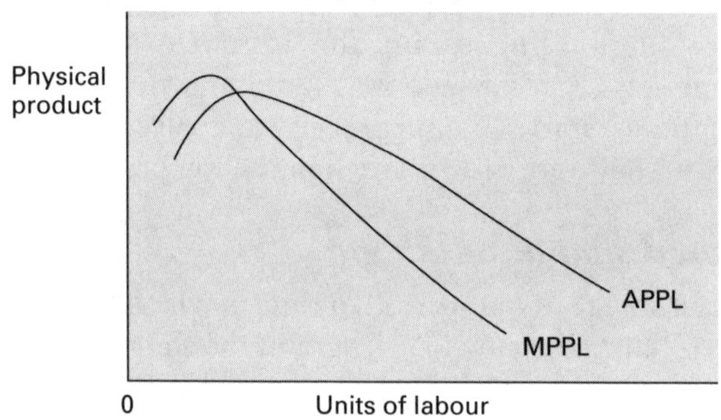

C Marginal and average revenue product of labour

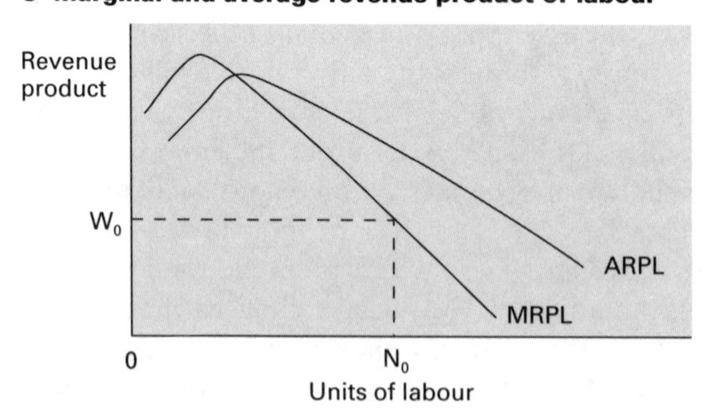

Figure 3.1 The derivation of the short-run demand for labour schedule of a competitive firm

From the TPPL curve we can derive two further curves, which are shown in part B of Figure 3.1. The first of these shows the average physical product of labour (APPL), that is the physical amount produced per worker. Thus at any point on the TPPL curve, such as A, the APPL is the slope of a ray from A to the origin. The second curve shows the marginal physical product of labour (MPPL), which is defined as the physical product of the last unit of labour employed, other factors constant. At any point, A, the MPPL is given by the slope of the TPPL curve, or, equivalently, by the slope of a line aa tangential to the TPPL curve at A.

Given the shape of the TPPL curve that we have drawn, the APPL and MPPL first increase with labour input and then decline. As we shall see shortly, it is only the downward-sloping sections of the curves that are relevant to the firm's demand for labour.

The final step is to express the physical products in value terms, and to do this we multiply the physical products by the corresponding measures of revenue to derive revenue products. Thus:

APPL × AR = average revenue product of labour (ARPL), and

MPPL × MR = marginal revenue product of labour (MRPL)

Now the firm is selling its product in a perfectly competitive market and faces a horizontal, or perfectly elastic, demand curve. Hence marginal revenue is equal to average revenue (price) and is the same at all levels of output. Thus as we are multiplying the physical products by the constants AR and MR, the revenue product curves, which are plotted in part C of Figure 3.1, have the same shape as the curves in part B.

In part C we can now derive the firm's demand for labour schedule. Hiring labour in a perfectly competitive market, it can purchase any quantity it likes at the going wage. If this wage is W_0, then the profit-maximising firm hires labour up to the point N_0 where the marginal revenue product of labour equals the wage. To hire less labour would mean the firm foregoing profit, for to the left of N_0 the last unit of labour hired adds more to revenue than it does to costs (the addition to costs being its wage). Similarly to the right of N_0 the last unit employed costs more than it adds to revenue, and would not be hired by a profit-maximising firm.

Were the wage to fall, more labour would be hired, and were it to rise, less labour would be hired. As the demand for labour is always where MRPL equals the wage, it follows that the demand curve for labour is determined by the MRPL curve and has an identical shape.

For the sake of completeness we ought to qualify that statement by saying that the demand for labour schedule is the MRPL schedule where the latter is downward sloping and lies below the ARPL schedule. Where the MRPL schedule is above the ARPL schedule, the firm would make a loss if it demanded labour from the MRPL, as labour's average product would then be less than its wage.

The general rule is then that the firm demands labour up to the point where the wage is equal to the marginal revenue product of labour. In the short-run case considered, the only way the firm could vary its factor proportions is by varying its labour input, as the capital stock is fixed. In the long run, inputs of capital can also be varied, and we now turn to an analysis of the demand for labour in the long run.

The long-run demand for labour

Engineers can design plants with various ratios of labour to capital and the firm chooses the plant that minimises the costs of producing any given output. The engineering relationship which links inputs and output is known as the 'production function,' and can be represented graphically, by an isoquant map, as in Figure 3.2.

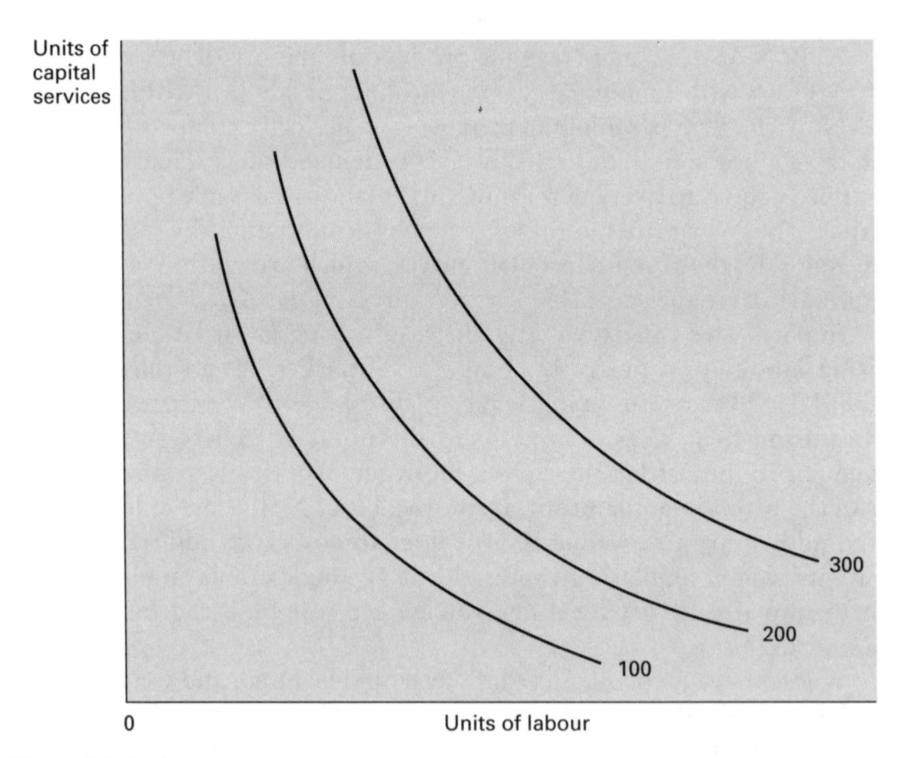

Figure 3.2 An isoquant map

The curves are known as 'isoquants'. Each isoquant represents the various combinations of inputs of capital services (vertical axis) and labour (horizontal axis) which can produce the same level of output. Isoquants, unlike the indifference curves of Chapter 2, can be labelled with a number, the level of output produced. The isoquants slope downwards from left to right because, as plants with smaller inputs of capital services are used, additional inputs of labour are required to produce the same output.

The absolute value of the slope of an isoquant at any point measures the marginal rate of substitution between labour and capital, that is, it tells us how many units of capital services are necessary to replace (say) one unit of labour to keep output unchanged. If, for example, the slope were half, then as this means that half a unit of capital is necessary to compensate for the loss of one unit of labour, it follows that the marginal physical productivity of one unit of labour is half that of one unit of capital. Thus we have that:

$$\text{the slope of an isoquant} = \text{marginal rate of substitution of capital for labour} = \frac{\text{MPPL}}{\text{MPPK}}$$

where MPPK is the marginal physical product of capital.

It is normally assumed that as one moves along an isoquant from right to left the slope increases and vice versa, as it is likely that as plants become (say) increasingly capital intensive it becomes increasingly difficult technically to substitute capital for labour. Hence the isoquants are convex, as in Figure 3.2.

Isoquants do not have to be convex. The two extreme cases are shown in Figure 3.3. Consider, first part A of the diagram. Here the isoquants are linear, that is their slopes are constant. Thus in this case the rate at which the two factors can be substituted at the margin is constant.

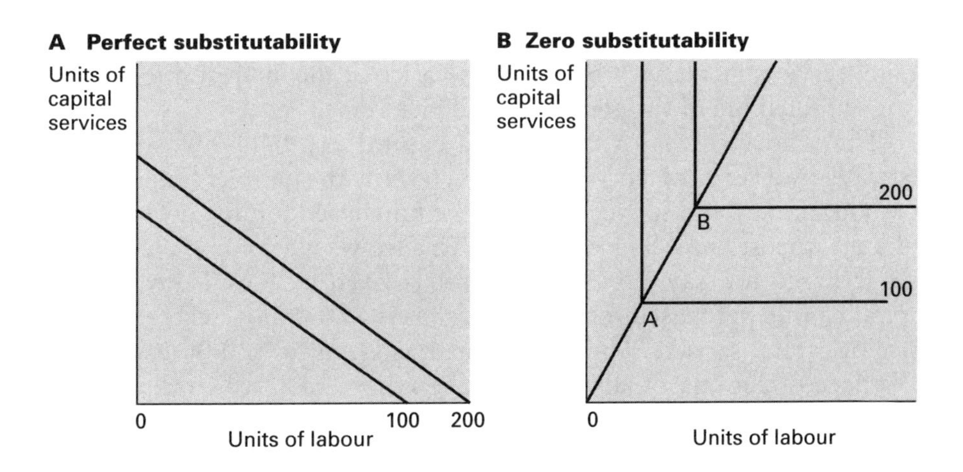

Figure 3.3 Extreme cases of substitutability

In part B of Figure 3.3 we show the opposite case. Here no substitution is possible. Take the isoquant labelled 100 units of output. This can be produced by the input combination represented by point A. If more labour is added to the same amount of capital nothing happens to output, and vice versa. One person flying a light aircraft would be an example. Clearly A represents the minimum input combination to produce 100 units of output. Similarly B, in our example two pilots and two aircrafts, represents the minimum input combination to produce 200 units of output. This is known as the fixed co-efficients case.

Returning to the normal diminishing marginal rate of substitution case (Figure 3.2) how does the profit maximising firm choose between the various alternative combinations of capital and labour which can produce any given output? It does so on the basis of the relative costs of labour and capital services. The cost of a unit of labour is its wage per unit of time but what is the cost of capital? Capital goods are not used up as they are purchased but last for a period of time—that after all is their main characteristic. That is why we have talked of inputs of capital services rather than of capital goods. If our unit of time is a year then in Figure 3.2 the horizontal axis is units of labour hired per year and the vertical axis is the part of the capital stock which is used up in any year. The cost of a capital service is made up of three main elements: first, the purchase price of the capital good; second, how long the good will last; and third, the cost of the funds used to purchase it. We will assume that the cost of finance is given by the interest rate.

Take a capital good costing $10 000 which is expected to last five years; the interest rate is 5 per cent. Then the annual cost of the good, or alternatively the cost of capital services per year, is given by the annual payments necessary to repay a loan of $10 000 over five years at 5 per cent interest, which is in fact $2310. We can see immediately that the price of capital services increases if the purchase price or the interest rate rises, or if the expected life of the good falls and vice versa.

The relative costs of labour and capital can be shown diagrammatically by a series of isocost lines which show the various combinations of labour and capital services that can be purchased for any given outlay. Take the isocost line AB in Figure 3.4. This shows what combinations can be purchased for, say $20 000. Point A is fixed by how many units of capital can be purchased for $20 000, that is $20 000/$P_k$ where P_k is the price of capital services. Similarly point B is given by $20 000/W, where W is the cost per unit of labour. Thus the slope of AB, which is:

$$\frac{OA}{OB} = \frac{\$20\,000}{P_k} \div \frac{\$20\,000}{W} = \frac{W}{P_k}$$

gives the ratio of the input prices.

At any given ratio of input prices there will be an infinite number of isocost lines each representing a different outlay. Lines further to the north-east represent larger outlays; thus the line CD shows a higher outlay than does line AD.

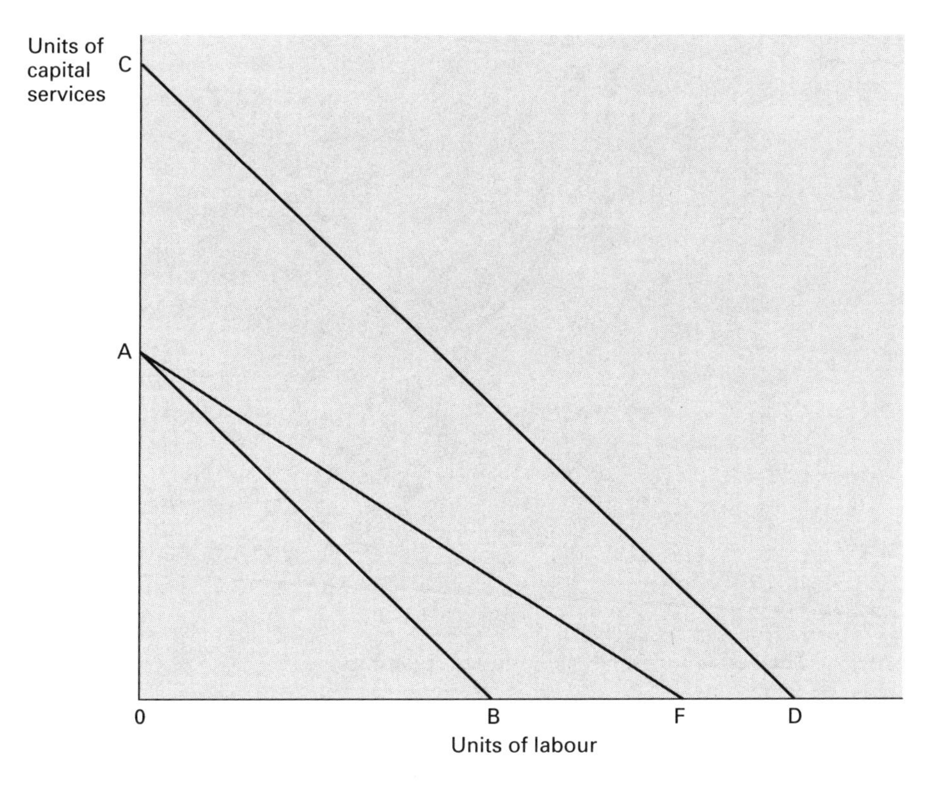

Figure 3.4 Isocost lines

If the price of one input changes relative to the other, the slope of the isocost lines change. Thus, for example, if the price of labour fell, and the price of capital services remained unaltered the isocost line AB would swivel to AF. If all expenditure was on capital services the same amount (OA) could be purchased as in the original case. If, however, all expenditure were on labour a greater amount (OF in the diagram) could be obtained.

Let us now bring the isoquant map and the isoquant lines together in Figure 3.5. Take the example where the firm wishes to produce 100 units of output. The cheapest way to produce them is given by the lowest isocost line that touches the 100-unit isoquant, and this is the line that is tangential to the isoquant. Thus the cost-minimising input combination is K_1L_1. At the point of tangency, E, the slopes of the isoquant and the isocost line are the same and hence, from our knowledge of what the slopes represent, that is the ratio of the marginal physical products of the two inputs and the ratio of the prices of the inputs respectively, we obtain:

$$\frac{MPPL}{MPPK} = \frac{W}{P_k}$$

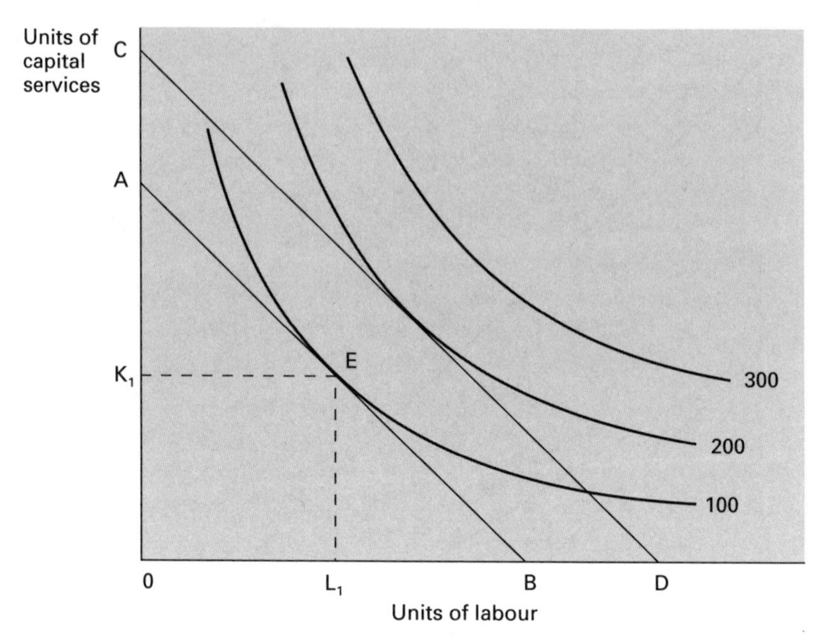

Figure 3.5 The derivation of cost-minimising input ratios

To minimise costs, inputs should be hired so that the ratio of their marginal physical products equals the ratio of their prices.

Our main concern is to see how the demand for labour varies with the wage, so starting from point E, which we reproduce in Figure 3.6, let us reduce the wage, other things remaining the same. The effect of a reduction in the wage is to reduce the slope of each isocost line, for example, from AB to AF. If the firm wishes to continue producing 100 units then the least-cost position is again at the point of tangency of the 100 isoquant with an isocost line, in this case at J. Thus, holding output constant, the effect of the wage reduction is to induce substitution of labour for capital: this is known as the 'substitution effect' of a wage change. Note that the magnitude of the substitution effect depends on the slope of the isoquants, that is on the marginal rate of substitution between labour and capital. This is intuitively appealing and requires no explanation, but we should draw attention to the limiting case where the isoquants are L-shaped. In this case E would be situated at the angle of the L, and following the wage change this would remain the cost-minimising way of producing that output. Hence in the fixed co-efficient case no substitution occurs.

Returning to the usual case of convex isoquants, the move to J described above is not the end of the story. For the reduction in costs per unit of output consequent on the substitution of the now cheaper labour for capital means that the firm is out of equilibrium in its product market.

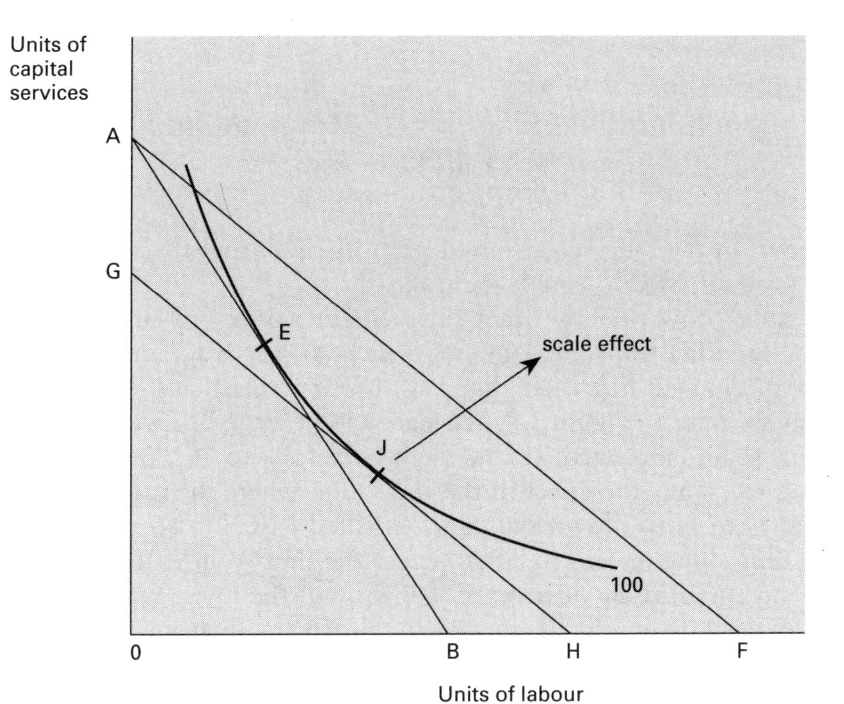

Figure 3.6 The effect of a wage reduction on input demands

At an unchanged product price it becomes profitable to expand output, and thus there will be a further increase in the demand for labour as a result. This is known as the 'scale effect' and is shown on Figure 3.6 as an arrow denoting a move somewhere to the north-east of J. As we have not specified the form of the production function nor the nature of the product market we cannot be more precise than that.

The demand for labour therefore increases as the wage falls, and we can easily show that in the long run, as in the short, the demand for labour schedule is given by the marginal revenue product of labour. The cost-minimising condition derived above implies that the marginal cost of expanding output through an increment of capital or labour must be the same. For it can be rewritten as:

$$\frac{W}{MPPL} = \frac{P_k}{MPPK}$$

The left-hand side gives us the money cost at the margin of producing one more unit of output using added labour and similarly the right shows the cost of using additional capital to produce one more unit. Thus the equation yields the marginal cost of production, MC. In equilibrium in the product market, firms produce where marginal revenue, MR, equals marginal cost. Thus we have:

$$MR = MC$$

$$\therefore\ MR = \frac{W}{MPPL}$$

$$\therefore\ MR \times MPPL = W$$

$$\therefore\ MRPL = W$$

Labour, in the long run, is hired up to the point where its marginal revenue product, MRPL, equals the wage.

We now show that the long-run demand curve for labour has a smaller slope than the short-run curve, thus at any wage the long-run elasticity of demand is greater than the short-run elasticity. To demonstrate this we refer to Figure 3.7. We start with a wage W_0, with N_0 units of labour being employed. If the wage now falls to W_1, other things remaining the same, the effect in the short run, where the capital inputs are fixed, is to move down the curve labelled $MRPL_0$. To remind the reader, diminishing returns to labour cause the short-run MRPL schedule (or demand curve) to be downward sloping, but the lower wage renders the employment of additional units profitable, so employment increases to N_1.

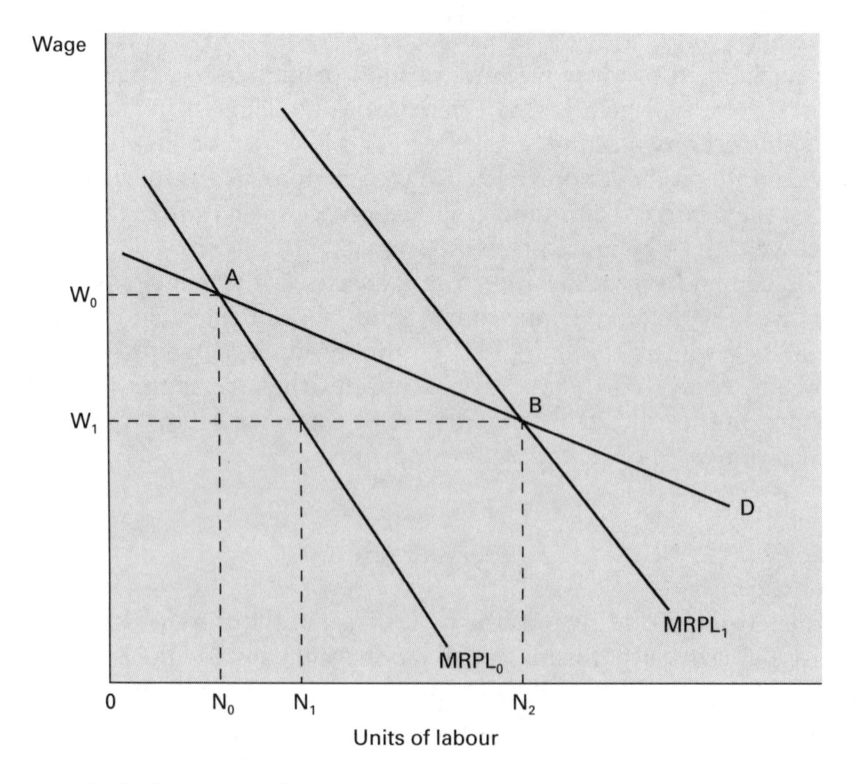

Figure 3.7 The long-run and short-run demand for labour schedules

In the long run, however, employment will increase further as substitution of labour for capital occurs and as, at a given output price, the scale of production increases. Thus after these adjustments have occurred a greater amount of labour is employed at a wage of W_1, say N_2 units. The long-run demand curve thus passes through points A and B and is more elastic than $MRPL_0$. Through B there now passes a further short-run demand curve which shows how demand varies with the wage, given the new capital stock. This is, again, an intuitively appealing result: the longer the time allowed for adjustment, the greater is the response of the demand for labour to a change in the wage.

Although we are only concerned with the demand for labour, it can similarly be shown that all factor inputs are demanded up to the point where their marginal revenue products equal their prices. The question then arises: Will there be, in the long run, enough revenue product to pay factors in this way? (The short run poses no problems, for capital, being the fixed factor, has no marginal product and receives any residual left after paying labour its marginal product.) It turns out that in the long run the total revenue product is just adequate to reward all factors in this way, with none left over, if the firm's production function exhibits constant returns to scale. Constant returns to scale exist if, when all inputs are increased in the same proportion, output increases in that same proportion.

To get a little more meaning into the proposition that firms generate enough revenue to pay all inputs their marginal revenue products consider a garage employing mechanics and other types of labour. If you take your car to be repaired you will be charged (say) \$40 an hour for the services of a mechanic. The mechanic, however, only gets paid (say) \$20 an hour. The rest goes to pay for the labour of the manager, the people who make up the accounts in the office, and for capital services. In long-run equilibrium, and if there are constant returns to scale, the remaining \$20 is just enough to remunerate these other inputs at their marginal revenue products.

3.3 The demand for labour of the competitive industry and the monopolistic firm

The results of the previous section enable us to discuss quite briefly the demands for labour of the competitive industry and of the firm which possesses some monopoly power, and it is to these that we now turn.

The competitive industry

To derive the demand curve for the competitive industry, we simply aggregate over the demand curves of the industry's constituent firms. Thus the essential elements of the foregoing analysis remain unaltered. There is one important difference, however, and this concerns the elasticity of the demand for labour, that is the proportionate change in the quantity of labour demanded in response to a proportionate change in the wage, other things remaining the same. In most circumstances the elasticity of the demand curve of a whole industry is less than that of each constituent firm. There are two influences on the demand curve of the industry which do not apply when we consider each firm in isolation.

First, and this applies in both the short and the long run, when we analysed the demand of the firm we held the price of the output of the firm constant. We cannot do this for the industry because as its output expands the price of its product falls, the proportionate extent of the fall depending on the elasticity of demand for the product. Whereas for the firm we multiplied MPPL by a constant marginal revenue we cannot do this for the industry, as product price is falling. Thus the industry short-run demand for labour curve is less elastic than that of each of the firms that make up the industry, and in the long run the decline in product price limits the size of the scale effect with similar effects on the elasticity of demand for labour.

Second, and this only applies to the long-run analysis, we were entitled when considering the firm to assume that the price of capital services remains constant, but at the industry level this may not be so. Let us refer back to Figure 3.6 to see the effect of a fall in the wage on demand for capital. The substitution effect (the move from E to J) leads to less capital being used, while the scale effect (the move outwards from J) leads to an increase in the demand for capital. The net outcome is not known and hence the demand of each firm, and hence by the industry, for capital may increase or decrease. This change may, depending upon the size of the industry and how specific to that industry the capital goods are, alter the price of capital services. To demonstrate the sort of effect that might occur let us say that the net effect is to increase the demand for capital and that this drives up the price of capital services. This then partially offsets the cost reduction due to the original fall in the wage and limits the scale effect on the demand for labour.

Hence, in the long-run situation the first influence, that of a decline in product price as output expands, always leads to the industry's demand for labour curve being less elastic than that of each constituent firm. The second influence, however, that of the change in the price of capital services, may operate in either direction. Although we cannot rule out the possibility that the second effect leads to the industry's demand curve being more elastic than that of the individual firms, and is also stronger than the effect of the decline in product price, this seems an unlikely eventuality. Thus, in general, the demand of the industry for labour can be expected to be less elastic than the demand of each individual firm in the industry.

We will not discuss further the determinants of the elasticity of demand for labour here. This elasticity is particularly relevant in the analysis of the power and effects of trade unions, so further treatment is postponed until we discuss unionism in Chapter 6.

In discussing the demand for labour of the non-competitive firm we shall confine our attention to situations where the competitive assumptions of Section 3.2 are broken on the product side of the market. A discussion of firms which hire labour in non-competitive markets and which thus face upward-sloping labour supply curves is deferred until Chapters 6 and 7.

Where firms are selling in less than perfectly competitive product markets, their demand curves are downward sloping. Consumers do not treat their product as indistinguishable from that of other firms and hence they possess some monopoly power, and the less elastic their demand curves the greater their degree of monopoly. How does that affect their demand for labour?

Let us take the short-run case. We derived the rule that labour demand is given by the marginal revenue product schedule and this is derived as follows:

$$\text{MRPL} = \text{MPPL} \times \text{MR}$$

In perfect competition MR is constant, and equal to price, so the decline in MRPL (which gives us our downward-sloping demand curve for labour) comes about solely due to the fall in MPPL. Where the firm faces a downward-sloping demand curve for its product the marginal revenue curve is below price and declines with output. Thus, the MRPL is dragged down by the decline of the MPPL and, additionally, by the fall in the MR, and hence the demand curve for labour is less elastic than under competition. Further, if we compare the demand for labour of a firm having some monopoly power with that of a number of competitive firms facing the same aggregate product demand curve, then at any wage the labour demand curve of the former lies below that of the competitive firms. This is the labour market reflection, of course, of the result that where monopoly elements are present output is lower than it is under competition.

The analysis of the demand for labour of the non-competitive firm in the long run proceeds as in Section 3.2, with the modification of a lower output and a falling marginal revenue that we have just noted. Thus both in the short run and in the long run the basic result of Section 3.2 carries over to firms which possess monopoly power in the markets in which they sell their goods and services; that is, that the demand for labour schedule is the marginal revenue product schedule. Therefore, as long as labour is hired in competitive markets it receives its marginal revenue product.

3.4 Criticisms of marginal productivity theory

From the formal analysis of the earlier sections of this chapter emerge two basic propositions: first that labour tends to receive a wage equal to its marginal product, and second that the lower the wage the more labour is demanded by a firm or industry. We should note immediately that the second proposition, although derived from the first, is not dependent on it. Thus wages may not equal marginal products but simply bear some fairly consistent relation to them. The second proposition would then hold although the first did not.

We will not attempt here to examine all the criticisms that have been made of the theory we have outlined, but rather we shall concentrate on a few objections that are important to our main concerns in later chapters.

Perhaps the most important point is that thus far we have assumed that firms aim to maximise their profits. What happens if that is not the case, and further how do we analyse the demand for labour of organisations, such as universities, which do not sell their products and who have no profits to maximise?

Over the last thirty years it has been increasingly doubted whether firms, particularly large firms, do aim to maximise their profits. The main reason for this doubt is that proprietary companies are run by managers who usually have negligible shareholdings and who therefore do not receive the profits. Is it not more plausible then to assume that managers aim to maximise something that gives them status or pleasure or utility? One of the earliest alternative theories, and one from which we can quite easily see the implications for labour demand, was that firms aim to maximise their turnover or sales revenue. This was advanced on the basis of the observation that managers' salaries seem to be related to the size of the firm rather than to its profits and that managers perceive their status to be similarly related to size. We can analyse the behaviour of such a firm using Figure 3.8.

The firm faces a downward-sloping demand curve for its product and thus total revenue rises then falls with output. Total costs rise with output. From these two curves we can plot the firm's profit curve, which is derived from the vertical difference between total revenue and total costs. The managers of the sales revenue maximising firm cannot ignore profits altogether for some minimum level of profit must be earned to keep shareholders content. Say this minimum level is OD, then we can draw a horizontal line showing the profit constraint.

Sales revenue is maximised at an output of OC, but as profits at that output are below the constraint the firm cannot achieve that level of output. The greatest revenue it can earn while meeting the constraint is that yielded by selling output OB. A profit-maximising firm in identical

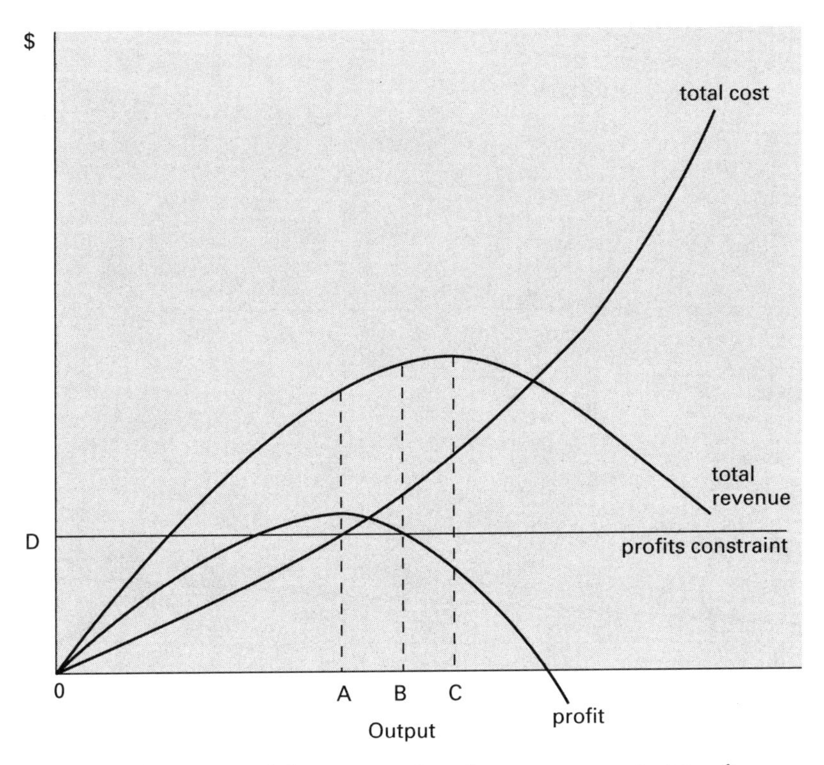

Figure 3.8 The derivation of the output of a sales revenue maximising firm

conditions would produce OA. Thus the sales revenue maximiser produces more, and sells at a lower price, than does the profit maximiser. The implications of this for labour demand are shown in Figure 3.9.

As we have assumed that the two firms (that is the profit maximiser and the revenue maximiser) possess the same revenue and cost schedules, the MRPL curve is the same for both. Given the wage W_0 the profit maximiser employs N_A units of labour. The sales revenue maximiser employs more labour as it is producing more and so goes to a point such as N_B where it pays labour a wage, W_0, in excess of its MRPL. It sacrifices profit to enable it to sell more.

There are alternative maximising models of corporate behaviour, for example, models in which managers maximise a utility function that contains variables other than sales. They tend to lead to the same basic result, that output is greater than it would be if profits were maximised and hence that labour is paid more than its marginal revenue product.

We should note, though, that in our example the demand for labour still varies inversely with the wage rate. Should the wage rate rise the effect in Figure 3.8 would be to shift the TC curve to the left, and move the profits curve downwards, so profits earned would be less than the constraint, and output and employment would fall. An opposite reaction

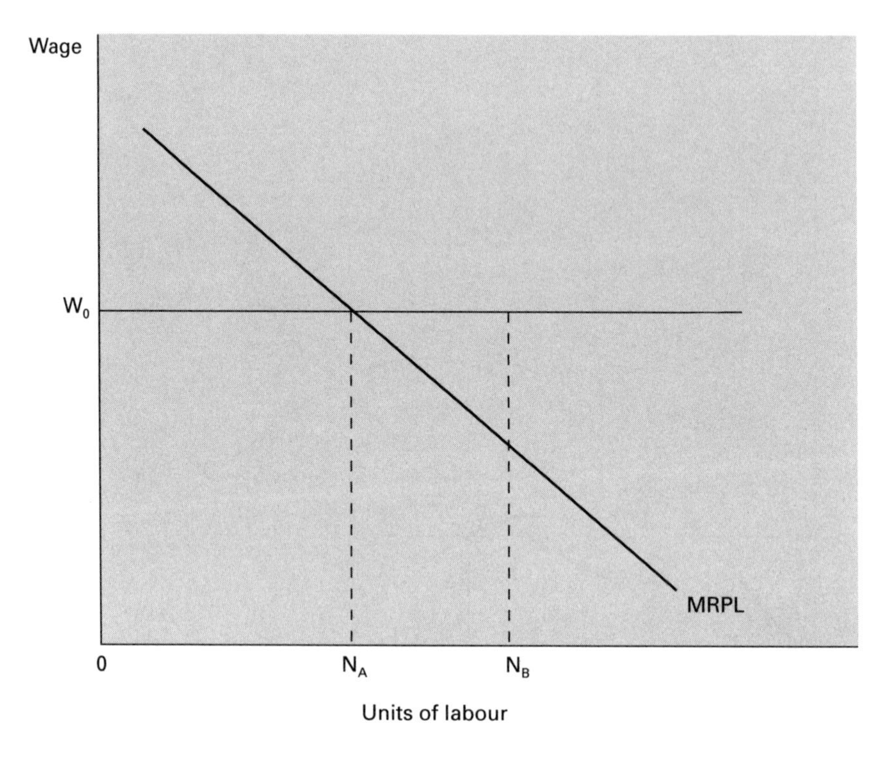

Figure 3.9 Employment under profit maximisation and sales revenue maximisation

would take place if the wage rate fell. Thus although wages do not equal MRP, the demand for labour does vary with the wage in the predicted way.

We now turn to the demand for labour of organisations whose output is not marketed. The non-market sector includes state education and health, other community services, and public administration and defence; currently about 20 per cent of employees are found in this part of the economy. Where there is no marginal revenue product then labour cannot receive it. In this sector, labour receives its average revenue product by conventional definition because in the national income accounts the whole output of such sectors corresponds to the total of wages and salaries paid—there being no profit. We have to abandon marginal productivity doctrine completely here but it still seems likely that employment by an organisation in this sector does vary with the wage. Most organisations are given annual budgets and as the wage of any type of labour increases there is an incentive to economise on its use. Admittedly this begs the questions of how wages are actually determined in this sector and how binding budgets are in practice, but as a general tendency labour demand should be expected to vary inversely with the wage. Studies which have estimated demand for labour equations for non-market sector public organisations have confirmed this. Thornton, for example, has studied the demand for public school teachers in the United States and found that it varies inversely with average teacher salaries, and that the elasticity of demand is in the range -0.6 to -0.8.[1]

A second set of criticisms centre on the determinancy of the marginal revenue product schedule. The most important question is whether firms really ever operate at maximum efficiency. The MRPL curves of Section 3.2 were drawn on the assumption that firms use all inputs in the most efficient way, that is the firm is on its production possibility frontier. It is a common observation that firms do not act in this way and that there is a lot of slack in their operation. This has come to be known as 'X-efficiency'. If a firm now faces an increase in the wage it has to pay its labour force, it may react not by reducing employment but by reducing inefficiency. The effect of this is to shift the MRPL schedule out to the right and thus the demand for labour is indeterminate.

Other objections are technologically based. A problem arises if there are increasing returns to scale. We showed in Section 3.2 that if there are constant returns to scale then the value of the output of the firm will just be enough to pay all factors their MRP. It can also be demonstrated that if there are increasing returns to scale the payment of MRP would not be possible as there would be inadequate revenue. We know that increasing returns to scale characterise many industries. A second technological objection is that in many firms the amount of substitution that can occur in the long run may be very limited, technology demanding fixed input co-efficients. In the short run, as capital is not perfectly divisible, only certain worker to machine ratios may be feasible. The demand for labour then takes the form of a step function rather than of a continuous curve.

By now we have discussed enough cases, in which marginal productivity theory is either inapplicable or inappropriate, to cast severe doubts on our ability to state that the demand for labour curve is derived from the MRPL schedule and whether labour is paid its MRPL. In most cases, however, we can say that the demand for labour varies in a systematic, inverse, way with the wage rate.

3.5 Conclusion

We have seen that, on its own terms, marginal productivity theory provides a precise explanation of the demand for labour. It does not, however, purport to explain wages because for that we need to include supply factors as well. As long as the marginal cost to the firm of a unit of labour is its wage, as it has been in the cases we have looked at, then wages and marginal products should tend to equality. Once the assumptions made by the theory are dropped or modified, however, this basic result is called into question. We have argued, though, that we should generally expect the demand for labour to be greater the lower the wage, and vice versa.

This proposition, that the demand for labour is inversely related to the wage, has received overwhelming empirical support. Various methods of estimation have been used and some studies have estimated the aggregate demand for labour while others have looked at the demand by industries or by broad occupational group.

Surveying a wide range of results, Hammermesh has concluded that in modern industrial economies the aggregate long-run elasticity of demand for labour is probably between -0.15 and -0.50.[2] Industry studies of labour demand tend to produce estimates that are of the same order of magnitude. Occupational studies suggest that the elasticity of demand for skilled labour is less than that of unskilled labour and that the degree of substitutability between capital and skilled labour is less than that between capital and unskilled labour.

Only relatively few estimates have been made of the demand for labour in Australia. Most recent studies of the aggregate elasticity of demand for labour tend to come up with rather higher elasticities than reported above for the United States and Western Europe.[3] Lewis and Kirby, for example, find that over the period 1967–87 the aggregate long-run elasticity of demand for labour is about -0.8.[4]

The results from an Australian industry study are more in conformity with those obtained overseas. Phipps has estimated the elasticity of demand for labour for seven industry groups over the period 1962–82.[5] The estimates vary between -0.15 and -0.50 and for all industry groups the elasticity is put at -0.25.

There is unambiguous empirical support, therefore, for the proposition that, whatever the relation of wages to marginal products, labour demand is inversely related to the wage. Further the elasticity of demand is invariably found to be less than unity.

Concepts for review

- Average physical product of labour
- Marginal physical product of labour
- Average revenue product of labour
- Marginal revenue product of labour
- Isoquant
- Iso-cost line
- Marginal rate of substitution of capital for labour

- Scale and substitution effects of a change in wages on the demand for labour
- Elasticity of demand for labour

Questions

1 Describe the main factors which determine the demand for a particular type of labour, considering both the short and the long run. (University of Adelaide).
2 Explain the derivation of a profit maximising firm's short-run demand for labour. Show the effect on the firm's long-run demand for labour of a decrease in the wage rate. (Macquarie University).
3 How realistic is the marginal productivity theory of labour demand? Discuss how the usefulness of the theory is related to the realism of its assumptions. (Macquarie University).
4 The elasticity of demand for labour in a firm may be very high, while the elasticity of demand for labour in the industry may be low. Explain. How do we expect a fall in the price of capital goods to affect labour demand? (Australian National University).

References

1 R.J. Thornton, 'The elasticity of demand for public school teachers', *Industrial Relations,* vol. 18, 1979, pp. 86-91.
2 D.S. Hammermesh, 'The demand for labour in the long run', in O. Ashenfelter and R. Layard (eds), *Handbook of Labour Economics,* vol. 1, North Holland, 1986.
3 B. Russell and W. Tease, 'Employment, output, and real wages', *Economic Record,* vol. 67, 1991, pp. 34-45.
4 P.E.T. Lewis and M. G. Kirby, 'A new approach to modelling the effects of incomes policies', *Economic Letters,* vol. 28, 1988, pp. 81-5.
5 J. Phipps, 'An examination of inter-industry differences in the relationship between output and employment in Australia', *Australian Bulletin of Labour,* vol. 13, 1986, pp. 36-50.

CHAPTER 4

Education and training

4.1 Introduction

So far we have abstracted from differences in skills possessed by individual workers, and in this chapter we remedy that important omission. The skills used by different people in the labour market, and the time taken to acquire those skills, clearly differ enormously. At one extreme there are jobs requiring little or no skill and at the other are jobs which require many years of training and experience. Although it is unlikely that any two people possess identical physical and intellectual skills we normally define skills broadly with respect to educational qualifications and/or to the type and length of training a person has undertaken.

As a first approximation we can identify three sources of the skills possessed by a worker: first, inherited personal characteristics such as strength and intelligence, which may be developed in the family prior to schooling; second, skills acquired through formal education and training; and third, those skills acquired through work experience and informal training in a work situation. There are interactions between these three elements and, as we shall see, these interactions make difficult the task of estimating the precise contribution made by any one of them. Thus a bright person is likely to receive an above-average amount of education and, as a result, to enter occupations with clearly defined patterns of informal training.

It is important at the outset, in spite of the foregoing caveat, to emphasise that for many workers training in a work situation, which is known as on-the-job training, is a very important source of work skills and may often be more important in this respect than formal education. Certainly estimates which have been made for the United States support this contention. Thurow, for example, citing the findings of the President's Automation Commission of 1964, reported that only 40 per cent of the workforce used skills acquired in formal education and training.[1] The remaining 60 per cent had acquired all their skills through informal training and experience. While the precise percentages quoted should not be taken too literally, they do indicate the importance of on-the-job training.

The main analytical framework we shall use is that provided by the theory of human capital. Although the idea that education may be seen as an investment is about as old as economics itself, it was not until around 1960 that it came to be formalised. The theory of human capital gives us many valuable insights into various aspects of labour markets. It is not without its critics, however, and we shall look at their arguments in some detail.

The chapter has four main sections. In Section 4.2 we outline the theory of human capital as applied to the individual's decision as to how much education to invest in, and Section 4.3 extends this to analogous decisions that the state has to make. In Section 4.4 training is analysed from the perspective of the individual and the firm, and we discuss government policy towards training. In the brief concluding section we present statistics on the overall educational attainment of the labour force.

4.2 Investment in education: the individual's decision

Investment in human capital

The reader will be familiar with the concept of investment in physical capital. A firm tooling up a factory, for example, incurs costs both now and during the installation. Subsequently, returns accrue from this expenditure in the form of the net contributions made to revenue from the sale of the goods produced on the new machines. The characteristic of investment is that it involves waiting: the costs are incurred now, the returns come later. By using techniques of investment appraisal the firm attempts to see whether the magnitude and timing of the returns relative to the initial cost make the investment worthwhile.

We can apply exactly the same procedure to what are termed investments in human capital. The investments with which we shall be concerned are those in schooling beyond the school leaving age (which we take to be fifteen years) as these are the only ones over which the individual has

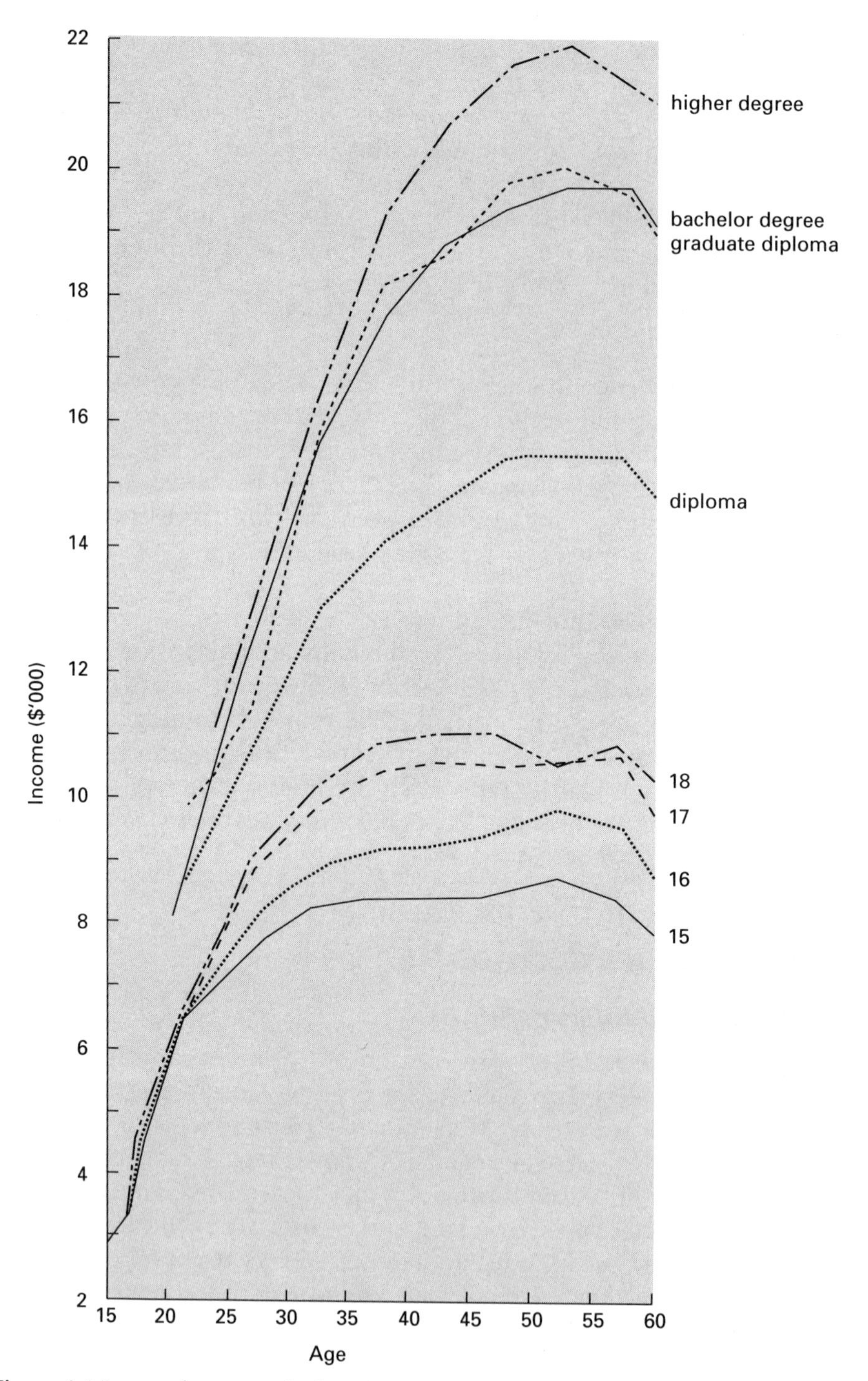

Figure 4.1 Income by age and education: Australian-born males, 1976
Source: P.W. Miller[2]

discretion. If a person stays on at school, or college, after the age of fifteen this will involve some costs. As we shall see the major cost takes the form of income foregone. That is, had the person not been in education then they could be working and earning. Thus they are 'investing' in their human capital.

Where do the returns to this investment in human capital come from? They come from the higher earnings that the person will receive during his or her working life.

Data are available on income by education and by age and from these we can plot what are termed lifetime income profiles. (If data existed on earnings, that is income excluding unearned income, then we could plot lifetime earnings profiles which would be preferable for our purposes. The inclusion of unearned income is most unlikely to distort the picture.) We could also include similar figures for females but it is convenient to discuss data for females in Chapter 7 where we deal with discrimination. The figures presented in this section thus are generally confined to males although the whole of the analytical material applies equally to males and females.

Lifetime income profiles for holders of various amounts of education are shown in Figure 4.1. It is important to understand what these age-income profiles represent. Take the top line which is labelled 'higher degree'. From the census it is possible to obtain respondents' age, educational qualifications, and income. We then plot, for all holders of higher degrees, their average incomes against their ages. Each of the other seven profiles can be interpreted in the same way, that is, they show the average incomes of each educational group by age in 1976. The lower four profiles, labelled '18' and so forth, refer to those who ended their formal education at the age specified.

These profiles have three important features. First, and most important, incomes increase with educational qualification. Although there are one or two intersections between profiles, particularly for younger age groups, lifetime incomes unambiguously increase with the amount of education received. Second, the age income profiles of the relatively more educated tend to be steeper, showing that income increases with age at a faster rate for the more educated. Third, there is a tendency for income to continue increasing with age for a greater number of years for the relatively more educated. It should be stressed that income data sets for various countries and various time periods all produce age income profiles with these characteristics.

What is the relevance of these profiles to the decisions of, say, young people who are seventeen and considering whether to end their education or to enter university? (We will assume that they are qualified to enter university.) The argument proceeds in two steps. First, it is assumed that in terms of the wage and price levels of 1976 all young people leaving school at seventeen have an average chance of following the earnings path labelled '17', whereas if they succeed in obtaining a degree they could expect to receive the graduate earnings pattern. Although the data represented in Figure 4.1 refer to incomes we will henceforth talk in terms of earnings, as only in a very indirect way does education affect income from assets other than education. It must be emphasised that these profiles show the average earnings of each group and there is considerable variation around them. Thus many who left school at fifteen earn more than those who left at some later age and some earn more than those with higher degrees. The average leaver at fifteen does, however, earn less than the average person who continued education beyond that age. Of course, as inflation proceeds, the actual earnings received would be higher than those shown, but all investment decisions should be made in terms of constant prices. Over time, however, real wages increase so that, even in 1976 prices, each of the profiles would tend to shift upwards. As we shall see, in some estimates of the profitability of education an arbitrary annual growth rate is applied to the earnings figures, reflecting the secular rise in real wages.

The second part of the argument is that the earnings difference between the graduate and the seventeen-year-old school leaver is due to the extra three years training undertaken by the graduate. In other words, the difference represents the monetary return to the investment in three years of education. From the point of view of the individual it does not matter why (say) graduates earn more than non-graduates but, as we shall see, from society's point of view the causal relationship is very important.

Thus, the basic principle is that individuals incur costs in undertaking education after the school leaving age. These returns to this investment take the form of higher lifetime earnings.

The estimation of rates of return to education

Whether it is profitable to undertake such an investment in human capital depends upon the rate of return to the investment and on the rate at which individuals discount the future. We begin by looking at the returns and costs in a little more detail and then explain how to calculate the rate of return to education. We shall continue the example of the costs and returns of taking a three year university degree.

In Figure 4.2 we show hypothetical age earnings profiles of a three year trained graduate and of someone who ended their education at the final year of high school, say at age seventeen.

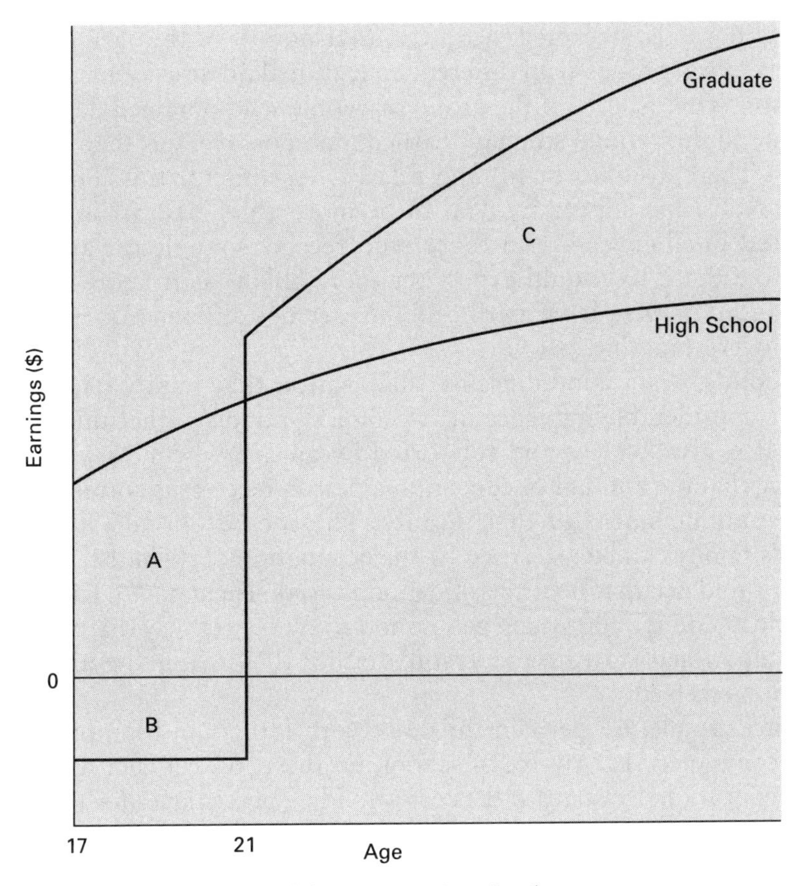

Figure 4.2 Costs and returns of three year university degree

The costs of taking a degree consist of earnings foregone (area A) and of direct costs (area B). Area A represents the earnings foregone as it is reasonable to assume that had the graduate entered the labour market after high school he or she would receive the average earnings of those who in fact did leave education at that point. In actual calculations of the rate of return the after tax earnings of those with high school qualifications are used. Those studying at university also incur direct costs such as expenditure on books and the Higher Education Contribution Scheme (HECS) charge. These can be represented by area B. Some students will be able to offset some of these costs by working part-time or by receiving Austudy awards.

The returns from a degree are represented by the area C, which measures the difference, after age twenty-one, between the earnings of the graduate and those with high school qualifications. The individual receives only the post-tax difference in earnings and therefore we should apply tax rates to each of the earnings profiles.

It is normally accepted, however, that not all of the earnings differences between groups with different educational qualifications are due to education. That is, even if the group of people who obtained degrees had not done so they would still have earned more, on average, than the other groups. There are two main, and related, reasons for this. First, those people who enter university tend to be more able—at least in terms of measured intelligence—than those who receive some lesser amount of education. Since we would expect the more able to earn more whatever their education then, if we ascribe all the earnings difference to education, we are overestimating its role.

Second, it is a commonsense observation that family background exerts a considerable influence on a person's earnings, other things being equal. It is also evident and supported by an overwhelming amount of evidence that the amount of education a person receives is correlated with socioeconomic status of their family. The socioeconomic status of a person's family can be measured by the occupation of the father. In Table 4.1 a six-fold occupational classification is used. The data are based upon a sample of about 2000 young people and show very clearly that the higher the occupational status of a person's father the greater the amount of education received.

For example, 66 per cent of those with fathers in the professional group completed year twelve of school. Of these, 64 per cent went on to higher education. By contrast the corresponding percentages for those with

Table 4.1 Participation rates by father's occupation, 1984 (%)

	Professional	*Managerial*	*White collar*	*Skilled*	*Semi-skilled*	*Unskilled*
Ever completed year twelve	66	50	42	27	26	24
Ever in post-secondary education	76	60	61	52	51	49
Ever in higher education: all persons	43	24	21	13	11	9
Ever in higher education: year twelve graduates	64	48	49	48	35	33
Ever in university	27	12	11	6	4	4

Source: T. Williams[3]

fathers in unskilled occupation were 24 per cent and 33 per cent. Of those with professional fathers 27 per cent went to university (in 1984 universities were distinguished from colleges of education) whereas 4 per cent of those with fathers in unskilled occupations did so. These are extreme cases but it is clear that a similar pattern is evident across all occupational groups.

The correlations between natural ability, family background, education, and earnings mean, therefore, that if we make no allowance for the effect of the former two variables, we will overestimate the contribution made to earnings by education. We shall be referring shortly to estimates of the rate of return to investment in education and shall see that in some cases this problem is simply noted but no attempt is made to allow for it in the estimates. In other work, a proportion of the average earnings differences is ascribed to education, the remaining part of the differences being held to be due to ability, background, and a miscellany of other factors. The proportion of the average earnings difference between groups with different educational qualifications that is attributed to education has become known, for reasons not clear, as the 'alpha co-efficient'. Although typically this is put at about two-thirds, it must be stressed that because ability, background, and education are themselves mutually correlated it is very difficult to disentangle their separate effects and that therefore the figure of two-thirds (or any other figure) must be taken as more or less arbitrary.

We have now discussed the returns and the costs of an increment of education and the final step is to use some form of investment appraisal to ascertain whether this would represent a profitable investment. To explain this it is easiest to take a highly simplified example. Consider a person deciding whether to leave school at age seventeen or to take a three-year university course (assuming she or he is qualified to do so). We will assume that, were the university course chosen, the student would be successful and obtain a degree, and on obtaining the degree earn $24 000 a year from age twenty to age sixty. On the other hand, if the person decides to leave school, he or she would, at constant prices, earn $20 000 a year until retiring at age sixty. (These sets of figures are assumed and not drawn from actual data.) To keep things simple we will assume that all of the $4000 a year earnings difference is due to education, that is the alpha co-efficient is unity, and that the student would not receive an education allowance nor incur any expenses on books, and we will also ignore income taxes. Thus the problem is, simply, does the extra $4000 a year from age twenty compensate for the three years of foregone earnings?

It would be convenient if we could do the sum as follows. The opportunity cost is $60 000 and the return is forty years additional earnings of $4000 a year which amounts to $160 000. Thus as the returns exceed the costs by $100 000 the investment looks to be worthwhile. This would not necessarily be the correct conclusion, however, as sums of money which accrue at different times are not worth the same amount. The reason for this is not the presence of inflation, for in our example all the sums are expressed at constant prices. Money receivable in the future is worth less than money receivable now because real interest rates are (normally) positive. Hence, before sums of money accruing at different periods can be added (or subtracted) they have to be discounted back to their present values.

For those not familiar with the principle of discounting, say the rate of interest is 5 per cent and we wish to compare $1000 receivable now with $1000 receivable in one year's time: $1000 invested for one year at 5 per cent will grow to $1000 (1 + 0.05) = $1050. Thus $1050 receivable next year is worth $1000 ($1050/(1+0.05)) now. What then is the present value of $1000 receivable in one year? It is $1000/(1 + 0.05) = $952.

Consider now the present value of $1000 due in two years' time. If we had the $1000 now and invested it at 5 per cent for two years it would grow to 1000 (1 + 0.05) + 0.05 [1000 (1 + 0.05)] = 1000 $(1 + 0.5)^2$ = $1102.50. Thus the present value of $1000 receivable in two years' time is given by $1000/$(1 + 0.05)^2$ = $907.

In the general case, the present value of $*P* receivable in *n* years, where the interest rate is *i*, is given by the expression $\$P/(1 + i)^n$.

There are two methods of appraising the profitability of investment in human (or physical) capital. The first is to calculate the rate of return to investment in education. If we denote the costs of the investment as C, and the returns as R, where R = the earnings of the graduate—the earnings of the seventeen-year-old school leaver, then to calculate the rate of return we solve for *r* in the following equation, remembering that the costs are spread over the first three years, followed by twenty years of additional earnings:

$$\sum_{t=0}^{2} \frac{C_t}{(1+r)^t} = \sum_{t=3}^{42} \frac{R_t}{(1+r)^t} \qquad (1)$$

In other words, we find the discount rate that equates the present value of the returns to the present value of the costs. This discount rate is known as the rate of return, *r*. Because we are considering only costs borne by, and returns accruing to, the individual, the calculation yields what is termed the 'private rate of return to education'. (The meaning and calculation of social rates of return are discussed in the next section.) The private rate of return has to be compared with the real rate of interest, *i*, as this represents either the return that is foregone by devoting funds to education or, if the individual borrows to finance the course of education, the costs of the finance. In practice, of course, borrowers' and lenders' rates do not coincide and given a wide range of financial assets and institutions there is no unique rate of interest. At any one time, however, there is some average rate of interest which we can take as representing the cost of finance. Say this is 5 per cent. The decision rule then is that the investment, in this case the three years of university education, is worthwhile if the private rate of return r exceeds the rate of interest i.

In our example we have therefore, from equation (1), to find the discount rate that solves the following equation:

$$\sum_{t=0}^{2} \frac{20\,000}{(1+r)^t} = \sum_{t=3}^{42} \frac{4000}{(1+r)^t} \quad (2)$$

In fact the solution is a discount rate of 5.58 per cent (that is, r = 0.0558). Comparing this with a real rate of interest of 5 per cent we find that the investment in the extra three years education is (just) worthwhile and those individuals who base their educational decisions on the monetary rewards would undertake a degree course.

An alternative way of appraising the investment is to calculate the present value of the two lifetime earnings flows, with a discount rate of 5 per cent. The earnings flow of the seventeen-year-old school leaver is obviously \$20 000 a year. We will not discount earnings in the first, or base, year and discounting then proceeds up to forty-three years hence, when the individual retires. As the first year is undiscounted the discount factor forty-three years ahead is $(1.05)^{42}$. The graduate earns nothing for the first three years and starts earning in the fourth year from the start, and we discount the annual earnings of \$24 000 in the same way. The calculation is thus as follows:

(a) End education at age seventeen:

$$\text{present value} = 20\,000 + \frac{20\,000}{(1.05)} + \frac{20\,000}{(1.05)_2} + \ldots + \frac{20\,000}{(1.05)^{52}} = \$368\,464 \quad (3)$$

(b) Take at three-year degree:

$$\text{present value} = \frac{24\,000}{(1.05)^4} + \ldots + \frac{24\,000}{(1.05)^{42}} = \$373\,353 \quad (4)$$

The decision rule using the net present value method is that the alternative which yields the highest present value is the preferred one. In our example the present value of the earnings flow of the degree option is the highest, and this would represent the best investment. Thus both methods of appraisal yield the same selection in our example and this is invariably the case in the appraisal of educational investments.

The example illustrates both the powerful effect of discounting and the possible sensitivity of the results to the rate of interest that is used. Recall that when the two lifetime earnings flows were undiscounted the graduate earnings flow exceeded the seventeen-year-old school leaver earnings flow by $100 000. We have just seen that discounting at 5 per cent the difference is a mere $4889. The reader should be able to confirm from the internal rate of return calculation that at a discount rate of 5.58 per cent the net present value of the two earnings flows will be equal and that at rates above 5.58 per cent the present value of the earnings of the seventeen-year-old school leaver will be greater.

In both methods of appraising the investment it is possible to include some allowance for risk which takes two main forms in this case. First, as we have emphasised, the earnings flows used are simply averages and there is considerable variation of individual earnings around the average. Second, the earnings in any year are only received, of course, if the individual is in employment. Thus some allowance is made in some estimates for the probability of being unemployed.

Rates of return to education in Australia

Let us now look at some estimates of the private rate of return to education in Australia. Miller has made estimates based upon the income data for 1976 that were presented in Figure 4.1. Although we have to refer the reader to the original source for the precise assumptions made in the calculation, the broad principles underlying the results of this study, which are shown in Table 4.2 are as follows: a growth rate of 2 per cent per annum is applied to all the income figures which in turn are adjusted for tax; 80 per cent of the income differentials are assumed to be due to education; and, on the costs side, earnings foregone are adjusted to allow for the average value of education allowances and part-time income.

Table 4.2 Private rates of return to education: Australian-born males, 1976 (%)

To	*From*	
	15 years	*17 years*
16 years	8.3	–
17 years	9.4	–
18 years	8.1	4.3
Bachelor degree	13.5	16.5
Higher degree	11.7	12.9

Source: P.W. Miller[2]

The figures in Table 4.2 are to be interpreted in the following way. The first column shows the rate of return to various educational alternatives compared with leaving school at fifteen and are thus average rates of return. For example to stay on until eighteen yields an average return over the three years of 8.1 per cent, to remain in education and obtain a first degree yields 13.5 per cent on the whole investment since fifteen, and so on.

Estimates for 1985-86 have been undertaken by Chia.[4] Unfortunately, data for this later year do not allow separate estimates for each type of degree. Thus the figures in Table 4.3 are based upon the incomes of those who completed the highest year in secondary school and of those who have a Bachelor degree or higher.

Table 4.3 Private rates of return to education, 1985–86 (%)

	–$660	*$980*	*$3130*
Males	9.7	10.8	12.6
Females	12.6	14.3	17.3

Source: T. Chia[4]

Three estimates are provided, each based on differing assumptions about the amount of income the degree holder received while studying. The direct costs (books and so on) of studying were $660 and hence someone with a monetary income of zero is shown, in column one, as having a net income of minus $660. It is evident that the rate of return to a degree is greater for females. This mainly arises because of marked differences in the participation and unemployment rates of graduate and non-graduate females.

What can we conclude from the figures in the two tables about the profitability of taking a degree? An investment in education is worthwhile, on a narrow monetary basis, if the private rate of return exceeds the real after tax rate of interest. While the estimates are sensitive to the assumptions made we can safely conclude that at the level of interest rates ruling in the 1970s and 1980s a degree represented a profitable investment.

We have described the estimation of the returns to education in some detail. Clearly very few people could have the information or the technique to make such estimates, and presumably very few graduates have ever seen the results reported here. It should also be remembered, as we argued earlier, that the monetary reward from following any educational course is only one influence on the decision to undertake it or not. For example, although study may not always seem pleasurable, it is likely that most students actually enjoy life at university. They thus gain consumption benefits from education which are ignored in the analysis which only includes investment benefits. It does seem plausible to argue, however, that at the margin there are people who, given other factors, are influenced by their perception of the costs and returns to education. This seems likely to be particularly the case where students make their choices between different subjects. The great growth in enrolments in accountancy courses that occurred in the 1970s and 1980s for example, seem, from casual observation, to have been related to the perceived high earnings of those with accountancy qualifications. Significant, and hence recognisable, changes in the profitability of pursuing education to certain levels (or of following certain courses) are likely then to lead to changes in the same direction in the number of young people undertaking such education. The sensitivity of the numbers of students to the net returns is not, however, known.

4.3 Social returns to education

Here we are concerned with the costs and benefits which accrue to society from investment in education. We will assume that society has decided the number of years of education that are compulsory and hence we are dealing with voluntary education above the school leaving age. In practice education within state schools beyond the leaving age has been supplied to all who qualify and who wish to continue, so we shall mainly be considering tertiary education. Virtually all tertiary education is supplied by the federal government and governments thus have to decide how many places to provide. They can also influence what sort of courses, or subjects, are offered.

Estimating the social rate of return

The technique of estimating the social returns to education is precisely the same as that described in Section 4.2 for the private rate of return to education to the individual. The difference in the calculation lies in which costs and returns are included. It is essentially an exercise in cost-benefit analysis, where the appropriate costs and benefits are those borne by, and accruing to, society as a whole.

We will take as our example the same case we discussed in Section 4.2, that is the benefits and costs of a three-year university degree course. The costs to society of providing the university place are, as in the earlier case, of two sorts. First, the opportunity cost, that is the loss to society of the potential output of the undergraduate while studying, reflected in this case by pre-tax (rather than post-tax) earnings. In this case any tertiary education allowances received by the student are not taken into account as they are transfer payments and not relevant to social investment appraisal. The second set of costs incurred by society are the direct costs of operating universities, that is staff salaries and all other running expenses including outlays, such as on books, made by students. As the

HECS charge has been set below the full cost of tuition, it follows that the social costs of providing tertiary education are considerably in excess of those incurred by the private individual.

What are the returns to society from higher education? It is held that the outputs of graduates when they are in the labour market are greater than those of non-graduates. That is, the knowledge and skills acquired in universities raise the marginal products of graduates over and above what they would have been had they terminated their education at the age of seventeen. In Chapter 3 we saw that people's earnings may approximate their marginal products and thus by comparing the lifetime earnings of the graduate with that of the seventeen-year-old school leaver we can arrive at an estimate of the difference between their marginal products over their lifetimes. Thus, as in the calculation of the private rate of return to education, the flow of returns is the difference between the earnings of the graduate and that of the seventeen-year-old school leaver. Here we use pre-tax earnings profiles, as it is these that reflect marginal products.

Note that in this case we have to make two assertions that were not necessary previously: first, that earnings reflect marginal products; and second, that the higher marginal products, and earnings, of the graduate are caused by the extra education received. We will shortly look at these assertions more closely.

The method of calculating the social rate of return is the same as described in the individual case. The difference, to repeat, lies in which costs and returns are included. The social costs are greater than the private costs, but as pre-tax rather than post-tax earnings differences are used the returns are also higher. The net effect is normally that the social rate of return to education is lower than the private return.

Miller has estimated the social rate of return to education in Australia based on the same data as were the private rates of return shown in Table 4.2. A sample of the results are shown in Table 4.4.

Table 4.4 Social rates of return to education: Australian-born males, 1976 (%)

To	*From*	
	15 years	*17 years*
Bachelor degree	13.6	14.7
Higher degree	10.5	10.4

Source: P.W. Miller[2]

In the previous section, we reported various estimates of the private rate of return for 1985-86. Chia has produced analogous estimates of the social rate of return. Assuming a net income while studying of $980 (see Table 4.3) the social rate of return to a degree is estimated to be 9.9 per cent for males and 11.3 per cent for females.

Thus, the social rate of return is slightly lower than the private rate. In order to assess whether, from this narrow economic point of view, tertiary education is a worthwhile social investment the social rate of return has to be compared to the social rate of discount. There is a vast amount of literature on how this rate is to be selected. In practice, the choice is made on pragmatic grounds and currently a (real) social rate of discount of around 10 per cent would be fairly typical in public sector project appraisal. On this basis as the social rate of return appears to be around 10–12 per cent tertiary education represents a worthwhile investment.

It has been argued that estimates of the social rate of return are too low because they ignore any external benefits of tertiary education. That is, the flow of returns is solely derived from the earnings of individuals and does not take into account benefits which accrue to others. These external benefits may take several forms. If higher education develops flexibility and adaptability, then in work situations where this is important other workers will derive benefit from the employment of those with tertiary education. In a similar vein the more educated a workforce the more quickly may innovations be diffused. More educated societies may be more tolerant, more law abiding and so on. These externalities are impossible to measure, so we obviously do not know the extent to which social rates of return are understated.

Chapman and Chia have argued that the level of the HECS charge can be used to provide a valuation of the externalities.[5] The HECS charge is set below the cost of providing tertiary education. If this difference was determined on grounds of economic efficiency then it can be used to provide the implicit valuation placed upon the external benefits by the federal government. While, as the authors acknowledge, this assumes a degree of rationalism unlikely to be possessed by politicians, it is quite an ingenious idea. At a discount rate of 10 per cent the externalities are calculated to be of the order of (in 1988 dollars) $2000 per student.

The human capital approach to educational provision has also been criticised on the grounds that the high correlation between ability, education, and socioeconomic background makes the estimation of the contribution of education to earnings difficult. We discussed this when we were looking at the private rate of return and will not comment further here.

The screening hypothesis

Perhaps the most fundamental criticism of social rates of return has come from what is termed the 'screening hypothesis'. We pointed out earlier that a crucial step in the argument linking education, productivity, and earnings was that a person receiving an increment of education became more productive because of the extra education. It is this link that the screening hypothesis challenges. We shall initially take the extreme case where education is held to have no effect at all on the individual's productivity and shall confine the argument, as do the exponents of this hypothesis, to higher education.

Although this view assumes that education does not in itself increase productivity, it is argued that it is used by employees and employers as a device for transmitting and receiving information about the individual's productivity. To the firm, the hiring of labour is an investment made under conditions of uncertainty. Firms know that they want individuals with high productivity, where we use productivity in the broadest sense as reflecting competence, responsibility, creativity, and initiative as well as the more narrowly defined cognitive and manipulative skills. After a period of time, of course, the worker's productivity becomes apparent. But the period may be quite long and in any event the act of hiring involves the employer in fixed costs which will not be recovered if a poor choice has been made.

How are employers to find out whether job applicants will be productive? Applicants are not indistinguishable:

> They come with various types of education and job experience, they come dressed differently, with different hair lengths, and of different sexes and races. Thus, although the employer does not know what he would really like to know about the individual he does have a quantity of potentially useful information in the form of observable characteristics...[6]

These characteristics may be divided into those such as race and sex which are unalterable and which are termed 'indices' and those, such as educational qualifications, which the individual can change and which are called 'signals'.

Say that employers come to learn that job recruits with higher educational qualifications do, on average, possess those characteristics which they value and that they do have higher productivities than those with lesser amounts of education. Then, although education per se has no effect on worker productivity, employers will use education as a screening device, that is they will select workers on the basis of their educational qualifications. Further, following the marginal productivity theory of the demand for labour, they will pay people on the basis of their education. As education becomes an important basis of pay, it becomes profitable for individuals to acquire education as a means of signalling their natural abilities to employers. Thus education is a way of providing information.

Take graduates as a group, for example. Their natural abilities are higher than non-graduates' so they get paid more. The only way for the individual to gain these high earnings is to take a degree and as a result the private rate of return is fairly high. But this view holds that higher education is economically worthless to society except in so far as it has an allocative function, that is it enables employers to fit people into the right jobs. It is argued that society could obtain these allocative benefits much more cheaply by, for instance, using psychological tests. Thus the amount of education provided, from society's point of view, is too great. Finally estimates of the social rate of return to education are totally misleading because there is no causal link between education and productivity.

We have set out here the screening hypothesis in its extreme form but, of course, nobody could take this seriously as higher education clearly does impart some job skills. The point at issue therefore is whether the screening role of education is a significant one. If it is, then the argument would still be that from society's point of view too much education is provided.

To fix ideas about the job role of education let us take the example of the average reader of this book, following a three-year degree course. Few readers will become professional economists, let alone labour economists, so how will a knowledge of the screening hypothesis or of labour economics help them in their future jobs? In a direct sense very little, if at all. In studying labour economics, however, the reader will, it is hoped, develop skills that are useful to employers, such as an analytical approach to problems, the ability to distil a lot of information into short essays or reports, a knowledge of where to obtain information, and so on. The reader may have friends reading history, philosophy or English and here the likelihood of making direct use of the material covered will be much less. Those taking more vocational subjects like engineering and accounting will use much more of their university-acquired information in job situations. It has to be said, however, that looking across all higher educational courses the direct use that will be made of subject matter is limited.

How are we to test the screening hypothesis? The problem is that both human capital theory and signalling models predict that the higher educated will earn more, as of course they do. How can we distinguish between them? We shall look briefly at some tests that have been made but should state at the outset that they are inconclusive.

Layard and Psacharopoulos have drawn attention to three unverified predictions of the screening hypothesis.[7] First, they argue that certificates (for example, degrees) received at the end of a course should represent a stronger signal than merely having undertaken a course for a number of years and hence that the payoff to a certificate should be greater than that to attendance. They report the results of various studies which show that in many, but not all, cases the rate of return earned by 'dropouts' from a course exceeds that received by those who completed the course. Second, they suggest that if the higher earnings of (say) graduates are due to screening rather than to differences in productivity caused by education, then the earnings of graduates should decline with age as employers learn more about their real productivity. In fact, as we saw in Figure 4.1, earnings differentials between graduates and others tend to increase with age. Against this it can be argued that if education is an effective screening device it will identify those with the highest productivity; if it is not effective then why do employers use it? Thus, it is not clear that this unverified prediction is a very sensible one to start with. Further, as we shall see in the next two chapters, there is a tendency for employers to put the highly qualified into different career structures and to provide them with more intensive on-the-job training. To the extent that this is so we would again expect, if education were used as an important screening device, that earnings differentials would rise with age. Layard and Psacharopoulos finally ask why employers do not use cheaper screening devices. The cost of using degrees as a screen is the net present value of the difference between the earnings of the graduate and an equally able non-graduate. It seems likely that some other screening device, like a day-long interview with psychological tests, would be cheaper. So why are such alternatives not used? A possible answer is that in a society where it is socially conventional for able young people to enter higher education it may be very difficult for an individual employer to break the usual pattern.

More formal empirical tests have been undertaken. Lang and Kropp analysed the effect of laws requiring compulsory attendance at school.[8] Under the human capital view of education such laws will not affect the amount of education received by those who would have stayed on at school anyway, as it will not affect the rate of return to voluntary schooling. The screening hypothesis would come up with a different prediction, however. Say the compulsory school leaving age was raised from fifteen to sixteen. Those who would have stayed on to sixteen anyway will now have to stay on to seventeen in order to signal their superior ability to employers. Similarly those previously staying on to seventeen will now have to stay on to eighteen to distinguish themselves from this later group and so on. From an analysis of time series material going back to 1920 the authors find that the raising of the compulsory schooling leaving age in the United States has had considerable effect on the enrolment rates of unaffected groups. There are, unfortunately, other possible explanations of increasing enrolment rates in voluntary schooling but, nonetheless this is another piece of evidence consistent with the screening hypothesis.

Another test has been proposed by Wolpin.[9] People acquire education to signal their abilities to potential employers. Those who are self-employed do not need to make such signals, however, and thus a simple test would be to compare the educational attainment, E_s, of the self-employed with the educational attainment, E_E, of employees. Screening would predict $E_E > E_s$. How would the difference be expected to vary with the average skill level of an occupation? The authors argue that the difference should increase with the skill level, it being likely that in high-skill occupations the intensity of the education signal is greatest. Various overseas studies have used this method and found support for the screening hypothesis but one application to Australian data by McNabb and Richardson proved inconclusive.[10] Other evidence produced by the latter authors was, however, consistent with the screening hypothesis.

Using Australian data Miller and Volker have attempted to discriminate between the screening hypothesis and human capital theory by applying a test initially proposed by Wiles.[11] Wiles argued that (for example) some economists directly apply their skills as economists in their jobs whereas others move into areas such as line management and do not exercise economic skills.[12] He suggested that under the human capital theory there would be an expectation that those exercising their acquired skills would earn more than those who were not, whereas under the screening hypothesis we would not expect any such difference in salaries. Miller and Volker estimated earnings functions for economics and science graduates separately and include a variable showing whether professional skills were used directly in their work. For both male and female economics graduates, and female science graduates (but not for male science graduates) there was no significant difference in earnings arising from the direct use of educational qualifications. The results are thus, in general, supportive of the screening hypothesis.

Finally, we can refer to the observation that the educational qualifications necessary to enter most occupations have increased over time. At a casual level this is consistent with the screen, for with the expansion of education more people possess (say) degrees and hence the strength of the signal given by a degree declines and individuals are induced to acquire additional qualifications. This tendency has become known as 'credentialism'.

We are forced to conclude that the available evidence does not permit us either to accept or to reject the screening hypothesis. The basic problem, to repeat, is that both the human capital view and the screening hypothesis predict that as individuals receive more education that they will, on average, earn more—as of course they do. Thus indirect tests of screening have to be devised but these are usually open to alternative interpretations.

4.4 Industrial training

We saw in the introduction to this chapter that many job skills are acquired in the context of a work situation. This method of skill acquisition can take several forms and we shall use the term 'industrial training' in a broad sense to refer to any form of training that is closely related to employment. The most formal type of industrial training is that provided off the job, for example, day-release training in a Technical and Further Education (TAFE) college, and the most informal is learning by doing or learning by experience. Between these two extremes is a variety of formal and informal on-the-job training. All industrial training has two characteristics. First, it is related to a particular work situation; and second, it involves costs. The costs of learning by experience, for example, are that the output of the worker while learning is less than that of an experienced worker.

General and specific training

The first question we consider in this section is who bears the costs of training? The answer will be seen to depend upon the type of training with which we are concerned. It is necessary to distinguish between general and specific training.

General training imparts skills which are useful in many firms beside the one which provides the training. Such training raises the worker's productivity equally in the training firm and in at least some other firms. Examples of general training abound—driving vehicles, operating word processors, teaching, most manual craft skills and so on.

Specific training on the other hand raises the worker's productivity only in the training firm, leaving productivity in all other firms unaltered. It is rare in practice to find cases of completely specific training. One largely hypothetical example would be training to operate a process patented by, and used by, only one firm. One very important form of specific training is the acquisition of knowledge about the operational procedures of a firm, who to ask about what, peculiar features of machines, or filing systems and so on. Thus in practice most training involves general and specific elements.

To understand the basic points, however, we shall first analyse the extreme cases of completely general and completely specific training. The issue of who bears the costs of training can best be illustrated with a diagram. Figure 4.3 takes a simple case where all training takes place in one year. The training has a once and for all effect on the worker's productivity. We assume the price level to the fixed.

If the worker were to receive no training assume his or her productivity to be MRP_1, and, from Chapter 2, we would expect that under competitive conditions this would be the wage paid. This wage would be paid throughout the person's period of employment, assumed to be OT years in the diagram.

If training is received then in the first year of employment, the worker's productivity would be some lesser amount, say MRP_0. Productivity is lower as the worker spends part of his or her time watching others and receiving instruction (either on or off-the job).

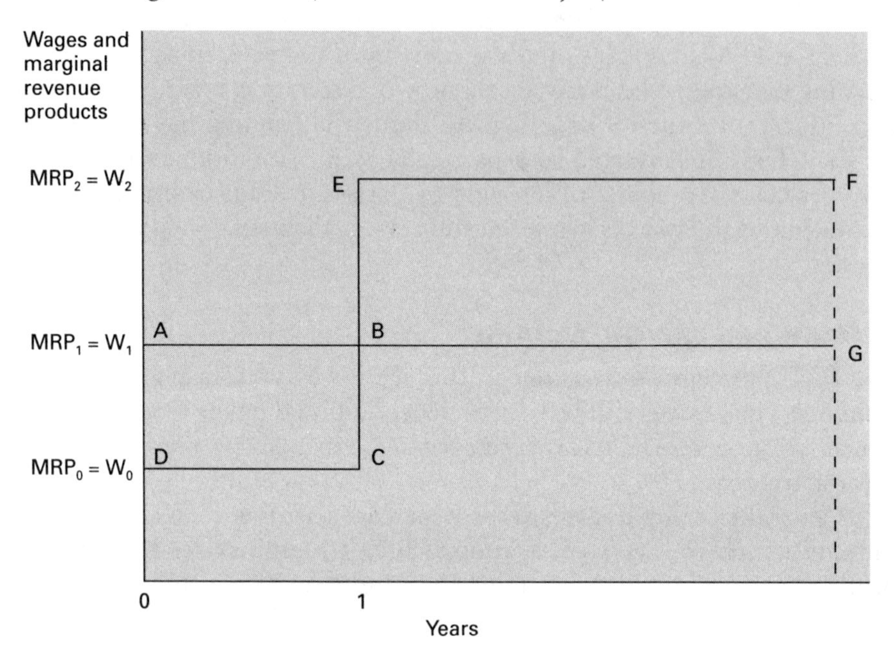

Figure 4.3 Training, wages and productivity

The effect of the training is, however, to raise the worker's productivity to MRP_2 in all subsequent years of employment.

Thus, the costs of the training comprise output lost during training, as shown by the area ABCD, and the returns take the form of higher post-training productivity (area EFGB). We leave aside for the moment how to evaluate whether the investment in training is worthwhile and simply assume it is.

Who will pay the costs? Take the general training case first. The training raises the worker's productivity in a wide range of firms, where he or she could command a wage of W_2 corresponding to his or her marginal revenue product. Thus unless the training firm raises the wage to W_2 on the completion of training the worker will leave. As the worker captures the benefit of the training it follows that the firm will not meet the costs. The firm will shift the burden of the costs on to the worker by paying, during training, a wage, W_0, which corresponds to the marginal revenue product during training. Thus workers bear the costs of general training.

Now consider specific training. In this case, remember, the worker's productivity in other firms does not rise after training and hence neither does the wage that he or she can earn elsewhere. Thus the training firm is under no pressure to raise the worker's wages. On the other hand, the worker would be unwilling to accept a lower wage during training as he or she would recoup none of the benefits of training. Thus the firm pays a wage W_1 during training and thus bears the costs as the marginal revenue product is a lower amount, MRP_0. It recoups by paying the same wage (W_1) after training by which time the worker's marginal revenue product has risen to MRP_2. Thus firms bear the costs of specific training.

The rate of return to training

Industrial training represents an investment in human capital in the same way as formal education. Similarly, it is possible to estimate a rate of return to training and it is reasonable to expect that the amount of training undertaken will depend upon its perceived profitability.

We will, again, consider general training first. The trainee, as we have seen, will bear the cost and receive the return. The question is whether the increase in earnings, after training—area EFGB in Figure 4.3 is enough to compensate for the costs of training—area ABCD.

The costs and returns come at different periods of time and hence we have to discount them back to present values (as explained in Section 4.3). Figure 4.2 is, of course, very simplified. In practice the costs of training will rarely be confined to one year and may comprise other items, such as tools and books, apart from foregone earnings. On the returns side, earnings may increase, over time as further experience is gained. The rate of return to training for the individual is thus given by r in the following equation:

$$\sum_{t=1}^{n} \frac{C_t}{(1+r)^t} = \sum_{t=1}^{m} \frac{W_{At} - W_t}{(1+r)^t} \qquad (5)$$

Here C_t denotes the cost of training (after tax income foregone plus direct costs) for each of the n years of training. On the right-hand side the returns comprise the after tax difference between the wage after training (W_{At}) and the wage that would be received with no training (W_t) in each of the m years of expected employment.

Under ideal conditions we would expect young people to acquire training up to the point where the rate of return came to equal the (real) interest rate. In practice we simply expect the number of people seeking training of a general sort to vary according to the perceived costs and returns. In some labour markets, particularly those for trades occupations, the arrangements for workers to bear the costs of formal training are institutionalised. The best example is apprenticeship schemes. Apprenticeships are formal legal contracts entered into between the apprentice, her or his parents, and an employer, and monitored by state authorities. The employer undertakes to provide training normally over a period of four years. The employer shifts the costs of the training on to the apprentices by paying them less than they could earn elsewhere. As these alternative earnings are, in general, not known, the institutional arrangement is to tie the apprentice's wage to some proportion of the fully qualified wage in the same trade. These proportions vary from around 40 per cent in the first year to around 90 per cent in the final year of an apprenticeship.

The evidence suggests that these proportions have been set too high. Miller has estimated that the private rate of return to a fifteen-year-old undertaking a four-year apprenticeship is about 44 per cent.[13] This is an extremely high figure; to put it in context compare it with the estimates of the private rate of return to higher education. It is not surprising that, invariably, the number of qualified applicants considerably exceeds the apprenticeship on offer.

Specific training can be evaluated in the same way. Here, remember, the firm bears the costs by paying the trainees a wage greater than their marginal products during training and attempts to recoup by paying them a wage less than their marginal products after training. Formally, the rate of return to the firm on specific training is given by r in the following:

$$\sum_{t=1}^{n} \frac{W_t - MP_t}{(1+r)^t} = \sum_{t=1}^{m} \frac{MP_{At} - W_{At}}{(1+r)^t} \tag{6}$$

W_t and MP_t denotes the wage and marginal revenue product during training, W_{At} and MP_{At} those after training. Where other costs of training, such as waste of materials and instructors time, are incurred these should be added to the costs side.

If we look at the rate of return equation (6) it will be seen that for any given level of costs, gross returns, and hence the rate of return, will be greater the longer the number of years (m) the worker stays with the firm after training. In the next chapter we shall examine various ways in which firms might induce workers to stay with them. One obvious method, however, is to pay a higher wage. Thus, in Figure 4.3, although the firm does not have to pay a wage higher than W_1 after training, it may in fact do so in order to reduce the risk of the workers quitting the firm and taking the firm's investment in training with them. Although, by definition, the training is of no use to the worker in other firms it nonetheless represents a loss of an investment to the firm giving the training. Thus, again in terms of Figure 4.3, the wage after training may lie between W_1 and W_2.

Government policy towards training

In Australia, as in most advanced countries, the level of industrial training is not left entirely to the free play of the market, but is influenced in various ways by government action. Evidently it is felt that firms and workers would not by their own actions provide the amount or distribution of training that society requires.

The government supports training directly through the provision of TAFE courses but also provides financial support to firms providing general training. Subsidies have been provided since 1977 to firms offering apprenticeships under a programme known as the Commonwealth Rebate for Apprentice Full Time Training scheme (CRAFT). The precise form of the CRAFT subsidy varies from time to time. In recent years, employers have received subsidies while apprentices are attending off-the-job training (invariably in TAFE). Employers who increase their effective intake over the level of the previous year have also attracted subsidies.

The Australian Traineeship System (ATS) is of more recent origin and was the major outcome of the (Kirby) Committee of Inquiry into Labour Market Programmes which reported in 1985. Traineeships last for one year and offer a combination of work experience and formal off-the-job training. A subsidy is paid to employers and a trainee wage is paid which is lower than the going wage in recognition of the training element. Traineeships are thus really a form of short-term apprenticeship, offered in employment areas where apprenticeships are not available.

Over the past couple of decades, a variety of other schemes have been devised by both state and federal governments to encourage firms to provide training. Most of these, for example the Special Youth Employment Training Program (1976–87), tended to be introduced in periods of high youth unemployment. Despite the training elements in them, they were really attempts to reduce unemployment among the long-term young unemployed.

Why does the federal government subsidise firms who provide apprenticeships or traineeships or simply training? One reason is that subsidies are necessary to compensate for the fact that the award system has set apprenticeships rates of pay too high. We have seen that although apprentices receive only a proportion of the tradesperson's wage, the rate of return to apprenticeship training is very high. While one solution would be to reduce apprentice wages (trainee wages were reduced in the Australian Traineeship System) an alternative is to provide subsidies to firms employing apprentices.

Were firms not constrained by the award system, and were there no subsidies, apprentice wages would undoubtedly fall dramatically. Trainees would finance their training through borrowing or by reducing consumption while being trained. At present there is no capital market to finance industrial training and thus it would have to be financed through reductions in consumption, which young persons may be unable, or unwilling, to make. Thus even if apprenticeships remained profitable for young people, the imperfection in the capital market could cause a reduction in the demand. Thus the CRAFT-type subsidy solution has its merits.

Those most likely to find it difficult to finance their general training are those from disadvantaged backgrounds. In terms of the investment appraisal methods we have discussed such individuals have relatively high rates of discount, or at least they act as if they do, and will forgo opportunities which would be worthwhile for those who discount earnings at a lower rate. From an equity consideration there is a case for discrimination in their favour, and, at least in conception, several past government schemes have favoured disadvantaged groups.

A further possible cause of market failure is ignorance. If potential trainees (and possibly firms) are ignorant of the payoffs from training then, again, a sub-optimal level of provision may arise. Subsidisation is again, however, a second-test solution for the most obvious remedy is to improve flows of information.

Finally, there is little doubt that in recessions individual employers act in a way that is detrimental to their longer term group interests. In recessions the apprenticeship intake is reduced. This happened in 1982–83 and in 1991, when the apprenticeship intake fell by 32 per cent over the previous year. The predictable result is that shortages of skilled workers emerge in the subsequent recovery years. The existence of CRAFT and the ATS allows the government to increase the level of the subsidy in recession years, as was done in 1992, in an attempt to reduce the scale of cuts to apprentice intakes.

Turning to specific training our analysis suggests that firms can recover the costs of such training through lower post-training wages and, unlike individuals, firms are not likely to have significant problems in financing their training. Thus, as many schemes have not drawn the distinction between general and specific training, it appears likely that specific training has been financially supported unnecessarily. It is possible, however, that the ability of firms to recover the costs of specific training is limited in Australia by the existence of minimum rates of pay laid down according to occupation and industry by the Industrial Relations Commission. On the other hand, many workers receive earnings in excess of the minimum award rate and, therefore, by paying only the award rate, or close to the award rate, the firm may in fact be able to depress rates of pay. This latter argument should perhaps be qualified by noting that union power may prevent such a policy. Another method of recovering training costs exists, however, and that is to place a worker on a lower skill classification than the individual's specific skills warrant. It is probable that firms have more flexibility in wage payments than the existence of minimum rates would suggest.

Since 1991, the government has encouraged training through the Training Guarantee Levy. Employers with a payroll of over $0.5 million per year are liable to pay a levy of 1 per cent of their payroll. If they can demonstrate, however, that training costing that amount (or more) has actually been provided, then no levy is payable. Similarly, if training costing less than the firm's liability under the levy has taken place, it can be credited towards the levy. Thus there is a incentive for firms to spend at least 1 per cent of their payroll, for otherwise they pay a levy. The levy has caused some debate. On the one hand, it is likely that it has raised the overall level of training. On the other, if the training was not previously undertaken perhaps it was not considered worthwhile.

4.5 Conclusion

Over the last thirty years or so there has been a great expansion in the number and proportion of young people who stay on at school, and proceed to university, or receive some other post-school education or training. As a result, the average amount of education possessed by the labour force has increased significantly. For example, in 1968 about 2 per cent of full-time workers had degrees, but by 1985 this proportion had increased to about 11 per cent.

We can give a picture of the amount of education and training possessed by the adult population. In Table 4.5 the educational attainment of the labour force is given by age using five classifications of educational attainment.

Table 4.5 Educational attainment of the employed population by age, 1991 (%)

	Age group				
Educational attainment	*20-34*	*35-44*	*45-54*	*55-69*	*Total aged 20-69*
Post-school qualifications					
Degree	11.2	12.7	8.4	5.0	9.9
Trade qualification	14.4	15.0	16.1	13.7	14.7
Other	21.8	24.0	21.2	14.5	20.1
No post-school qualifications					
Attended highest level of schooling available	17.3	9.9	7.8	6.5	11.7
Did not attend highest level of schooling available	35.0	38.2	45.9	60.0	42.6

Source: *Labour Force Status and Educational Attainment*, 1991, (ABS, cat. no. 6235.0).

Note: Columns do not necessarily sum to 100.0 because some people with unknown qualifications are shown in the original totals.

The table reflects the increases in education we have just commented on. The first and final rows are particularly interesting: 11.2 per cent of people aged between twenty and thirty-four possess degrees, whereas in the highest age group the proportion is 5.0 per cent. Only 35 per cent of the youngest age group left school before the final year, whereas in the fifty-five to sixty-nine age group no less than 60 per cent did so. On present trends the stock of human capital possessed by the whole population will of course continue to increase over time.

Concepts for review

- On-the-job training
- Human capital
- Investment in human capital
- Lifetime incomes profiles
- Private rate of return to education
- Social rate of return to education
- Discounting
- Present value of an earnings flow
- External benefits of higher education
- Indices
- Signals
- The screening hypothesis
- Credentialism
- General training and skills
- Specific training and skills
- Apprenticeships

Questions

1 Explain what effect you would expect the following to have on the stock of human capital:
   a) the Higher Education Contribution Scheme (HECS);
   b) a change in the wage structure which makes it more compressed (that is, reduces the differences in pay between high paying and low paying jobs);
   c) reduced job opportunities for youth (University of Adelaide).
2 What is human capital? Discuss the effect of a minimum wage law on the level of investment in human capital (University of Melbourne).
3 What is the relation between the private rate of return to investment in higher education and the social rate of return? Are there any conditions under which fees should be charged for higher education? (University of New England).

4 Why do graduates earn more than non-graduates? (Murdoch University).
5 According to a certain textbook, employers are unwilling to pay for general training. Explain the reasoning on which this statement is based and critically evaluate its applicability. (Curtin University).
6 Does the screening hypothesis represent an alternative to the theory of human capital or is the theory of human capital sufficiently elastic to accommodate the screening hypothesis? (University of Western Australia).
7 'The Australian wages system leads to poor training outcomes, which means that changing it will improve training outcomes.' Discuss. (Australian National University).

References

1 L.C. Thurow, *Generating Inequality,* Macmillan, Melbourne, 1975, p. 78.
2 P.W. Miller, 'The rate of return to education', *Australian Economic Review,* no. 3, 1982, pp. 23-32.
3 T. Williams, *Participation in Education,* ACER Research Monograph, no. 30, Hawthorn, 1987.
4 T. Chia, *Returns to Higher Education in Australia,* unpublished PhD thesis, Australian National University, 1990.
5 B.J. Chapman and T. Chia, 'Financing higher education: private rates of return and externalities in the context of the tertiary tax', *Australian National University,* Centre for Economic Policy Research, Discussion Paper, no. 213, 1989.
6 A.M. Spence, *Market Signalling,* Harvard University Press, Cambridge, 1974, p. 8.
7 R. Layard and G. Psacharopoulos, 'The screening hypothesis and the returns to education', *Journal of Political Economy,* vol. 82, no. 5, 1974, pp. 985-98.
8 K. Lang and D. Kropp, 'Human capital versus sorting: the effects of compulsory attendance laws', *Quarterly Journal of Economics,* vol. CI, no. 3, 1986, pp. 609-24.
9 K. Wolpin 'Education and screening', *American Economic Review,* vol. 67, no. 5, 1977, pp. 949-58.
10 R. McNabb and S. Richardson, 'Earnings, education and experience: is Australia different?', *Australian Economic Papers,* vol. 28, no. 52, 1989, pp. 57-75.
11 P.W. Miller and P.A. Volker, 'The screening hypothesis: an application of the Wiles test to graduates from Australian universities', *Economic Inquiry,* vol. 22, no.1, 1984.
12 P. Wiles, 'The correlation between education and earnings: the external-test-not content hypothesis', *Higher Education,* vol. 3, no. 1, pp. 43-58, 1974.
13 P.W. Miller, 'The rate of return to education: the evidence from the 1976 Census', *ANU Centre for Economic Policy Research, Discussion Paper No. 25,* 1981.

CHAPTER 5

Internal and local labour markets

5.1 Introduction

This, and the following chapters, are concerned with how individual labour markets operate. In this chapter we proceed as follows. In Section 5.2 we analyse how a competitive labour market might operate. This analysis is an application of standard supply and demand analysis. As in the case in markets for goods and services, the conditions of the competitive model are far from fully met in labour markets and hence the results of the analysis have to be qualified. Most of the rest of the next four chapters are devoted to analysing the results of market imperfections and to alternatives to the competitive model.

In the introductory chapter the concept of an internal labour market was explained. In Section 5.3 we describe internal labour markets in more detail and look at the reasons why most firms operate some form of internal labour market, and in the fourth section we look at empirical work on internal labour markets in Australia.

The final section of this chapter is devoted to a discussion of local labour markets and to how workers acquire information about jobs and how they conduct their search for jobs.

5.2 The analysis of competitive labour markets

Assumptions

Let us take the case of the labour market for a particular occupation, for example, accounting clerk. Assume the labour market for accounting clerks has the following characteristics. First, there are a large number of firms employing accounting clerks and a large number of clerks and that neither employers nor workers combine together in a trade association or in trade unions. Second, all accounting clerks are exactly identical and third, there are no obstacles preventing them leaving or joining any employer. Fourth, both employers and workers are very well informed about job opportunities and the availability of workers and about the wages paid by all firms. Fifth, the non-wage conditions of employment, such as fringe benefits and working conditions, are identical in each employing firm.

The equilibrium wage

In such a market, an equilibrium wage will be established for accounting clerks which clears the market, leaving no excess supply or demand. In the following analysis, we assume all other wages (and prices) in the whole economy are constant.

We have already analysed the demand for labour (Chapter 3) and have established that the total demand for clerks will be derived from the marginal productivity of clerks and will be inversely related to the wage. If the demand for accounting clerks is at all typical, it is likely that it will have an elasticity of less than unity (not that this affects the subsequent analysis).

In the first instance, let us take the supply in the short run, which we will define in this context as the period of time in which the number of accounting clerks being trained cannot be altered. In this short-run period the supply of accounting clerks will be positively related to the wage offered. If the wage rises where do additional accounting clerks come from in the short run? It is important to understand that not all people trained for a particular occupation actually work in it. For example, roughly one-half of all people with trades skills work in an occupation other than the trade in which they are qualified. Thus as the wage of accounting clerks rises some will transfer from other employment. Similarly, some people qualified as clerks will be out of the labour market, perhaps raising children. The higher the wage, the greater the number of these that will seek work as clerks. In this short-run period the supply of accounting clerks is likely to be relatively inelastic. Supply and demand will interact in the normal way, as shown in Figure 5.1.

The equilibrium wage will be W_0 and at this wage N_0 clerks will be employed, a number exactly equal to the number of clerks seeking employment at that wage. This equilibrium will be disturbed if either the supply or the demand curves shift.

Take the case where the demand for accounting clerks increases, perhaps due to a change in tax legislation. The demand curve shifts, in

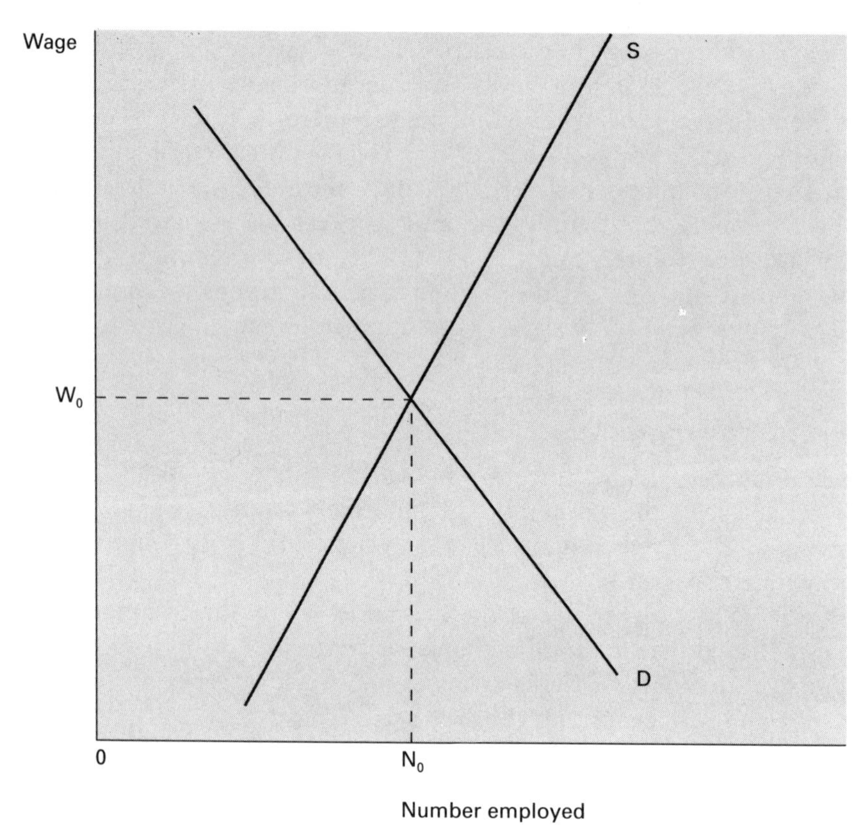

Figure 5.1 Short-run equilibrium in a competitive labour market

Figure 5.2, to D_1 and in the short run a higher equilibrium wage of W_1 is established and more people are now employed as accounting clerks.

As time elapses, however, the supply curve of accounting clerks will also tend to shift to the right. This effect will occur, because the increase in the wage of accounting clerks will have increased the private rate of return to education (or training) courses which lead to an accounting clerk qualification. Thus the number of people entering such courses will increase and hence after a period of time, the length of which will depend on the duration of the courses, there will be an increase in the number of people entering the labour market seeking employment as accounting clerks. As this occurs, and the supply curve shifts to the right, the wage of clerks will tend to fall below W_1 (see Figure 5.2) and in the long run, other things remaining constant, will tend to settle around W_0.

An opposite sequence of events will occur were the demand for accounting clerks to decline, causing the demand schedule to shift to the left. In the short run the wage and the numbers employed would fall. The workers who left accounting would be those for whom the wage fell below

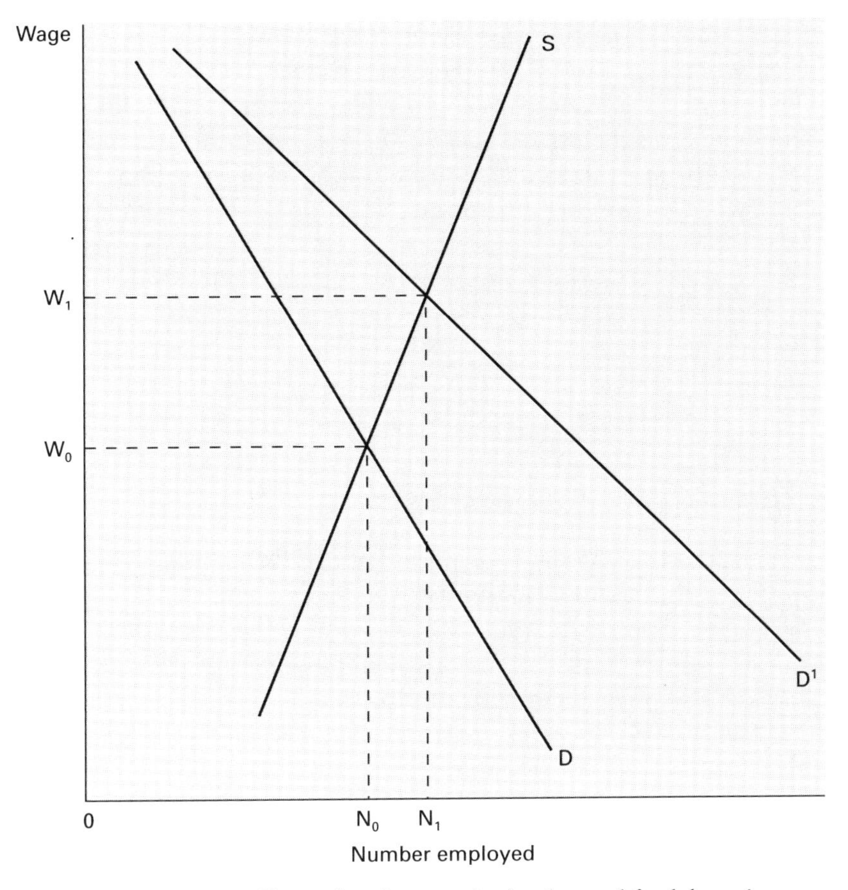

Figure 5.2 The short-run effects of an increase in the demand for labour in a competitive labour market

their supply price. In the long run the decline in the wage in accounting would cause the rate of return to accounting qualifications to fall and the numbers obtaining such qualifications would tend to decline, causing the supply curve to shift to the left, and the wage would tend to increase back towards W_0.

This analysis of a competitive labour market will provide a useful framework, but a glance back at the assumptions it rests upon tells us that it may have to be amended if it is to describe actual labour markets.

In some labour markets there are few buyers. Some (or all) of whom then come to possess what is termed 'monopsony power'. The market for school teachers would be a good example. Over one half of teachers in each state is hired by the Ministry of Education. In many labour markets the sellers of labour join to form trade unions and the employers form employers associations to bargain with unions.

We assumed all accounting clerks to be identical. In practice, clerks, like other workers, come in different sizes, shapes, colours and gender and differ in their willingness to work hard, take initiatives, get on with fellow workers and so on. Partly because of these factors, the assumptions that there are no obstacles to joining a firm, as long as one is willing to work at the going wage, or leaving a firm, often do not hold. The reasons for this are the subject matter of most of the rest of this chapter. As we shall see, in the final section, workers and firms are often ill-informed about wages and vacancies. Finally, jobs vary enormously in their non-wage conditions of employment.

At various places in the next six chapters we look at how these conditions affect the operation of labour markets.

5.3 Internal labour markets

A key characteristic of the vast majority of labour markets is that the person presently occupying any job has rights over those who do not occupy the job. These job rights may, in ways we will shortly describe, be institutionalised by trade unions or by employers, but they exist even in the absence of institutional rules. Employers and workers form attachments for each other and a job is normally not open to competition from outsiders as long as its occupant performs satisfactorily. A crucial distinction then exists between the 'ins' and the 'outs', with those in particular jobs enjoying preferential treatment over those who are not in those jobs.

Where this distinction exists, and its existence is very widespread, it follows that we can envisage each employing unit as constituting a labour market of its own. Such markets are known as 'internal labour markets'.

The main features of internal labour markets

Although the notion of an internal labour market can be traced back to around 1940, the analysis of such markets was advanced considerably with the publication in 1971 of a book by Doeringer and Piore.[1] In it they define an internal labour market as:

> an administrative unit, such as a manufacturing plant, within which the pricing and allocation of labour is governed by a set of administrative rules and procedures. The internal labour market, governed by administrative rules, is to be distinguished from the external labour market of conventional economic theory where pricing, allocating, and training decisions are controlled directly by economic variables.

The internal labour market is insulated from the 'external' market where economic variables, perhaps operating in the way described in Section 5.2, determine the wage and the allocation of labour. Internal labour markets can never be completely insulated from the external market, and the forces operating in it, because movement from the external into the internal market has to take place. The job classifications at which such movement occurs are known as 'ports of entry'. Jobs which do not constitute ports of entry are always filled by internal promotion.

In an internal labour market there will be a set of jobs arranged in hierarchies. These hierarchies then provide a set of job ladders which workers can ascend. Most, and sometimes all, recruitment takes place in lower level jobs, that is, the ports of entry into the internal market are at the lowest job classifications. Workers entering an internal labour market are normally subject to a probationary period, but once this is passed they will not face competition from outsiders for their jobs, even if outsiders would be willing to accept a lower rate of pay. The 'ins' are insulated from competition from the 'outs'.

Workers progress up job ladders by acquiring on-the-job skills and, more generally, experience. The length of the job ladder will depend upon the nature of the job. For blue-collar workers, job ladders may be quite short, ending at some supervisory level. For white-collar workers, particularly those with post-school qualifications, job ladders may be very long with individuals having the potential to gain promotion for much of their careers. How far up the ladder any one individual will progress will depend upon their perceived performance. Some will make significant progress, some will not progress beyond the first few steps of a job ladder.

Consider the following two examples of job hierarchies and of internal labour markets. The first is that found in vehicle building plants and is portrayed in Figure 5.3.

The vehicle factory is divided into many job sections, one of which is shown in Figure 5.3:

> Each job section has a few dozen workers. The lowest positions in the section are made up of ordinary manual workers, and one ordinary worker is usually engaged at one job. The next level is comprised of relief operators, whose job it is to take the place of ordinary workers in the section when the latter take a rest or are absent. One relief operator is expected to cover several jobs, so one job section has a few relief operators. The next position is that of leading hand. There are one or two leading hands in each section, and they cover about ten to twenty jobs. Their work mainly involves trouble-shooting and assisting the foreman. The next position is that of foreman. Foremen supervise the workers and production in their sections and are regarded as white-collar workers. There are a few general foremen in a factory, with a responsibility for several job sections and a large job area. All of these workers are occasionally promoted to the higher positions of officers in such managerial sections as personnel or industrial relations.[2]

The main port of entry is 'ordinary worker'. While it is possible to enter the other job classifications from outside a company, the majority of these jobs are filled by internal promotion. In his case studies, Matsushige

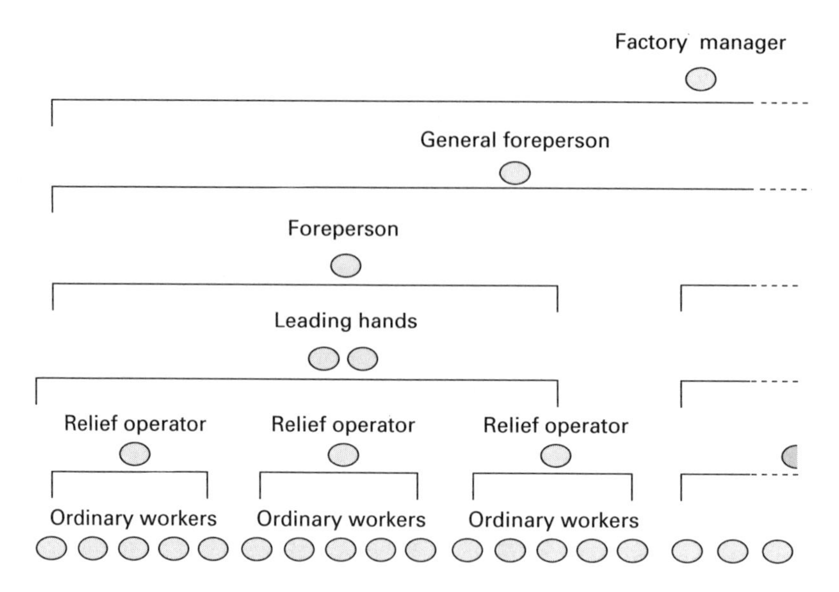

Figure 5.3 The job hierarchy in vehicle building companies
Source: Matsushige 1989

found that over three-quarters of promotions were internal to the company concerned.

A second example is the internal labour markets operated by trading banks. Nowak has undertaken a case study of such a bank and found that the bank has different recruitment policies for the general retail function area and for specialists such as lawyers and electronic data processors.[3] While the latter groups are recruited at several job classifications, recruitment for the general area places employees on a job ladder stretching from the most junior clerical position through to senior management. Over three-quarters of those joining this job ladder do so at the bottom, as school leavers. In recent years some mature-age recruitment has occurred, almost invariably to relatively junior positions. Thus virtually all middle and senior positions are filled by internal promotion in internal labour markets.

As advancement will depend at least in part on the number of years spent with the employer, labour turnover will tend to be relatively low. For reasons we will discuss shortly, employers may reinforce this tendency with other mechanisms designed to reduce turnover, such as non-portable superannuation schemes.

A final and very important feature of internal labour markets is that wages are tied to jobs rather than workers. That is, a clerk grade 3, or a manager grade 2, for example, will have a salary, or a salary scale, tied to it and whoever occupies that job will receive that salary. This is an apparent contradiction to traditional theory, as set out in Chapter 3. As we shall see, marginal productivity must ultimately influence pay but in a broader sense, either over several periods of time or among a group of workers, than marginal productivity theory would suggest. The internal pay structure once evolved will, as we shall see, change only slowly, but will tend to be relatively unresponsive to changes in the external labour market.

As we shall see there is convincing evidence that internal labour markets are widespread in Australia, as they are in all industrial economies. Why do firms choose to operate internal labour markets? There are several forces which favour the generation of internal labour markets. The first is the existence of fixed (as well as variable) costs of hiring labour which has led to the notion of labour being what is termed a quasi-fixed factor of production.

Labour as a quasi-fixed factor of production

In orthodox theory, as in Chapter 3, labour is viewed as a variable factor of production whose employment can be varied by the firm in line with variations in the level of production. Correspondingly, labour costs are counted as variable costs. In fact some of the costs of hiring labour are invariant with output (or with the period for which labour is employed) and hence, like those of capital, are fixed costs.

Thus labour is a quasi-fixed factor of production, some costs of which are fixed with respect to output while other costs vary directly with output. This idea was first developed by Oi and the material in this section is based upon his pioneering work.[4] The analysis is similar to that of on-the-job training, which was covered in Chapter 4.

The variable costs of employing labour are the wages paid. The fixed costs are of two types. First, the cost of hiring labour, which includes the costs of advertising vacancies, screening applicants, and other recruitment costs. We would expect these costs to be positively related to the skills and qualifications required by, and thus the wage attached to, the job to be filled.

Second, there are the costs of any training that is given to new employees. We saw in Chapter 4 that the costs of specific training tend to be borne by the firm while the costs of general training are met by employees. Assuming that to be the case, it is the costs of specific training that constitute the second element of fixed labour costs.

The total cost, C, in present values, of hiring an additional worker is thus the discounted sum of the wages, W, over the expected period of employment, T, plus hiring costs, H, plus the cost of training, K. For simplicity, we will assume all training to occur in the first year of employment. The total cost of an additional worker can therefore be written as:

$$C = \sum_{t=0}^{T} \frac{W_t}{(1 + i)^t} + H + K$$

The present value of the returns, V, to employing an additional worker is, of course, that of the worker's marginal product over the expected period of employment. Thus:

$$V = \sum_{t=0}^{T} \frac{MP_t}{(1 + i)^t}$$

Profit maximisation demands that people are employed up to the point where marginal costs equal marginal returns, that is where:

$$\sum_{t=0}^{T} \frac{W_t}{(1 + i)^t} + H + K = \sum_{t=0}^{T} \frac{MP_t}{(1 + i)^t} \quad (1)$$

In order to derive some implications from equation (1) it is convenient to simplify it. First, say that the firm assumes that the wage and the marginal product will be the same in each period, where W^* and MP^* represent these constant values. Second, we convert the fixed costs into annual terms by amortising them over the expected period of employment, using the method described on p. 52, and call this annual sum the periodic rent R. This represents the fixed cost, in annual terms, of hiring an additional worker. Equation (1) can therefore be presented more simply as:

$$W^* + R = MP^* \quad (2)$$

On the marginal worker to be hired, marginal products thus have to exceed wages by the amount of the periodic rent. We can use the left-hand side of (2) to measure the degree of fixity of a factor as:

$$\frac{R}{W^* + R}$$

Fixity will vary: from zero for a perfectly variable factor, which has no periodic rent, to unity for a perfectly fixed factor which has no variable cost, when W^* would be zero.

The simple result shown in equation (2) is a very useful one, and we shall draw on its implications in subsequent chapters. While it is in front of us, let's digress for a moment to derive an important result before demonstrating how the fixed costs of employing labour can offer one explanation of the widespread existence of internal labour markets.

Take a firm in long-run equilibrium satisfying equation (2). Now say there is a decline in the demand for its product. Thus marginal product declines, so that:

$$W^* + R > MP^*$$

Should the firm lay off workers to restore the equality? The theory of the firm tells us that in the short run, sunk costs, that is those already incurred, are irrelevant to decisions. As long as labour covers its variable costs it should continue to be employed, as any contribution to sunk costs is better than none. Thus in the short run labour is employed up to the point where $W^* = MP^*$ (which is, of course, the basic result of Chapter 3 in which labour was treated as a purely variable factor).

As long as there are some fixed costs of employing labour these therefore cushion workers from the effects of cyclical downturns. Further, the greater the degree of fixity, the stronger is the cushioning effect. This proposition enables us to test the quasi-fixed hypothesis for we would predict that skilled workers, who are likely to have relatively high periodic rents, would experience greater stability of employment than unskilled workers. The latter would have relatively low periodic rents and hence in a cyclical downswing soon reach the point where $W^* = MP^*$, and they are laid off. When we look at the evidence we find that this proposition is very well founded.

The periodic rent is the fixed costs of employing labour, amortised over the expected period of employment. It follows from equation (2), or in capitalised terms from equation (1), that the firm would at least wish to ensure that the worker stays for this period. Furthermore, if the worker stays beyond the period in which the fixed costs of employment are recouped then the firm may earn a surplus on its investment in hiring and training. The firm thus has an incentive to reduce turnover and we shall see shortly that one of the characteristics of internal labour markets is the existence of devices which have the effect of inducing workers to stay with the firm for long periods. Further, in hiring labour, firms may wish to attempt to select those workers whose characteristics suggest that they will wish to remain for extended periods. We cannot, of course, deduce that such measures would be necessarily profitable for they will incur costs which have to be set alongside the benefits of extended employment.

Specific and idiosyncratic skills

As we have just seen, the existence of firm-specific skills gives the firm an incentive to extend the period of employment to protect its investment in specific training. We should emphasise that the term 'specific skills' needs to be interpreted broadly for there are few machines or processes that are used in only one firm. However, Doeringer and Piore, for example, went to some lengths to argue that specific skills are very common and that 'there are no true examples of a completely general skill'. Their examples were drawn largely from production processes and the argument is basically that every piece of machinery is more or less unique, that its operation gets modified over time so that standard manuals are inadequate, and so both technology and the associated jobs become specific. In non-manual occupations, specific skills should be interpreted to include a knowledge of procedures and of organisational structures, personal contacts with, for example, customers and people in supplying organisations and so on.

Whatever the definition of specific skills, it is clear that they can only be acquired through on-the-job training. For if skills are related to a job or a machine or a procedure it follows that they can only be learnt in a work context. As we have seen, the distinction between on-the-job training and learning by doing is blurred but the help and advice of fellow workers has a crucial role to play in both. In order that this assistance be given freely it is necessary that workers be assured that those whom they help to train do not pose a threat to their jobs in the future. Protection from such a threat takes various forms. The most important is that once a worker passes a probationary period his or her job is secure as long as some minimal level of competence is displayed and as long as product market conditions allow. If product market conditions deteriorate workers are normally protected from those who they train by a system of seniority rights which include first-in-last-out redundancy rules.

A further explanation of the role that the existence of specific skills plays in the promotion of internal labour markets has been offered by Williamson.[5] His argument is that most tasks are 'idiosyncratic', an adjective which broadly corresponds to our term 'specific'. In the absence of some sort of institutional framework a lot of time would have to be devoted to individual bargaining but the internal market, with its set procedures, and with its tendency to attach wages to jobs rather than individuals, avoids the need for such costly bargaining.

Information

A third reason why many firms operate internal labour markets is that they provide information about workers and lead to efficient recruitment. Consider a firm wishing to appoint an office supervisor. It can either appoint someone from within the organisation or it can recruit from outside. If it does the latter it can gain information on applicants from various sources. It can examine applicants' educational qualifications, and their career records as provided in their resume. In some cases it may be possible to gain written or oral references from an applicant's previous employer although information of this sort has sometimes to be viewed with suspicion, for obvious reasons. Some applicants will be interviewed and further information about them—what they look like, how they speak, their views on certain matters—can be obtained.

If, however, the appointment is made from among existing employees it is likely that better information will be available. Management will have greater knowledge of the skills, behaviour and other characteristics of its existing workforce than of applicants from outside. This will be particularly so of characteristics like willingness to work hard, show initiative, and the ability to get on with people.

Thus there will exist a clear tendency for firms which operate internal labour markets to recruit, at job classifications higher than ports of entry, largely (but not entirely) from within. This tendency may be stronger the higher up the job hierarchy the job in question lies. We saw earlier that the banking case study found that external appointments to managerial positions are confined to junior levels. Blandy, in a survey of executives, found that 80 per cent of chief executive officers and 60 per cent of all senior executives were recruited from within their respective organisations.[6]

Custom and practice and worker preferences

Doeringer and Piore, in their analysis of internal labour markets, placed some emphasis on custom and practice, a phenomenon which has received more emphasis in the literature of industrial relations than in labour economics. The term is used to summarise the rules, usually unwritten, governing all aspects of the work relation. Although unions, in the form of shop stewards, may often be the vehicle through which such rules are interpreted and enforced, custom predates unions and exists in the absence of unions. The main point for our purpose is that custom-and-practice, which governs the actions of members of work groups, imposes structure on the labour market. More generally, the actions of workers seem to suggest that they value the stability offered by employment in internal markets. Employment itself is more stable than in unstructured markets and the allocation of jobs and prospects for advancement are determined by seniority rules and by custom rather than at the sometimes arbitrary whim of supervisors and management. Doeringer and Piore argued that workers should thus be willing to accept lower wages to gain these benefits and consequently there is a gain to the firm. While this may well be so, it is a difficult proposition to substantiate for, as we shall see, wages in structured markets tend to be higher than those elsewhere and the pay and stability offered often result in queues of workers wishing access to such employment. Perhaps alternatively we might argue that the premium placed by workers upon internal markets is reflected in morale and the gains come from subsequent improvements in industrial relations and in productivity. (We shall explore in more detail the relation between wages and worker productivity in Chapter 8 when we discuss the concept of efficiency wages.)

A classification of internal labour markets

We have identified three potential sources of gain to employers from operating an internal labour market. The first comes from reduced labour turnover. In the competitive model of the labour market described in Section 5.2 turnover has virtually no costs, for workers are identical and easily replaceable. Once there are fixed costs in employing labour then turnover brings costs with it. We saw in the previous section that the greater the fixity of labour as a factor of production, the more costly turnover is. In particular, the more specific are skills, the greater are the rewards from measures designed to reduce labour turnover.

What measures can firms adopt to reduce labour turnover? First, the existence of job ladders gives workers an incentive to remain with firms for long periods of time. Second, employers often provide seniority rights (apart from the increased possibility of promotion). Such rights will include, as we have seen, first-in-last-out layoff rules and first choice of overtime opportunities. Third, firms may provide superannuation schemes that are only worth their full value if the employee stays with the firm until retirement age. These can provide very powerful incentives to remain with a firm. Fourth, turnover is inversely related to the level of earnings and so can be reduced by the payment of above average wages. The various wage strategies that may be followed are discussed further in the final section of this chapter.

The second source of cost reduction comes from the contribution of internal markets to efficient recruitment. We have seen that internal recruitment is efficient because management has greater knowledge of the skills, behaviour and work characteristics of its existing workforce than of applicants from outside. Third, workers seem to prefer stable employment patterns and hence gains from improved morale may accrue.

These are the returns to operating internal labour markets. Costs, higher wages for example, are also incurred. To the extent that such markets seem to characterise large sectors of employment in advanced economies we must assume that there are net gains to be made. These gains would not be equal in all markets and therefore we would expect internal markets to differ in their degree of openness, the greater the gains the more closed the internal market.

A three-fold classification of internal labour markets can be used—open, manorial and guild. 'Open' labour markets are those in which there are ports of entry at all job classifications so that the line drawn between the internal and external labour market is very thin. From our analysis we would expect to find such markets operating where specific training is unimportant and where little capital or machinery is used. Here the costs of labour turnover are low with correspondingly little incentive for the firm to internalise the labour market. In open labour markets 'ins' do have preferential rights over 'outs', but the existence of many ports of entry implies that such internal labour markets are very exposed to conditions in the external market.

'Manorial' or 'enterprise' labour markets are those which can be described as closed internal labour markets with few ports of entry and with well-defined promotion or progression lines. For manual workers the boundary of such markets is normally the plant whereas for administrative and managerial workers the unit is the firm.

The third classification is the 'guild' labour market. Such markets exist in occupations in which general training is important and where skills are recognised by certificates. Examples would be craft workers who have served an apprenticeship and, in white-collar occupations, accountants and lawyers. Their general skills allow them to move between firms but rarely between occupations or industries. Seniority rights for such workers normally depend upon experience in the occupation rather than within the firm. From their analysis Doeringer and Piore conclude that pricing and allocation within guild markets are subject to administrative rules and thus, despite the potential mobility of such workers, they are to be treated as internal labour markets.

It should be emphasised that firms may adopt a strategy of operating one type of labour market for some worker groups and another for others. For example, in the banking industry, most employers have manorial labour markets for those engaged in branch banking and in general management and guild labour markets for electronic data processors, lawyers and other professionals. Another example arises in retailing. Here it is common for a manorial labour market to be operated for a core of supervisory and managerial staff and for a large number of casual workers to be employed on an open labour market basis.

5.4 Internal labour markets in Australia

In this section, we review the evidence on the extent of internal labour markets in Australia. The evidence can be divided into three types. First, the direct evidence of those who have undertaken case studies in individual firms. Second, we can use material on how long people remain in their jobs, for if internal labour markets are common we should expect to find jobs lasting for quite long periods of time. Third, there exist studies of how employers adjust to changing labour market conditions; the relevance of this material is that in internal labour markets we would expect the wage responsiveness to changing conditions to be weak. Our discussion of the third set of evidence will be relatively long as it provides valuable insights into broader aspects of labour market behaviour.

Case studies

Some case study work on internal labour markets has been undertaken in Australia. Maglen and Daly investigated the employment of engineers in ten organisations; they developed various criteria to identify internal labour markets and found that in general the criteria were satisfied.[7] Turnover rates were found to be low, and in all but one firm over half the employees had been with the organisation for the whole of their working lives. Most ports of entry were near the base of the job hierarchy and clearly defined promotion patterns were easily identified. Although on-the-job training was seen by employers and employees as important, the sorts of skills imparted tended to be general rather than specific. Finally, the ways in which firms were adjusting to the then current surplus of engineers, and had adjusted to shortages in the past, were consistent with the existence of a formalised internal labour market. Relative wage changes were eschewed, although we should note that the existence of a basic award rate for engineers would in any event constrain downward adjustment to some extent. There was, in the firms studied, clear evidence of rigid internal wage structures. When there were surpluses of new recruits, hiring standards were tightened, graduates being employed rather than diplomates. Where shortages occurred recruitment standards were relaxed with a corresponding increase in training, and positions were reclassified with, for example, technicians filling jobs normally occupied by junior professional workers.

A study of qualified workers in Western Australia similarly confirmed the existence of internal labour markets.[8] In the nineteen organisations studied it was common to find only two ports of entry, one for school leavers and one for graduates, with most other posts then being filled internally. The common rationale for such a procedure was the importance of on-the-job training and the desire to minimise turnover. Ports of entry for those with specialist skills of a general nature, for example, lawyers, were commonly found at all levels, suggesting a guild-type market for such workers.

Nowak has studied the labour market operated by a trading bank.[9] General management employees were in a very closed manorial internal labour market with clearly defined job ladders and with few ports of entry. The labour market for specialist employees was characteristic of a guild market, with a greater level of labour mobility. In the case of specialists internal promotion was quite common, however, and jobs were not fully open to the external market. We can also refer again to the study by Matsushige of labour markets in the vehicle building industry.[10] We showed the job hierarchy in Figure 5.3 and reported there that the majority of post-entry level jobs are filled by internal recruitment. The authors of both of these latter case studies suggest that a major motivation of management in operating closed manorial labour markets was the information gained about the skills and other characteristics of workers.

Nowak and Crockett have analysed labour markets for all types of employees in three firms.[11] Their findings showed in each case that fairly closed internal labour markets existed. Most recruitment took place at the lowest job classifications, well-defined job ladders existed with standard entry requirements for each job ladder, and firms stressed the importance of skills acquired through experience.

Thus, the work so far undertaken confirms the existence of internal labour markets with few ports of entry in the cases studied. We suspect that similar conclusions could be drawn elsewhere, and certainly casual empiricism indicates, for example, the operation of internal labour markets in much of public sector employment.

Job durations

The relevance of estimates of how long people stay in jobs is that we would expect labour turnover to be low in internal labour markets and, correspondingly, that people would stay with their employers for relatively long periods of time. This expectation arises because, on the one hand, employers wish to protect their investment in firm specific skills and on the other because workers will wish to progress up job ladders.

The length of a job is defined by the Australian Bureau of Statistics as a continuous spell of employment at a specific location with one employer. From an annual survey undertaken by the ABS one can estimate the durations of two sets of jobs. As we shall see there is an enormous difference between the two sets, a difference which gives us a powerful insight into how the labour market works, and we must be careful to understand the basis of the two sets of estimates.

Consider all those people who were occupying a job, at the time of the ABS survey in 1990. We can calculate how long these jobs will last from when they began in the past until when they will end some time in the future. (The reader may wonder how, without a crystal ball, one can foresee how long a job is going to last into the future, but in fact the method is very simple.[12]) In Table 5.1 this estimate is referred to as the completed length of jobs held in the survey week.

During 1990 a large number of people will have entered a job. That is, a large number of job durations will have commenced in 1990. Thus the second estimate is of how long the jobs that began in 1990 will last from their starting date in 1990 until their occupant leaves them. In Table 5.1 this estimate is referred to as the completed length of jobs starting in 1990.

Table 5.1 Job durations, 1990

	Completed length of jobs held in survey week (years)	*Completed length of jobs starting in 1990 (years)*
Males	14.9	2.1
Females	10.1	1.9

Source: Calculated from *Labour Mobility*, (ABS, cat. no. 6209.0).

Consider the first column which shows the durations of those jobs that were occupied at the time of the survey. These jobs last a very long time, nearly fifteen years in the case of males. Jobs held by females tend to have shorter durations as most females leave their jobs at some stage to have children. Bearing in mind that these job durations are averages, they imply that many people stay in one job for much of their working life. How are we to reconcile this with the estimates, in column two, of how long jobs that started in 1990 will last? Because the probability of leaving a job declines with the length of the period for which it has been held. Those males who have held a job for less than three months, for example have about a 60 per cent chance of leaving it in the next year. Males who have held a job for between fifteen and twenty years have about a one in fifty chance of it ending in the next year. These declining probabilities are themselves the result of two tendencies. First, due to different characteristics and attitudes, as job durations increase those who remain are increasingly likely to be stayers whose individual probabilities of leaving jobs are low. Second, and very relevant to our main theme, as duration increases the chances of leaving decline because job attachment increases, job ladders are climbed, and the firing practices of employers favour stayers.

So the picture we gain is one of a large number of short jobs co-existing with long job durations for those who have been termed as the 'hard core of the employed'. We shall return in subsequent chapters to look at some implications of this but the point at issue here is that the very long job durations of those currently employed at any time are totally consistent with, and a logical outcome of, the widespread existence of internal labour markets.

Adjustment to changing conditions

The third set of evidence supporting the proposition that internal labour markets are typical comes from studies of how labour markets adjust to changing conditions. We have seen that the internal labour market is, to some extent, insulated from changes in the external labour market. We would expect then that the more closed an internal labour market is, the weaker would be the wage response to changing circumstances and, correspondingly, the greater the burden of adjustment that would be carried by quantities and qualities. For labour markets have to adjust in some way. If there is a change in the relation between the demand for, and supply of, labour then, if the wage does not change, either the quantity of labour employed or its quality must.

The main conclusion reached by a series of case studies of Australian labour markets was that:

> ...imperfectly flexible wages are a persuasive feature of a range of labour markets in Australia. We summarise this condition as one in which labour markets work—a bit. The current wage did change as would be predicted by changes in supply and demand but a significant part of the burden of adjustment was carried by non-wage changes.[13]

We discuss this broad conclusion, which is in conformity with those of similar studies in the United States and Britain, in two parts. First, why is the wage responsiveness low? And second, what forms do non-wage adjustments take?

To discuss the first question we need to investigate the structure of wages in an internal labour market. There are two main points to be made. First, there is a range of indeterminacy in relative wages in internal labour markets. This arises because the typical worker occupies several jobs during her or his employment, which normally lasts many years. For this reason, even at ports of entry, wages need not be equal to those offered elsewhere. What the new entrant is concerned with is the wage over the expected period of employment and over the various jobs which that may encompass. More formally the entering worker is interested in the net present value of the expected earnings stream. But there are many possible combinations of wages at different job classifications which can yield the required present value of the earnings stream.

Specific training also introduces indeterminacy. Where specific skills are quantitatively important then both employers and workers are given an element of monopoly power. Existing workers are the only suppliers of the specific skills while the firm is the only buyer of such skills. The standard analysis of bilateral monopoly, with which we shall deal in Chapter 6, leads to the conclusion that only upper and lower limits on the wage can be set.

The upshot of this is that there are a considerable number of internal wage structures that are consistent with those constraints. In fact what little we know of internal wage structures suggests that internal wage structures (the relationships between the wages for different jobs) are more or less unique—there being as many wage structures as there are establishments. It may be that in Australia the degree of flexibility is reduced by the existence of minimum award rates of pay for many job classifications. We shall see in the final section of this chapter that there is a considerable variance in the earnings of similar workers in different plants, however, and this indicates that over-award pay, overtime earnings, and different piece-rate systems do provide considerable flexibility.

The second point is that an internal structure of pay, once arrived at, tends to become rigid. This is what the role of custom would lead us to expect, for a wage relativity once established becomes customary and tends to be perpetuated. This then limits management's ability to adjust to changing labour market conditions. For if the entry rate of pay is increased there will be pressure for other rates to increase to maintain internal relativities, which makes wage adjustment relatively costly. Similar results would follow from an attempt to reduce quits at a certain job level by increasing the pay there.

The upshot is that maintaining internal pay relativities is a management priority. A former compensation director at Eastman Kodak in the United States has stated that

> ...there is always some degree of conflict between internal and external pay equity. The position taken by most salary administrators is that internal relationships should be given first priority and external pay relationships for certain jobs must be compromised on occasion.[14]

The second question to be discussed is what forms non-wage adjustments take. First, there occur variations in hours of work. Upward variations will normally, but not always, involve the payment of overtime premia (or penalty rates of pay), which were discussed in Section 2.3 of Chapter 2. It should be clear by now that the attractiveness of increasing hours will depend upon how important are the fixed costs of employing labour, and in particular how important are firm-specific training and experience.

Second, variations in recruitment rates can be made. The simplest way for a firm to bring about reductions in its labour force is to lower its recruitment rate. The high turnover rates we discussed earlier in this section will then lead to its workforce declining. We might note here that it then follows that in cyclical downsavings, when large numbers of firms are acting in this way, the burden of unemployment will fall disproportionately on new entrants to the labour force, notably the young.

Firms wishing to increase their rate of recruitment will often be in labour markets where there is a shortage of labour. Assuming that wage rates are not increased, then something else will have to be varied if the firm is to secure the desired number of recruits. In these conditions it is common for firms to relax their customary hiring standards, that is, to hire into certain grades workers with lesser qualifications than are normally sought. Blandy and Richardson found this to be a particularly important adjustment mechanism in professional occupations. If hiring standards are relaxed in firms where specific skills are important a normal corollary will be an increase in training expenditures. In weak labour markets employers will tend to increase their hiring standards.

A third non-wage adjustment mechanism is changes in promotion rates. Workers, especially in white-collar occupations, have an expectation of being promoted from time to time. However, the rate of promotion is rarely, if ever, specified. Thus, variations to the speed at which people are promoted provide a means of adjusting to changing conditions which is unlikely to have any serious effects on morale.

Finally, firms may resort to sub-contracting. We saw that a major reason for avoiding raising the pay of a group in short supply is that this will disturb internal pay relativities and lead to pressure for all wage rates to be increased. It appears that this pressure does not materialise if the work is sub-contracted, for those who do the work are not part of the internal labour market.

We conclude our discussion by emphasising that, because wage adjustments are less used than non-wage adjustments, it does not mean that labour markets are inefficient. If firms prefer to make quality and quantity adjustments we must presume that they find it efficient to do so. A major reason for this is that the costs of non-wage adjustments to labour shortages are confined to marginal workers and do not generalise to intra-marginal employees. For example, the firm does incur costs by relaxing hiring standards either through increased training or through new recruits being less productive. If, however, wages were to be increased this higher cost applies to both new and existing workers.

5.5 Local labour markets

The mobility of workers between the different regions of Australia is fairly limited. This is the case in most countries but for obvious geographic reasons it is particularly so in Australia. Thus, for example, keyboard operators and their employers in Brisbane have to be seen as comprising a different labour market from their counterparts in Perth.

The country thus has to be seen as being made up of a number of what are termed local labour markets. A perfectly defined local labour market is that area from which all firms in the locality draw their workers and in which all the area's workers work for those firms. Although some isolated country towns may meet this definition, the borders of most local labour markets, particularly in metropolitan areas, are not easy to define. Cities are best viewed as consisting of a continuum of overlapping local labour markets. Those who investigate local labour markets thus have to fall back on some arbitrary rule of thumb to define their boundaries.

The competitive model of the labour market that we outlined in Section 5.2 of this chapter might, at first sight, suggest that workers of similar skills would earn more or less the same amount in different firms in a local labour market. When we look at the facts, however, we observe a considerable variation in earnings. At this stage of the chapter, of course, some variation should not come as a surprise to us for the existence of internal labour markets leads to such wage differences. There are other factors at work, however, and after presenting the evidence we shall discuss the various reasons for the existence of a wide dispersion of earnings of similar workers.

Studies of wages in local labour markets are not very common as the data have to be collected by survey. Fortunately, although perhaps surprisingly, the amount of variation in wages that is found is very similar across time and countries. The main results we report here were obtained from a survey carried out in 1974. The survey was undertaken in Adelaide and was of the earnings of fourteen occupational groups in 101 manufacturing industries. For each occupation average standard weekly earnings (that is, earnings excluding the effect of overtime and short-time working) in each plant were calculated. The spread of earnings between plants for each occupation was then measured by the co-efficient of variation (the standard deviation divided by the mean). In Table 5.2 we present the results for the whole sample and for the metal trades industry group.

It is evident that for apparently similar workers there is considerable variation in pay between employers, whether we consider all manufacturing or only those plants in the metal industry. To demonstrate this let us assume that a similar dispersion occurs today and assume the average wage of general clerks is $30 000. The co-efficient of variation of 12.8 per cent in all manufacturing (see Table 5.2) means that the standard deviation is $3840. This in turn would imply that 95 per cent of all general clerks earn between approximately $22 320 and $37 680 which is a surprising amount of variation. The authors of the study made comparisons with similar investigations in Britain and in the United States and found that the degree of dispersion was very similar.

These persistent findings of a wide dispersion of plant earnings suggest that it is not the case that investigators have simply come up with point-of-time snapshots of local labour markets in disequilibrium. No labour markets are ever in complete equilibrium, of course, but there is no suggestion that we would have observed a much smaller dispersion had these markets been examined at some other date. Some studies have in fact

Table 5.2 Inter-plan earnings differences: Adelaide, 1974

	Co-efficient of variation (%)	
Occupation	*all manufacturing*	*metal trades only*
Unskilled		
Factory cleaner	11.2	9.4
Semi-skilled		
Driver 3-6 ton truck	15.5	–
Forklift truck driver	13.5	12.1
Storeperson	12.9	11.3
Trade worker's assistant	10.8	–
Skilled		
Fitter and turner	7.5	8.1
Machinist (first class)	9.9	9.2
Welder (first class)	10.8	12.3
Die setter	8.2	9.5
Electrical fitter	7.5	6.8
Sheet-metal worker	11.3	12.3
Clerical		
Clerk (general)	12.8	8.2
Ledger machinist	11.4	10.6
Typist	12.9	14.6

Notes: All workers in clerical group were female; all other groups comprise males only. Two entries omitted because the sample size was too small.
Source: W. Brown et al.[15]

gathered evidence from the same local labour market at different dates and they find little change in wage variation and further that the rank order of plants in terms of average wages is fairly constant. We can, therefore, be reasonably confident that there still exists today a wide dispersion of earnings within local labour markets. Some indirect evidence on this can be obtained from data on the incidence of over-award payments. In the Australian system of wage determination the main way in which differences in earnings for workers with identical skills can arise is through over-award payments. The amount of over-award pay in different firms in the whole of the private sector is shown in Table 5.3.

Respondents to the survey on which Table 5.3 is based were asked the average over-award pay received by the largest group in receipt of over-award pay at the work place. Table 5.3 shows that at nearly 30 per cent of work places there were no over-award payments. At the other extreme in 0.5 per cent of work places over-award payments were no less than 75–100 per cent of the award rate of pay. It is not known from this data how over-award pay varies within local labour markets.

How are we to explain the large differences in wages that are found for members of the same occupational group in the same local labour

Table 5.3 Frequency distribution of over-award pay as a percentage of the award rate, 1990

Range	*Per cent*
0	29.2
1–5	11.9
5–10	20.3
10–15	11.7
15–20	10.0
20–30	8.4
30–50	6.5
50–75	1.5
75–100	0.5

Source: F. Gill[16]

market? We can immediately dispose of one possible explanation of the wage differences, that they compensate for differences in non-wage conditions of employment such as fringe benefits and congeniality of surroundings. All the evidence suggests that wages and non-wage conditions are positively associated.

In the literature on local labour markets three possible, and not necessarily exclusive or independent, explanations of wage differences have received the greatest attention. These are that they are explicable through imperfect information, through differences in worker quality, and through the existence of internal labour markets. We will look at them in turn but the reader should be aware that there is some dispute as to whether these wage differences are the outcome of random or chaotic influences, or of more-or-less rational behaviour on the part of workers and employers. An eclectic view is also permissible.

To isolate the role of imperfect information let us take a group of reasonable homogeneous workers in an area where employers operate open labour markets and hence where the conditions of competitive theory approximately hold. Neither buyers nor sellers would have complete information and this leads to a dispersion of wages.

On the worker's side it is not worthwhile to carry out enough search for the best (highest paid) job to eliminate all wage differences. We know that the distribution of wages for similar workers in local markets is roughly normally distributed and we can use the properties of the normal distribution to investigate the returns to the search undertaken by a worker. If the average wage in the distribution is W and the standard deviation is σ_w, then it can be shown that the expected maximum wage offer, W_m, a worker would come across in n searches is:

$$W_m = 0.65 n^{0.37} \sigma_w + \overline{W}$$

This expression, which we will ask the reader to take on trust, is approximately true for between three and twenty searches.[17] It shows that as the number of searches increases the expected maximum wage offer (not the maximum possible offer, for this would of course simply be the highest wage in the market) increases, but at a decreasing rate. We can see the implications of this more fully if we differentiate the term with respect to *n* to derive the marginal gain from one more search:

$$\frac{\delta W_m}{\delta n} = \frac{0.24\sigma_w}{n^{0.63}}$$

To put some numbers in, let us take the case where δ_w is one-tenth of the average wage (giving a co-efficient of variation of 10 per cent, which is fairly typical of the figures in Table 5.2), which in turn is $30 000 (approximately its level in 1992). The results of applying the above formula are shown in Table 5.4.

The gains from additional searches are quite small in absolute terms and trivial in terms of the assumed average wage of $30 000. Further, searching, whether the worker is presently in or out of employment is a

Table 5.4 Gains from search: numerical example ($ p.a.)

Number of searches (n)	*Marginal wage rate gain* ($\delta Ww/\delta n$)
5	257
10	167
15	131
20	109

Note: For assumptions see text.

far from costless activity. In deciding to continue searching for a better wage workers weigh up the probable marginal returns and marginal costs. The returns in our realistic example are so small that for many workers it is just not worthwhile engaging in much searching. Thus even in competitive labour markets lack of information will give rise to wage differences.

Before leaving Table 5.4 we should note one obvious implication, which is that the longer the prospective period of employment the greater, in absolute terms, the returns from additional search. Therefore, the returns from searching for jobs which are ports of entry into internal labour markets are, other things being equal, relatively high. A further information problem is introduced, however, in that it may be difficult to ascertain the present value of earnings in such markets as these are likely to rise over time with experience and promotion.

Exactly how much information about job opportunities and wages workers do have is not clear. Evidence suggests that most workers who are in employment do not even attempt any systematic evaluation of alternative jobs. Some workers in jobs do undertake searches, as do, of course, the unemployed. It is customary to divide the channels through which information is obtained into formal and informal. Formal information networks include the Commonwealth Employment Service (CES), private employment agencies, newspaper and journal advertisements and, in some occupations, union agencies. The relative importance of these varies from occupation to occupation. The CES tends to offer vacancies in the range of jobs which do not require many qualifications. Highly qualified staff, on the other hand, are normally recruited through advertisements in national newspapers and specialist journals or through private employment agencies. Trade unions which operate closed shops in effect run their own job agencies.

Informal information channels include job notices posted at factory gates, casual conversation and, most important of all, information gained from friends and relatives who are already employed in the firm where the vacancy exists. Hirings that result in this way are termed 'employee referrals'. Employee referrals, have advantages for both workers and employers, and they arise from the fact that qualitative information can be transmitted in this way. If an employer is happy with the present workforce then that employer tends to get recruits who are similar to existing workers. Job searchers, on the other hand, can obtain information informally about the nature of the job, attitudes of supervisors, and working conditions, that is unlikely to be available through formal sources.

The Australian Bureau of Statistics undertakes a survey which provides data on the relative importance of the main methods of obtaining a job (cat. no. 6245.0). In the year up to July 1990, 1.9 million people started a job; 0.8 million moved from another job; while 1.1 million were previously not working.Of these people, 25 per cent were approached by employers, a surprisingly high 35 per cent got their jobs by approaching an employer without prior knowledge that a job was available, and the remaining 40 per cent applied for a job vacancy that they knew existed.

Of this latter group, 11 per cent obtained the information from the CES, 37 per cent from job advertisements, 41 per cent from friends and relations, while the remaining 11 per cent used some other means of obtaining information about the existence of a vacancy.

The wage relativities that exist in local labour markets are known, at least in a broad way, to employers. Most employers belong to employers' federations and many of these organisations disseminate, in varying degrees of detail, information about wage levels. In the Adelaide labour market, metal trades employers swap data and probably have fairly fragmentary information. In other metropolitan labour markets the Metal Trades Industries Association holds systematic wage surveys, the results of which are distributed to members; hence firms know exactly where they stand in the wage ranking. It seems probable then that firms make conscious decisions to be relatively high-wage or relatively low-wage employers, which leads us to the other two explanations of the wage dispersion that we observe in local labour markets.

The first rests upon the fact that workers are not homogeneous. If we look again at the occupational classification used, for example, in Table 5.2, we see that in many cases the investigators have had to use fairly broad job descriptions and hence some of the observed dispersion arises from a comparison of what are in effect different jobs. This problem is less acute here, where we are comparing average plant earnings, than would be the case if we were measuring the spread of individual earnings, but nevertheless we are likely to pick up some spurious dispersion. More fundamentally workers in an occupational group differ in the sense that they do not equally possess the characteristics which employers seek, where these characteristics include, as well as skill, keeping time, attendance and sickness records, co-operativeness, willingness to work hard, and so on. It seems plausible that high-paying employers are able to recruit workers with more desirable characteristics and who are more productive. The idea that the payment of above average wages leads to productivity gains has been formalised in the notion of efficiency wages. Efficiency wage models of the labour market, and their implications, are discussed in Section 8.5 of Chapter 8.

A further gain accruing to firms which pay relatively high wages is that they have lower turnover rates, for this inverse relation is well established. We have seen in preceding sections of this chapter that turnover costs are directly related to the magnitude of the fixed costs of employing labour. We have also seen that where such costs are high there is an incentive to develop relatively closed internal labour markets, and it is the existence of such markets that is the third explanation of the observed wage variation in local markets. The reasons for this were set out in Section 5.3, but the basic point is that the insulation of the firms' internal markets from the external market and the likelihood of a worker performing several jobs during the period of employment means that competition does not set a unique rate for any job classification.

To sum up, the evidence consistently demonstrates a wide variation of the earnings of apparently similar workers between different plants in the same local labour market. Imperfect information can explain some of this variation but is not a complete explanation as firms, at least, seem to have considerable knowledge of wage structures. High-paying firms attract better quality labour and they also gain from having lower turnover rates. Our analysis of internal labour markets would also lead us to expect wage differences. This is not an exhaustive list of explanations, for example, the power of union bargaining for over-award payments is not equal in all plants and there is some evidence that establishment variables such as plant size have some influence. The three factors we have looked at enable us to explain, or at least to rationalise, some of the wage differences that we observed within local labour markets.

Concepts for review

- Internal labour market
- External labour market
- Port of entry
- Job ladders
- Job hierarchies
- Seniority rights
- Fixed costs of employing labour
- Quasi-fixed factor of production
- Open labour markets
- Manorial (enterprise) labour markets
- Guild labour markets
- Local labour markets
- Formal and informal information channels
- Employee referrals

Questions

1 What are internal labour markets? Why do they exist? What implications do they have for labour market analysis? (University of Western Australia)
2 How can search activity in labour markets be explained? What factors are likely to affect the extent of search? Is there a rationale for public involvement in the search process? (University of New England)
3 How do labour markets adjust to an increase in the demand for labour? (Curtin University of Technology)
4 Explain why pay differs within firms and between firms in local labour markets. (Macquarie University)
5 Is it sometimes said that the concepts of fixed employment costs and specific training have revolutionised our view of labour markets. Discuss. (University of Western Australia)
6 'The major effect of large organisations, both public and private, upon labour market outcomes is to reduce the allocative role played by market wages.' Discuss. (Murdoch University)

References

1 P.B. Doeringer and M.J. Piore, *Internal Labour Markets and Manpower Analysis*, D.C. Heath and Co., Lexington, 1971.
2 H. Matsushige, The internalisation of the labour market in the Australian vehicle building industry, unpublished PhD thesis, Australian National University, 1989.
3 M.J. Nowak, The role of information in internal labour markets, unpublished PhD thesis, Murdoch University, 1989.
4 W.Y. Oi, 'Labour as a quasi fixed factor of production', *Journal of Political Economy*, vol. 70, no. 6, 1962, pp. 538-55.
5 O.E. Williamson, *Markets and Hierarchies: Analysis and Anti-trust Implications*, The Free Press, New York, 1975, ch. 4.
6 R. Blandy, 'The senior executives', in R. Blandy and S. Richardson, *How Labour Markets Work*, Longman Cheshire, Melbourne, 1982.
7 L.R. Maglen and C. Daly, 'Internal labour markets for skilled manpower: some Australian evidence', mimeo, 1980.
8 M.J. Nowak, 'Internal labour markets and the market for highly qualified labour', *Journal of Industrial Relations*, vol. 21, no. 1, 1979, pp. 20-34.
9 M.J. Nowak, op. cit.
10 H. Matsushige, op. cit.
11 M.J. Nowak and G.V. Crockett, 'The operation of internal labour markets: three case studies', *Journal of Industrial Relations*, vol. 25, no. 4, 1983, pp. 445-64.
12 K. Norris, 'Job durations in Australia', *Journal of Industrial Relations*, vol. 26, no. 2, 1984, pp. 188-99.
13 R. Blandy and S. Richardson (eds), *How Labour Markets Work*, Longman Cheshire, Melbourne, 1982.
14 Cited in L. Katz, 'Efficiency wage theories: a partial evaluation', in S. Fischer (ed.), *NBER Macroeconomics Annual*, MIT Press, Cambridge, 1986.
15 W. Brown et al., 'Occupational pay structures under different wage fixing arrangements: a comparison of intra-occupational pay dispersion in Australia, Great Britain and the United States', *British Journal of Industrial Relations*, vol. 18, 1980, pp. 217-30.
16 F. Gill, 'Over-award payments: an analysis of the AWIRS data set', University of Sydney, mimeo, 1992.
17 G.J. Stigler, 'Information in the labour market', *Journal of Political Economy*, vol. 70, no. 5, part 2, 1962, pp. 94-105.

CHAPTER 6

Trade unions

6.1 Introduction

One of the most striking differences between the competitive model of the labour market that we described in Section 5.2 of the previous chapter and reality is that in many industries and occupations workers join together to act in unison in their negotiations with their employers. These organised associations of labour are known as trade unions and have characterised industrial societies for long periods of time. For all intents and purposes, we can treat members of professional organisations, such as the Australian Medical Association, as trade unions. Although they are not called trade unions, and are not classified as such, or included in the statistics below, their aims and objectives and their methods of attempting to attain them are virtually the same as those of trade unions.

Union density

In statistical analyses of trade union membership it is conventional, and convenient for comparative purposes, to write in terms of union density. In Australia union density is measured as the proportion of workers who are members of unions in their main job as a proportion of total employees. In 1990 union density across all employees was 40.5 per cent.

Union density varies considerably across industries, occupations, and sectors of employment as can be seen from Table 6.1.

Table 6.1 reveals enormous differences in union density. Perhaps the most striking is that between the public sector (68 per cent) and the private sector (31 per cent). This difference is, in turn, partly responsible for the differences between industries. Thus in agriculture, a very weakly unionised industry, few employees are in the public sector whereas the opposite is true in some highly unionised industries such as electricity, gas and water, communications and (obviously) public administration and

Table 6.1 **Trade union density, 1990 (%)**

Employment category	*Employees in unions*
Agriculture etc.	13
Mining	63
Manufacturing	46
Electricity, gas, water	79
Construction	45
Wholesale, retail trade	23
Transport, storage	58
Communications	76
Finance, property, business services	29
Public administration, defence	60
Community services	49
Recreation, personal services	25
Males	45
Females	37
Public sector	68
Private sector	31
Full-time	42
Part-time	35
Permanent	46
Casual	19
Total	41

Source: *Trade Union Members, Australia*, (ABS, cat. no. 6325.0).

defence. Note also, the relatively low union density among female workers and among casual workers.

In international comparisons, Australia occupies an intermediate position in terms of union density, although the difference between the public and private sectors is rather greater than in most other industrial countries.

The fall in union density in Australia

The membership of trade unions as a proportion of all workers is declining in Australia. Union density was 51 per cent in 1976, 45.6 per cent in 1986 and, as we have seen, 40.5 per cent in 1990. From these proportions it can be seen that the rate of decline of union density is accelerating.

What has caused this decline in union intensity? In a statistical sense there are two possible explanations. First, the structure of employment may have changed, such as to bring about a decline in the overall level of union density. To take an obvious possibility, there may have been a shift away from public sector employment (where union density is high) towards private sector employment (where it is relatively low). Second, within each industry, sector, or occupation, there may have been a decline in the propensity to join trade unions.

This issue has been investigated by Peetz.[1] His conclusions are that changes to the structure of employment have, since 1982, brought about a decline in overall union density. Private-sector employment has increased relative to public-sector employment and there has been a tendency for weakly unionised industries, such as recreation and personal services, and finance property and business services, to increase their share of total employment. The growth of casual employment, that we discussed in Section 8.3, has also reduced overall union density as such workers are difficult to unionise.

Important though these structural changes have been, however, the main explanation of the decline in union density is a fall in the propensity to join unions. That is, within industries, occupations, and sectors, people are simply less likely to join unions now than they were previously. To give some idea of relative magnitudes, consider the period 1976–88, when union density declined by 2 per cent a year. Peetz suggests that about 0.6 percentage points of this was due to changes in the composition of employment while the remaining 1.4 per cent decline was due to the fall in the propensity to join unions.

It is not clear why there has been a fall in the tendency for people to join unions. An adverse change in public attitudes may have occurred and in some states legislative changes worked against unions. The decline in union density began as early as 1976, but since 1983, it has coincided with the period in which wage determination was dominated by the Accord. The Accord gave the union movement the greatest influence over economic policy that it ever had but it also substantially reduced the role of individual unions.

The effect of the Accord on union membership has been investigated by Kenyon and Lewis.[2] Their method was to estimate a model of union membership over the period between 1948–82 and to use this to predict what would have happened to union membership in the absence of the Accord. The difference between actual and predicted membership is then held to measure the effect of the Accord. The main results are as follows. First, union membership is found to be positively associated with the rate of growth of real wages and with the rate of unemployment. Second, although the fall in real wages and in unemployment that occurred between 1983 and 1990 would have been expected to reduce union membership the actual decline was significantly greater than predicted. Thus Kenyon and Lewis conclude that the Accord has reduced union membership. They suggest that the reason is that the benefits of union membership have been perceived as low as virtually all workers have received identical wage increases through National Wage Decisions, and, further, the union movement, through the Accord, has delivered real wage reductions.

The plan of the rest of this chapter is as follows. In Section 6.2 we look at the goals of trade unions and the extent to which they conflict. In Section 6.3 we discuss some models of the way unions bargain with employers, and in the following section we describe estimates of the effects that unions have upon relative wages. Section 6.5 discusses the exit-voice view of trade unions which suggests that unions have beneficial effects on the level of productivity.

6.2 Union goals

Unions are organisations with multiple objectives. Thus, unions may aim to secure increases in wages, reductions in the standard working week, improvements in working conditions, increased security of employment, improved grievance procedures, and increased employment of union members. This latter objective will often conflict with several of the others.

To simplify things, in this section we will concentrate on wages and employment, assuming hours and the other conditions of employment to be constant. The analysis will generalise, for the achievement of shorter weekly hours, for example, is almost the same as an increase in wage rates for the same weekly hours. The payment of penalty rates for overtime slightly complicates things but does not fundamentally alter the principle. In this section, as in Chapter 3, the analysis of which we shall draw upon here, we shall take the overall level of prices and wages to be constant. Thus when we speak of an increase in the wages of a group we imply an increase in its wage relative to other groups. (In an inflationary context, relative wage gains are of course made by winning an increase greater than those gained by others.)

Unions would be unable to pursue these objectives in a competitive industry with identical firms. For any firm which paid more than the market wage would go out of business. Unions can only prosper in industries where economic rents, in the form of monopoly profits, are earned. Thus it is no coincidence that union density is, in Table 6.1, very low in agriculture, probably the most competitive industry.

One obvious example of economic rent is the economic profit earned by a monopoly firm and we frame our discussion of union objectives around this example. We shall initially assume that the union has the power to bargain a wage above the competitive level but that once that wage is set the level of employment is determined by the firm. Later we shall look at cases where unions are able to negotiate over employment levels.

Where do unions get the power to act in this way? Union power comes from two sources. First, some unions control the long-run supply of labour to an occupation and by restricting supply they can increase wages. The most obvious cases of this are professional associations which can control the number of people who gain the necessary certification. In general, however, this source of union power is likely to be quite limited and the province of a few craft unions and professional associations. The main form of union power is the ability to impose losses on employers through strikes and other forms of industrial action, such as the work-to-rule.

Four union goals

Here we will assume that a union has the power to raise wages above the competitive level but that the level of employment is solely determined by the employer. These are sometimes termed 'right to manage' models, where the outcome always lies on the firm's demand curve for labour. We can identify, in Figure 6.1, several goals that unions might seek to achieve.

The line D is the firm's demand for labour curve (as derived in Chapter 3). To this demand curve will correspond a marginal revenue (MR) curve. In this case the union is a seller of labour and the MR curve shows how much will be added to the revenue of the union, that is the total wage bill, if one more (union) worker is employed.

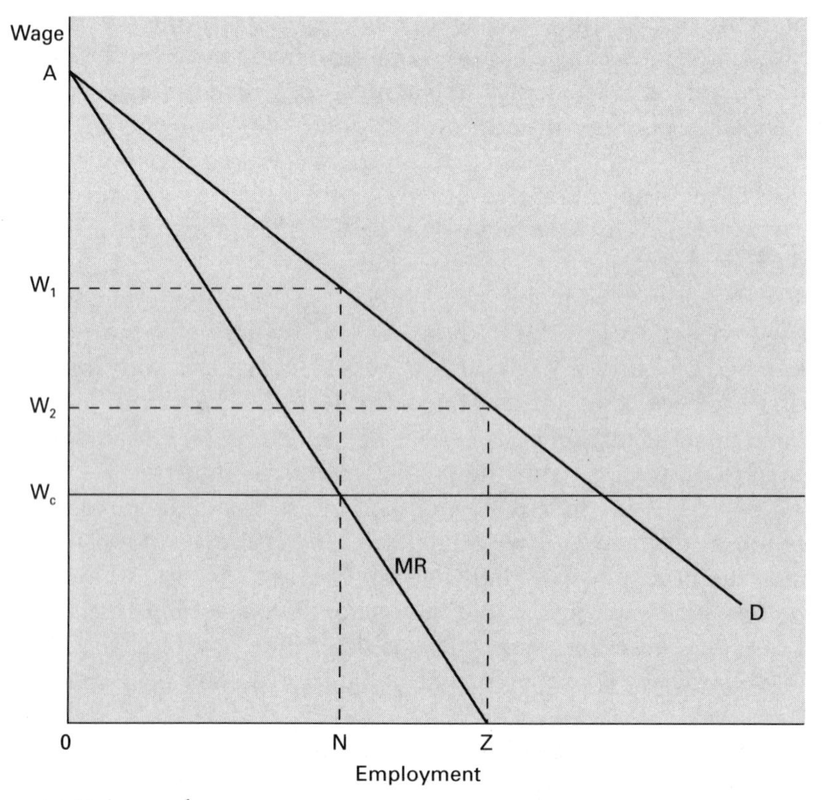

Figure 6.1 Union goals

The wage, W_c, is the wage that would obtain in the absence of a union. Alternatively it can be viewed as the highest wage the workers could obtain elsewhere. One orthodox approach (analogous to the orthodox analysis of firms' objectives) would be to argue that unions are trying to maximise something. There are four possibilities. The first is that it tries to maximise the wage. This would lead to a wage fractionally less than OA with one worker employed, an absurd outcome. The second is that the union attempts to maximise the employment of union members. Employment is at its greatest at W_c. But this is the competitive wage and the union wage must surely be higher than this otherwise, presumably, nobody would bother to join the union. Thus these first two possibilities can be ruled out. A third possibility is that the union attempts to maximise the economic rents, that is total payments over and above the supply price of labour, W_c. These represent economic (or monopoly) profit of the union viewed as a monopoly seller. The union would set the wage at OW_1 and the firm would then choose the profit maximising employment level, ON.

Finally the union could aim to maximise the wage bill of its members. (This is analogous to the case of a firm maximising sales revenue, that was discussed in Section 3.4 of Chapter 3.) As the marginal revenue curve shows, the addition to the wage bill brought about by the employment of additional workers it follows that this objective is achieved where the MR curve cuts the horizontal axis, thus the wage is W_2 and 0Z workers are employed.

While wage bill and rent maximisation are not implausible objectives it is not clear why a union would choose one or the other of the resulting wage outcomes, W_1 or W_2 rather than choosing some point in between (or indeed some other wage in the entire range A-W_c). The wage ultimately will depend on the preferences of union organisers and members. Compare the latter two outcomes for example. Wage bill maximisation gives a lower wage (W_2) than does the maximisation of economic rents, but employment is higher. More union members are employed but at a lower wage.

Union utility maximisation

This suggests another approach in which we see union members as deriving utility from both the wage and the level of employment. Thus there are various combinations of wages and employment levels that yield union members equal utility. In the same vein as we drew individual workers' preference maps between goods and leisure in Section 2.2 of Chapter 2, we can draw union preferences between wages and employment, as in Figure 6.2.

As both the level of employment of union members and the wage received give utility, the indifference map will exhibit the normal features.

Any indifference curve, U_1 for example, shows the combinations of wages and employment between which the union is indifferent. Higher indifference curves, U_2 for example, represent combinations of wages and employment which are superior outcomes to those represented by U_1.

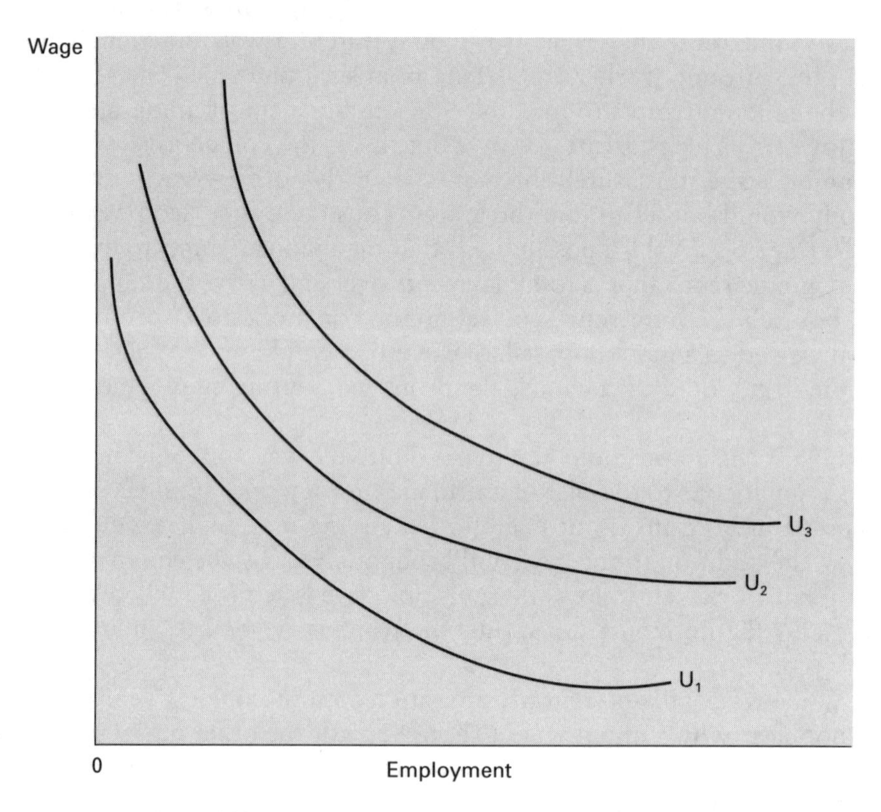

Figure 6.2 Union indifference curves between wages and employment

The precise shape of the indifference curves will depend on the preferences of members. Not all members will have the same preferences. Union members who are unemployed will presumably tend to give more weight to employment than would someone in employment. There is a further problem of how a union leadership ascertains the preferences of their members. We will overlook these issues and take the case where all members have identical preferences, as portrayed in Figure 6.3.

In right to manage models where the outcome is on the demand for labour curve the optimum is to bargain a wage W_1. The firm will then employ N_1 people and thus the outcome is at point A, which is on the highest indifference curve that can be attained. At point A, at the margin the actual trade off between wages and employment, as given by the slope of the labour demand curve, is equal to the unions willingness to substitute wages for employment.

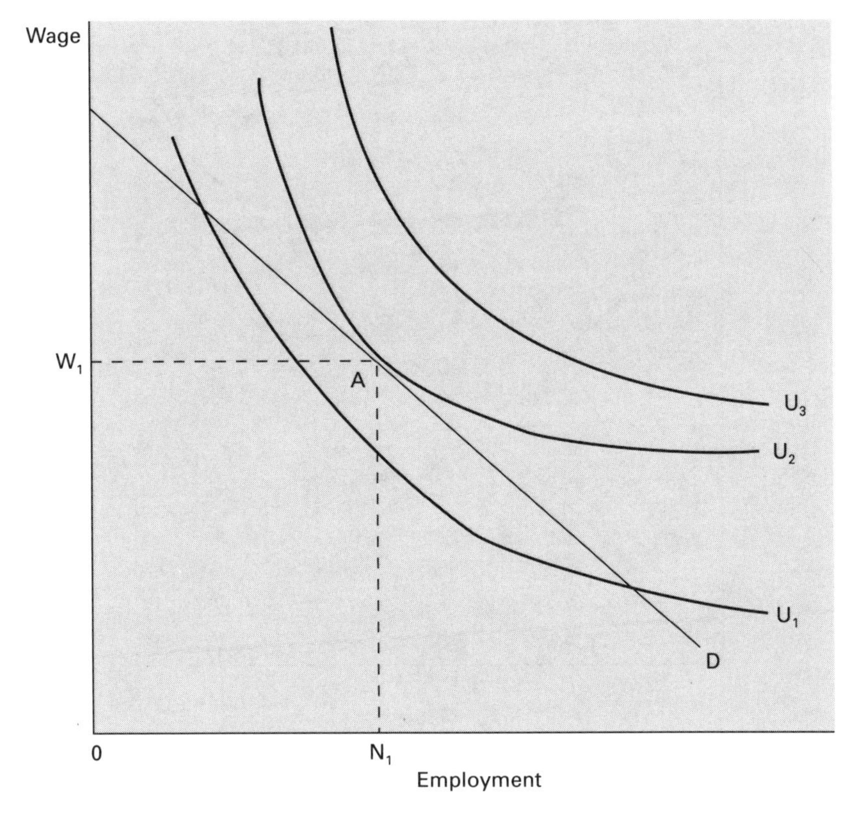

Figure 6.3 Union utility maximisation

In right to manage models, if the union raises wages above the competitive level then there will be a cost in terms of reduced employment.

Unions and monopsonistic employers

There is, however, one exception to this rule. This exists where the employer has monopsony power. This arises where, in the absence of a union, the firm cannot obtain as much labour as it wishes at the competitive wage but has to increase wages to obtain more labour. This could arise in a town where employment of a certain type of worker was dominated by one employer. In some occupational labour markets, that for teachers for example, government employers are dominant. Wage determination in a monopsonistic firm is demonstrated in Figure 6.4.

The firm, as explained above, has to raise the wage to obtain more labour and thus faces an upward sloping supply curve of labour. If this is the case, the marginal cost of labour is greater than the wage. A simple example will demonstrate this.

Initially 100 workers are employed at a daily wage of $100 giving a wage bill of $10 000 a day. To attract one more worker the wage has to

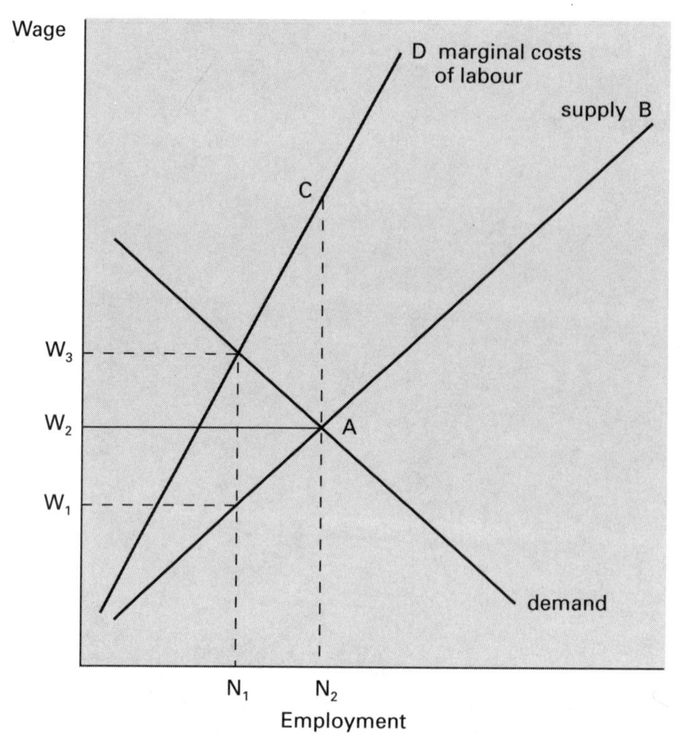

Figure 6.4 The effect of a union in a monopsonistic firm

be raised to \$102 a day. Employment is now 101 at a wage of \$102 giving a daily wage bill of \$10 302. Thus, the extra worker has added \$302 to the wage bill and that is her marginal cost, although the wage she receives is \$102. This effect arises because the increased wage of \$102 has to be paid to the 100 workers previously employed. Thus in Figure 6.4 if we start with no unions then employment is N_1 (fixed by the intersection of the demand and marginal cost schedules) and that supply of labour is secured by paying a wage of W_1. Thus we get the result that under monopsony, labour is exploited in the sense of receiving less than its marginal revenue product.

Now a union is formed and it can be demonstrated that at any wage up to W_2 the union may increase both the wage and employment. Take the limiting case where a wage of W_2 is bargained. The supply curve now takes the form W_2AB and the marginal cost schedule becomes W_2ACD, being discontinuous between A and C. Thus as monopsony power has been eliminated, the marginal cost and supply schedules coincide in the section W_2A. The profit-maximising firm hires N_2 labour at the wage W_2 and both employment and the wage have increased.

If the wage is now raised above W_2 then the basic result once again holds, that wage gains can only be won with the expense of employment losses. The reader will note that up to a wage of W_3 employment would still be higher than at the original wage of W_1, but nevertheless any wage gain above W_2 brings associated employment losses.

As there is reason to suspect that in many labour markets employers, in the absence of unions, would have monopsony power or would collude to act as if they did then the elimination of monopsony may have been an important source of gains to unionised labour. Once that power has been eliminated, however, wage gains can only be won at the expense of employment losses. This statement rests, we should remind the reader, on the assumption that the union is unable to bargain over employment levels. We shall discuss bargaining models in the next section. Here, however, we can gain more insights into union behaviour by asking under what conditions the employment losses consequent on a wage gain will tend to be relatively small.

The Marshallian rules

Obviously unions are in a favoured position if, for a given wage gain, the employment losses are small. The terms of the trade off between wages and employment are determined by the elasticity of the demand curve for union labour, which is itself influenced by four factors. These were first identified by Alfred Marshall about 100 years ago and have become known as the Marshallian rules. A union will be more favoured in gaining a wage increase:

1. the lower is the ability of employers to substitute other inputs for union labour;
2. the less elastic is the demand for the product;
3. the smaller is the proportion of total costs comprised by union labour;
4. the lower is the elasticity of supply of other inputs.

Rule 1 is straightforward. It must be difficult for the employer to substitute from the now more expensive labour, either by employing non-union labour (which means that the union must control supply) or by using more capital equipment. Formally, the elasticity of substitution between labour and alternative inputs must be low.

Rule 2 is also intuitively obvious. Raising wages raises costs and hence product prices rise and demand falls. The employment losses are less the lower is this decline in demand, that is the lower is the elasticity of demand for the product. Although it might appear that unions can do little to influence the elasticity of product demand they can do so by reducing the amount of competition from imports, and hence are usually to be found on the side of those arguing against further reduction in the tariff protection of Australian industries.

Rule 3, the 'importance of being unimportant', needs closer consideration. It seems quite plausible that if union labour is a very small proportion of total costs then any change in the wage would have a very small influence on prices and hence demand and employment. Hicks demonstrated long ago, however, that this rule only holds as long as the elasticity of demand for the final product is greater than the elasticity of substitution in production. We can see the sense of Hicks' result from the following example. Say product demand is inelastic and unionised labour wins a wage increase, then there is little adverse effect on demand and hence on employment. However, if it is relatively easy to substitute other factors for unionised labour then unionised labour would be in the best position if it accounts for a large proportion of total costs, the reason being that the scale of the necessary substitution may deter the firm from attempting it. Therefore in this case it is 'important to be important'.

We do not, in general, know the magnitude of these two elasticities but it is normally assumed that the Hicks' condition is likely to be met and thus the rule as formulated by Marshall is appropriate. A good example of a group favoured by this condition, and by rule 1, is that of air pilots. The salary of a pilot is a minute proportion of the costs of operating a plane and substitution is difficult (but not impossible as second pilots can be substituted by flight engineers). Pilots as a result are among the most highly paid trade unionists.

One further problem with rule 3 is that where there are traditional interrelationships between the pay of different groups in an industry then there is a tendency for wage increases to be generalised. In this case it is the proportion of total costs which is made up by all labour costs rather than the costs of the particular union group that is relevant. The high wages of pilots have, for example, pulled up the salaries of all flight crew.

The last of the Marshallian rules is that unions are favoured when the elasticity of supply of competing inputs is low. In this case, even if the elasticity of substitution in production is high, as substitution towards other factors occurs their price would be driven up and this would limit the scale of profitable substitution.

The 1989 pilots' dispute

We argued earlier in this section that unions seek to gain a share in the rents earned by firms with monopoly power. Where the degree of monopoly power falls, so do the total rents. This might then be expected to influence bargaining over wages and conditions. A good example of this occurred shortly prior to the deregulation of the domestic airline industry in Australia.

We have seen above that two of the Marshallian conditions favour pilots. Since the Second World War Ansett and Australian Airlines enjoyed a duopoly position in interstate flights, a duopoly bestowed by the federal government. The consequent rents were shared between the companies and airline staff in the form of profits, wage levels and overstaffing. This cosy arrangement was to come to an end in late 1990 when new entrants would be allowed in to the industry. In the latter half of 1989 the Australian Federation of Air Pilots (AFAP) began to pursue a 30 per cent wage claim. In previous such episodes employers tended to cave in, secure in the knowledge that they could simply raise prices to recoup. This time, however, this prospect was unlikely and a stern resistance followed involving the cancellation of pilots contracts and the employment of overseas pilots. By any standards the AFAP were defeated. New contracts involved changed working conditions and the impact effect on the employment of pilots by the two airlines was a decrease of about a quarter. Thus the change in the market conditions for domestic travel had repercussions for the demand for pilots—which is just what our analysis would lead us to expect.

6.3 Bargaining models

In the previous section we examined cases where the union set a wage and left the level of employment to the firm. In other words the eventual outcome always lay on the firm's demand for labour curve. Here we analyse the case where there is bargaining over both the wage and the level of employment. We shall consider two such models. The first is the bilateral monopoly model which is of some antiquity but which gives some useful insights. The second model we shall discuss is of much more recent origin and is what can be termed an 'efficient bargaining model'.

The bilateral monopoly model

In the bilateral monopoly model a monopsonist bargains with a trade union monopoly seller of labour. To understand this model we simply need to bring together two previously separate discussions. The first is that of the behaviour of monopsony buyers of labour (p.130). The second is that of a union which has the objective of maximising the collective economic rents of its members (p.127).

The model is diagrammatically represented in Figure 6.5. We analyse the preferred positions of the union and the firm respectively and these then set the limits to the bargain. The union's preferred outcome is where the employer can exercise no monopsony power and where economic rents are maximised. This occurs where the marginal revenue of union members curve intersects the supply of labour curve (which reflects the supply price of labour). Thus the union's best outcome is determined by point C, with N_2 labour being employed at a wage W_2, the area AW_2BC representing economic rent. Labour is paid a wage equal to its marginal product but in excess of its supply price.

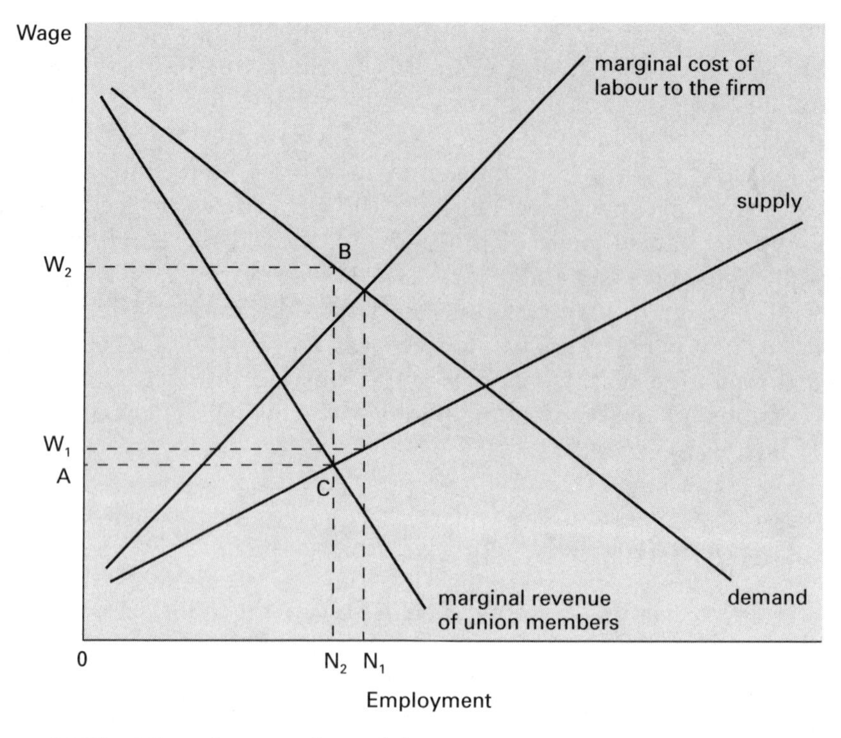

Figure 6.5 The bilateral monopoly model

Now take the case where the monopsonist has all the power. We discussed this case in the previous section, where we saw that the firm's best outcome would be where the demand for labour curve intersects the curve representing the marginal cost of labour to the firm, at point D. That is, an outcome of a wage of W_1 with a level of employment of N_1.

Thus, the optimal outcome for the union is a wage of W_2 and an employment level of N_2. For the firm the best outcome is, predictably, a lower wage, W_1, but a higher level of employment N_1. The final outcome is indeterminate. All we can say is that it will lie between these two limits. The actual outcome will depend on perceived bargaining strengths and upon the skills of the negotiators.

The final outcome in this model is a point either on the firm's demand for labour curve or beneath it. This is not so, however, in the next model we consider.

An efficient bargaining model

To put efficient bargaining models into context refer back to Figure 6.3. This represented a situation where a union, with a utility function consisting of employment and wages as its two components bargained with a single firm. Once the wage was settled the firm determined the level of employment. Thus in Figure 6.3 the optimal outcome for the union was a wage of W_1. Given that wage the profit maximising employment level for the firm was N_1. The major insight given to us by the efficient bargaining model, as developed by McDonald and Solow, is that there will be other combinations of employment and wage levels that will be preferred by both parties.[3] To explain this we need to introduce a further construct, the iso-product curve. A set of such curves is shown in Figure 6.6.

The demand for labour curve is derived from a profit maximising decision and represents the firm's marginal revenue product of labour curve, as we saw in Section 3.2 of Chapter 3. The shape of each iso-profit curve is intuitively obvious. It peaks on the demand for labour curve, say point A on iso-profit curve I_3. To employ more labour than is represented by point A the firm, in order to maintain profit levels, would need to pay a lower wage. Similarly, and remembering that A represents a profit maximising point, were less labour to be employed (given the level of other inputs) a lower wage would be necessary to generate the same level of profit.

Less obvious is the proposition that as we move to iso-profit curves that are higher up the diagram, the level of profit is lower. Thus I_3

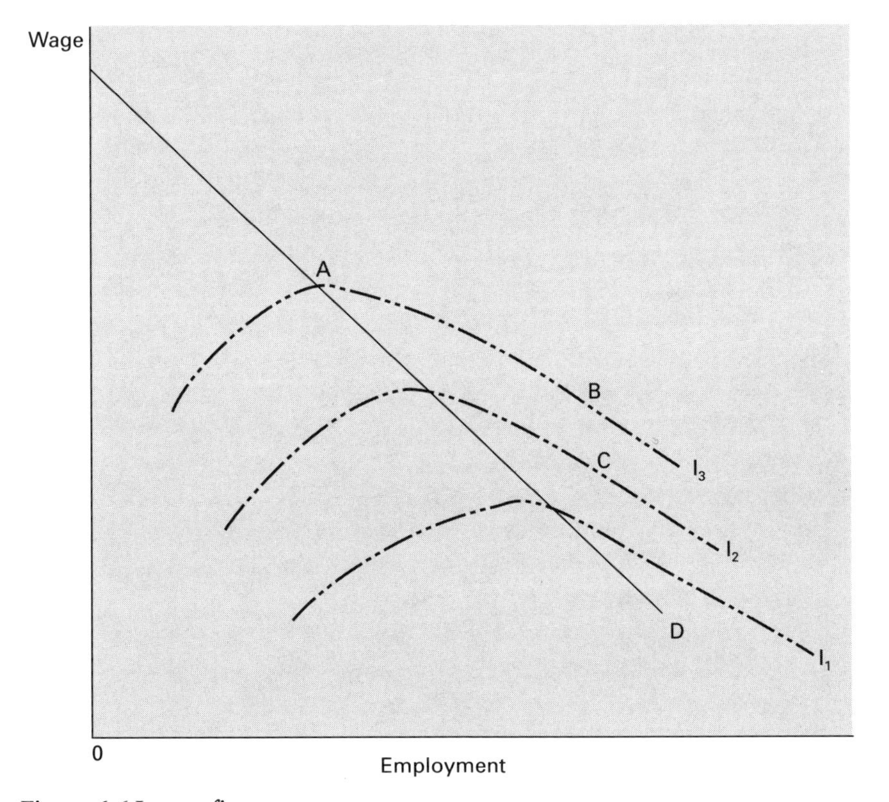

Figure 6.6 Iso-profit curve

represents lower profits than I_2 and so on. The explanation for this is as follows. Consider points B and C. B lies vertically above C and hence represents the same level of employment, and hence of output, than does C. Hence, as output and revenue are the same at both points, C must represent higher profits as wages are lower than at B.

Let us now bring the union indifference map (see Figure 6.3) and the firm's iso-profit curves together, as in Figure 6.7. In the situation where the firm determined the level of employment we saw previously that the union would go to the point, represented by A in Figure 6.7, where the union indifference curve was tangential to the demand for labour curve.

In Figure 6.7 we now see, that if the union can also bargain over employment levels there are other combinations that would be preferred either by the union, or by the firm, or by both. Take the two limiting cases, represented by points B and C. First consider the combination of wage levels and employment represented by point B. The firm is indifferent between points A and B as both are on the same iso-product curve. The union, however, prefers point B to A as the former lies on a higher indifference curve.

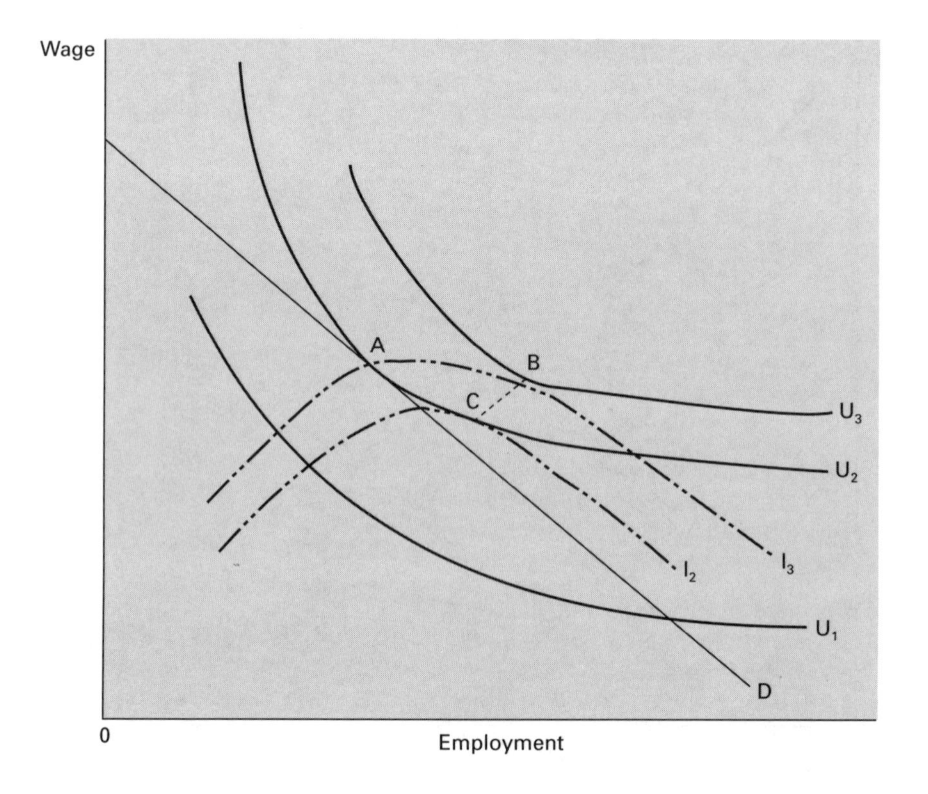

Figure 6.7 Efficient bargains

Now consider point C. The union is indifferent between A and C as both lie on the same indifference curve. The firm however prefers C to A as the former lies on a curve that represents higher profits. It thus follows that there are points between B and C which both the union and the firm would prefer to point A. The locus of points at which at least one of the partners would be better off than at point A, on the firm's demand for labour curve, is shown as the line BC in Figure 6.5 and is known as the contract curve.

Thus far we have shown just one segment of the contract curve. There will be other combinations of wages and employment, lying to the south-west of C and the north-east of B that would be preferred by at least one party to a point on the demand for labour curve (the other party being indifferent).

There will, however, be an upper and lower bound to the contract curve as each party to the bargain will have a limit beyond which they will not go. Consider first the union. It will not agree to a combination which represents a wage below the competitive outcome. For, as we saw in the previous section, if that were the case there is no reason why anyone would join the union. Similarly, the firm will have in mind some minimum acceptable level of profit. Perhaps, as we argued in the context of the sales revenue maximisation hypothesis in Section 3.4 of Chapter 3, this is the minimum level of profit necessary to satisfy shareholders.

These limits are shown in Figure 6.8. This may look a little forbidding at first sight, but is merely an extension of Figure 6.7.

The positioning of the points A, B and C is as explained in the previous diagram. It is evident that there will be many other points of tangency between union indifference curves and firm iso-product curves—a few of which are shown here. The contract curve does not, however, stretch beyond point X and point Z. Why not? Z lies on the iso-profit curve which represents the minimum acceptable level of profit. Iso-product curves which lie above I_4 represent unacceptable levels of profit and the firm will not conclude a bargain that results in such profit levels. The competitive wage is represented by W_c and any wage below this will see the likely demise of the union. Thus the contract curve between X and Z is the locus of all efficient bargaining outcomes.

Compare those results with that of the right to manage model. In the latter case, we saw the result of the bargain would be at A, where a union indifference curve is tangential to the demand for labour curve. Under efficient bargaining we end up somewhere on the line XZ. Thus we can say that employment will be higher than at A but we do not know whether the wage is higher or lower than at A. Remember that as we move from X towards Z the utility of the union increases while the profits of the firm fall. Whereabouts the final bargain is struck will depend, as in the bilateral monopoly model, upon the bargain skills and strengths of the two parties.

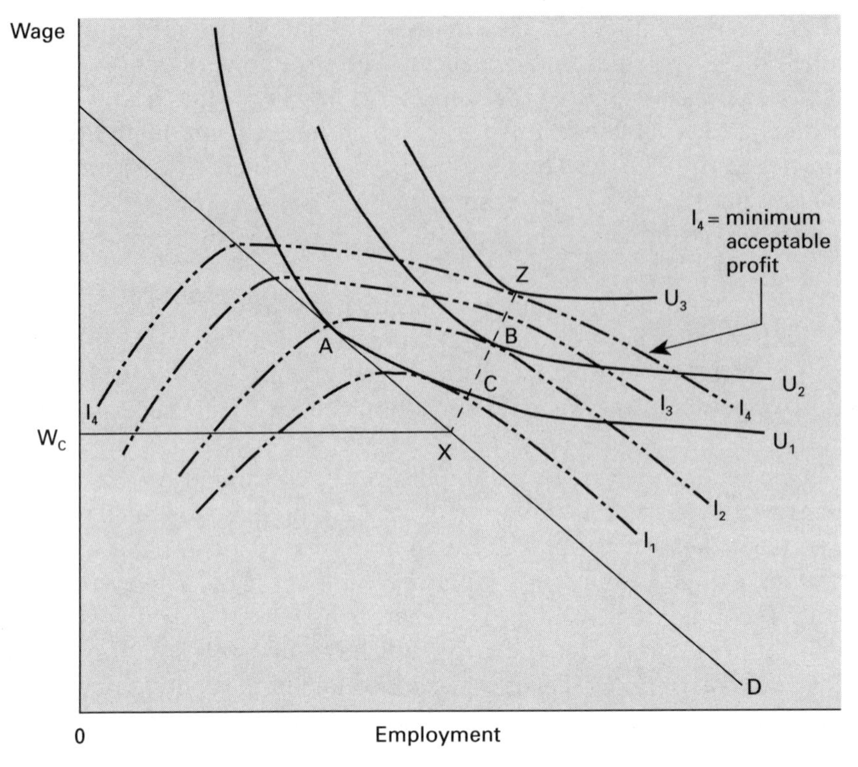

Figure 6.8 The limits of efficient bargaining

Compared to the competitive outcome of X we can see that the wage will be higher under competitive bargaining and so also will the level of employment. (This latter proposition will not always hold. Backward sloping contract curves will result from certain patterns of union preferences between employment and wages).

What in effect is going on in this model is that the firm earns some profit in excess of the competitive level (or an economic rent), usually because it enjoys some monopoly power in its product model. The union now gains some of this rent, taking some of it in the form of higher pay per worker and some of it in the form of extra workers who are not really needed. The technically most efficient method of producing any given output lies on the demand for labour curve; in this model the outcome is always to the right of the demand curve.

The term 'feather-bedding' is commonly used to describe conditions in industries which are overstaffed. These are invariably highly unionised and at the level of casual empiricism they lend credence to the model. Unions will rarely if ever be able to formally negotiate a precise volume of employment at a given wage. They can, however, negotiate staffing levels. For example that every train must have a guard as well as a driver, or the number of people in a flight crew. More generally unions can feather-bed through restrictive working practices that are condoned by management. A well-known example in Australia would be the overstaffing on the waterfront which is now belatedly being tackled.

It is not easy to devise formal empirical tests to distinguish between right to manage models and efficient bargaining models of union behaviour. The few tests that have been undertaken overseas have, so far, proved inconclusive.

6.4 The union mark-up

Throughout the previous two sections we have seen that whatever goals unions pursue the resulting wage is always higher than it would be in the absence of the union. It would seem logical to deduce from this that union members must earn more than workers who are not in unions. Unfortunately, it is not possible to make such an a priori deduction because unions affect the earnings of workers who are not members. These influences on the wages of other workers can be positive or negative. How do they arise?

First consider a negative effect. We have seen that when a union raises the wage above the competitive level the effect is often to reduce the level of employment. These displaced workers seek employment in other firms or industries and shift the supply curve of labour there to the right thus depressing the wage. Thus the union raises members' wages, lowers those of non-members, and hence creates a union wage differential.

There are two other effects at work, however, which tend to raise the wage of non-union workers. The first is known as the threat effect. Many firms wish to have a non-union workforce not for the direct financial gain that comes from lower wages but because they do not want any union imposed limits on the management decision-making process. Thus in an attempt to forestall unionisation they pay their workers the union rate. IBM is the classic example of a firm that has behaved in this way.

The second positive influence that unions may have on the wages of other workers arises from the spillover effect. In many industries, and firms people who are non-union members work alongside union members. It would be administratively costly to pay them differently and to do so would have adverse effects on morale. The firm thus pays all workers the union rate. In Australia this spillover effect tends to be formalised through the system of industrial awards. Thus, although about 40 per cent of workers are in unions, 80 per cent of workers get paid under awards, and hence receive the award pay negotiated by unions. (In the same way as union density has declined so too has award coverage. In 1985, 85 per cent of workers were covered by awards.) Given that unions will raise the pay of non-union members in some circumstances and lower them in others the net effect is a matter for empirical investigation.

Estimates of the union mark-up

Empirical work has attempted to identify what is termed the union mark-up. The union mark-up is equal to:

$$\frac{\text{Wages of union members} - \text{wages of identical non-union workers}}{\text{Wages of non-union members}}$$

The mark-up is usually expressed in percentage terms. It is important to note that we are concerned with identifying differences in pay between unionists and non-unionists who are identical in all other respects. That is, we wish to compare sets of people whose human capital and other characteristics are such that we would, in the absence of unions, expect them to earn the same amount.

Three methods of estimating the union mark-up have been used. Investigators working before the 1970s had to rely upon cross-sectional analyses, comparing earnings in different industries with different union densities. It was difficult to control for differences in worker characteristics. The most careful sifting of this evidence for the United States was undertaken by Lewis who concluded that the mark-up was around 15 per cent and that it tended to become greater in recessions and smaller in economic upswings.[4]

In the 1970s what are termed unit record data came to be available and the second method of estimation uses these. Unit record data provide information on individuals. In this context the relevant information relates to earnings and the various characteristics such as age and education, that determine earnings. If there is information on a large number of individuals it is possible to estimate what are termed statistical earnings functions. These are potentially powerful tools of empirical analysis, the results of which we shall also refer to in subsequent chapters. It is thus useful to give a brief explanation of earnings functions here. The next few paragraphs are, therefore, a digression from our main theme, to which we shall shortly return.

Statistical earnings functions

The purpose of this section is to explain the principles underlying earnings functions and how to interpret the resulting empirical findings. It is not our intention to go into any detail or to explain how to estimate such functions. (A good exposition is provided by Berndt.[5])

The analysis in Chapters 4 and 5 suggests two factors that are likely to have a strong influence upon the earnings of an individual. The first is the amount of education they have received. In practice both the type and the amount of education will influence earnings. It is rarely possible to take the former into account, however, and earnings are thus held to be a function of the number of years of schooling, which we will denote by S.

A second major influence of earnings is the amount of on the job training a person has received. Data on this are rarely available and the number of years of labour market experience, X, is used instead. The longer a person has been in the labour force the more training he or she is likely to have received. Experience is usually measured as age minus years of schooling minus five, it being assumed that schooling begins at age five. Earnings tend to increase with experience at a declining rate and thus it is common to also include experience squared (X^2) as an explanatory variable.

Thus far we have an earnings function that relates the earnings (E) of an individual to three variables:

$$E = a + rS + bX + cX^2 + u \tag{1}$$

where a is a constant term, r, b, and c are co-efficients to be estimated and u is an error term. The co-efficients can be estimated, using a technique known as multiple regression analysis, for any group of individuals for whom the required information is available. Each of the co-efficients tells us the quantitative influence of that variable on earnings, holding all the other variables constant. Thus r reflects the rate of return to schooling and b reflects the rate of return to experience. As argued above we would expect the co-efficient c to be negative.

We know however that many other factors, apart from the three included in equation (1), will influence earnings. A widely used method to capture the effect of many other influences is the inclusion of what are termed dummy variables.

Our main concern in this chapter is the effect of trade unions on earnings. We wish to know the difference in pay between people, identical in other respects, who are in unions and who are not in unions. To identify this we add a dummy variable, which we shall denote by T, to equation (1) which thus becomes,

$$E = a + rS + bX + cX^2 + mT + u \tag{2}$$

For any individual who is a union member T will assume the value of unity and for any individual who is not in a union T will take on a value of zero. The union mark-up can be derived from the co-efficient m. It can be appreciated that statistical earnings functions are ideally suited to the purpose of estimating the union mark-up as they, in principle, allow us to hold the other influences on earnings constant. Other dummy variables can be included in earnings functions to capture the effect of say the industry a person works in or the region in which they reside. Thus it is common to find a whole string of dummy variables included in the regressions.

Earnings functions have now been estimated on a large number of data sets covering different countries and different time periods. At some risk of over-generalising the included variables typically account for about 40 per cent of the observed variation in earnings. This is a little disappointing. Nonetheless, the statistical earnings function is a very useful tool of empirical labour market analysis.

The union mark-up again

Returning to our main theme, Mulvey has made estimates of the union mark-up from unit record data resulting from a survey of Australian households undertaken in 1982 by the Australian Bureau of Statistics.[6] Mulvey found the union mark-up to be 9.6 per cent for males and 7.4 per cent for females. Miller and Rummery have made estimates of the mark-up for male workers using the 1985 Australian Longitudinal Survey.[7] This survey is confined to young workers, aged between nineteen and twenty-five. The union mark-up in this case was estimated to be 13.1 per cent. The authors argue that this is quite consistent with Mulvey's results as the largest union effects tend to operate for young workers. Rather higher estimates of the union mark-up have been obtained by Christie from a survey of males and females in 1984.[8] She estimates the mark-up to be 15.4 per cent. Thus from these three studies based on earnings functions it is correct to conclude that there is no doubt that a positive union mark-up exists and that it seems to be in the range 7–15 per cent.

As we have seen, 80 per cent of workers receive award wages and so it is likely that the main way that unions raise wages is through increasing the other components of earnings, notably over-award pay and overtime. Miller and Mulvey have investigated the role of trade unions in the allocation of overtime, using the 1985 Australian Longitudinal Survey referred to above.[9] Their main conclusions were as follows. First, unions influence the incidence but not the extent of overtime working. That is, union members have a greater chance of working some overtime but, once a person is working overtime, being a union member does not influence the hours of overtime. The authors suggest that about 1 per cent of the union mark-up of 13 per cent for young workers is explicable through this overtime effect.

Miller and Mulvey have subsequently investigated, using the same database, the effect of unions on the level of fringe benefits.[10] They find that union members do tend to enjoy a higher level of fringe benefits and the inclusion of the value of fringe benefits increases the union mark-up by about 1 per cent.

We can place the Australian union wage mark-up of 7–15 per cent in the context of overseas studies based upon statistical earnings functions. It seems that the mark-up here is very similar to that in Britain, where the level of union density is also similar, but lower than that in the United States, where union density is much lower. Literally hundreds of estimates have been undertaken on unit record data in the United States and it is difficult to summarise them. Perhaps 15 per cent might represent a central estimate.

The basic problem with the earnings function approach is that the data are never precise enough to enable researchers to compare precisely similar workers. This difficulty can be overcome where unit record data are available on a longitudinal basis. Here one can trace what happens to the earnings of the same people over time. In this context the task is to see how people's earnings change as they move from unionised to non-unionised jobs and vice versa. Longitudinal studies suffer from small sample sizes as such job changes are not all that common. In the United States estimates of the union mark-up derived from longitudinal studies tend to come up with rather lower estimates than those based on earnings functions. The limited evidence suggests that this is also true of Australia. Kornfeld has estimated the union mark-up for young workers using the longitudinal method from the Australian Longitudinal Survey.[11] He finds a wage premium of around 7 per cent for union workers, which is substantially less than the 13 per cent estimated from the same data by Miller and Rummery, using the earnings function approach.

We can thus conclude that unions do raise the pay of their members relative to that of non-union workers. The precise size of the mark-up is difficult to determine but appears, in Australia, to be of the order of 7–15 per cent.

The existence of a union mark will tend to lead to a misallocation of resources, as can be demonstrated in Figure 6.9.

Take a firm possessing some monopoly power but purchasing labour initially in a competitive market so that it can hire as much as it needs at the wage, W_0. Thus employment will be at N_0. Now a union is formed and bargains a wage of W_1. In a 'right to manage' situation employment will fall to N_1. This leads to a welfare loss represented by the area of the triangle ABC. This reflects the fact that the units of labour (N_0—N_1) that have been displaced had marginal products greater than their opportunity cost (which is equal to their wage). These are not the only welfare losses. The displaced workers will seek employment in other firms, depressing the wage there and increasing employment. We can 'represent' the situation in one of these other firms in the same diagram. Initially the wage was W_0 with N_0 labour being hired. Now the wage falls to W_2 and employment rises to N_2. This causes a further welfare loss for workers previously employed in the first firm with marginal products of at least W_0 now are employed in the second firm where their marginal products are lower (between W_0 and W_2). Christie has undertaken a rough calculation of the magnitude of these static welfare losses and suggest that they may be of the order of 0.5 per cent of GDP.

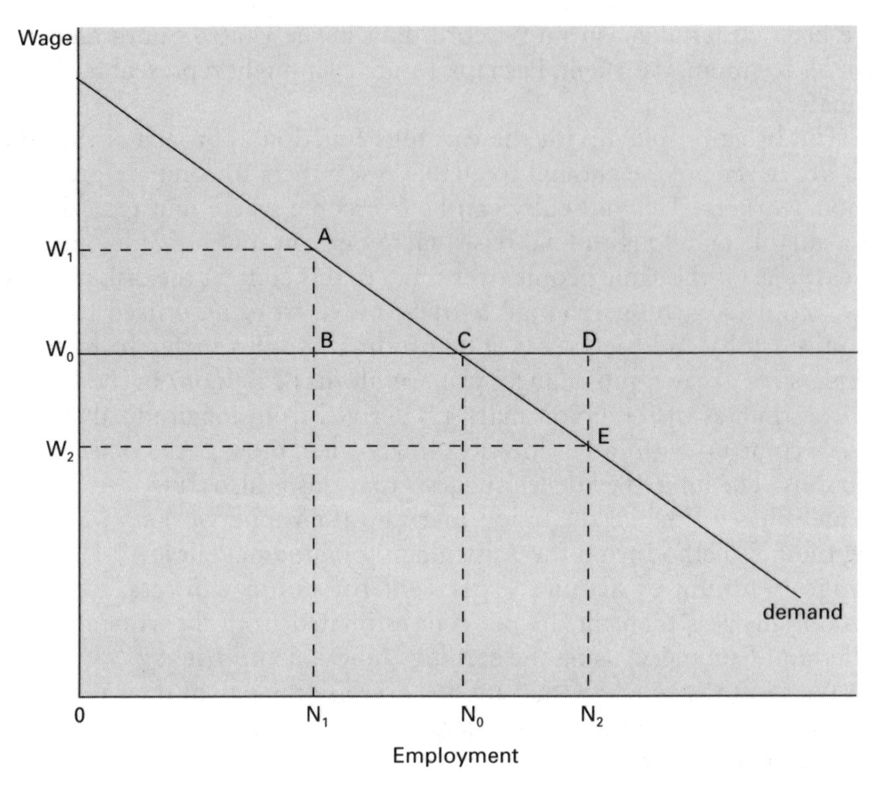

Figure 6.9 Allocative effects of unions

6.5 The exit-voice model of union behaviour

We have been discussing what has been termed 'the monopoly face' of unionism. This is not favourable to unions for we have seen that it leads to allocative inefficiencies and consequently to welfare losses.

In an influential book Freeman and Medoff have argued that there is a favourable result of trade unions which has to be set alongside their monopoly face.[12] This second effect is termed the 'voice response face of unionism' which, it is argued, raises productivity.

Consider how dissatisfaction is shown. There are two alternative methods, exit and voice. In product markets, exit consists of consumers changing products or services. If you go to a restaurant and are served a poor meal or receive poor service you do not go there again. If many people act in the same way the restaurant either improves or goes out of business. While this may well be a description of how many of us do behave if we get a bad meal there is a more efficient way of acting and that is to complain to the management of the restaurant. This may not only result in immediate improvement—an overcooked steak being replaced by a medium rare one—but will be far more effective in informing management of consumer dissatisfaction. This latter method of showing dissatisfaction is termed 'voice'. What are the analogous alternatives in labour markets? Exit simply consists of quitting. If you do not like the terms or conditions of work you leave and join another employer. The alternative is to use voice, that is to let management know of your dissatisfaction.

Freeman and Medoff argue that voice is the most likely response in unionised employment and exit the most likely response of non-union workers. There are two reasons for this. First many employment conditions such as safety, have some characteristics of public goods. They are non-excludable in the sense that no-one who works in a given factory or office can be excluded from benefiting from the conditions. Many conditions of work are also non-rival; one worker's benefit from the observance by a firm of stringent safety regulations does not mean there is less benefit for other workers. As a result each worker has only a very weak incentive to complain and try to get conditions improved. Unions, however, provide a collective voice. Note, that as in the case of public goods there is a free-rider problem—workers will benefit irrespective of whether they are in the union or not. Unions may try to stop free-riding by operating a closed shop but usually have to accept it as inevitable. The second reason for expecting individuals to be less likely to use voice and more likely to exit is because individuals will fear victimisation if they complain. They may be dismissed or their future promotion prospects may disappear. No such risks are faced by a trade union.

Unions are more likely to use the voice mechanism and quit rates will be lower in unionised firms. This, as we saw in the previous chapter, will be efficient from the point of view of the firm, notably where firms have made investments in firm-specific training and where the fixed costs of hiring are relatively high. Further unions are likely to negotiate a set of industrial relations procedures which are valued by workers and which are also likely to increase efficiency and productivity. Unions are also able to impose restrictive working practices and to restrict the scope of management decisions. Freeman and Medoff recognise this possibility, of course, and argue that which outcome results depends upon the prevailing industrial relations atmosphere. It is possible that this explains the different empirical findings in Britain and the United States. In the latter there is little doubt that the weight of the evidence finds that quit rates are lower in union firms and that productivity is higher, and in many studies substantially higher. In Britain, however, empirical analysis has tended to produce contrary results. It is widely thought that industrial relations attitudes are more adversarial in Britain than in the United States, with unions and management being more concerned with the division of a static level of company output rather than seeking ways, improved working methods for example, to increase output.

Thus the basic proposition is that unions raise output per worker, largely through reducing quit rates. There are few studies which have addressed this question in Australia. Miller and Mulvey have analysed the relation between quit rates and unionisation in the labour market for young workers, using data from the Australian Longitudinal Survey.[13] They find that while unions tend to reduce quit rates (by around 10 per cent) and are consequently associated with longer job durations (of around 20 per cent) they also reduce layoffs, that is they reduce job terminations which are at the discretion of the employer. This latter effect will tend to reduce productivity whereas the lower quit rates will tend to raise productivity. Thus the overall effect of unions on productivity is not clear, at least in the labour market for young workers.

Drago and Wooden have attempted to throw some light on this issue from the results of a mail survey of large firms accounting for about a third of total employment.[14] They note that conditions in Australia do not, a priori, appear to be favourable to the exit-voice model, which will be most effective when unions are organised along enterprise or industrial lines. In the former case, the union speaks for all its members employed by the firm. In Australia, however, unions tend to be organised along craft or occupational lines and hence any one employer has to deal with several unions. In these circumstances voice is likely to be relatively ineffective. The authors find that quit rates are not negatively associated with unionisation in large firms. Some other aspects of union presence, for example the existence of joint union-management committees do seem to be linked to reduced quit rates. Thus some indirect support is given to the proposition that unions lead to lower rates of turnover.

A more direct test has been carried out on the data gathered in the Australian Workplace Industrial Relations Survey that was undertaken in 1989–90.[15] This provides data on employer perceptions of productivity in their plants relative to others and on union density. Crockett and his colleagues find that trade unionism tends to be associated with lower relative productivity.

Thus these three Australian pieces of research have not, on balance, produced results supportive of the exit-voice model although more research is needed before we can reach definite conclusions. A tentative conclusion is perhaps that the exit–voice model, like some wine, does not travel too well and that it best explains outcomes in its country of origin, the United States. Nonetheless, it has proved very influential in discussion of the effects of trade unions and has drawn attention to the possibility that there are potential gains to be set aside the welfare losses associated with the monopoly face of unionism.

Concepts for review

- Union density
- Economic rent
- Right to manage models of union behaviour
- Union marginal revenue curve
- Union utility maximisation

- Monopsony power
- Marginal cost of labour
- Marshallian rules
- Bilateral monopoly
- Iso-profit curve
- Efficient bargains
- Feather-bedding
- Union mark-up
- Threat effect
- Spillover effect
- Earnings function
- Exit/voice responses

Questions

1. Why is unionism declining in Australia? Is it true that trade unions are becoming less effective in achieving their objectives? Would it matter if they were? (La Trobe University)
2. 'Unions reduce employment and lessen productivity.' Discuss theory and evidence. (Australian National University)
3. Many employers argue that although they are prepared to negotiate with unions about wages and conditions, they are not prepared to relinquish their 'right to manage' which includes the freedom to hire and fire workers as they see fit. How would you convince such an employer that this may not be the best way of going about things? (Curtin University)
4. Is the empirical evidence that trade unions raise their members' wages relative to those of non-members convincing? Does it take adequate account of the impact of unions on non-union wages? (University of Western Australia)

References

1. D. Peetz, 'Declining union density', *Journal of Industrial Relations*, vol. 32, no. 2, 1990, pp. 197-223.
2. P. Kenyon and P.E.T. Lewis, 'Trade union membership and the Accord', *Australian Economic Papers*, 1993 (forthcoming).
3. I.M. McDonald and R.M. Solow, 'Wage bargaining and employment', *American Economic Review*, vol. 71, no. 5, 1981, pp. 896-908.
4. G. Lewis, *Union Relative Wage Effects: a Survey*, University of Chicago Press, Chicago, 1986.
5. E.R. Berndt, *The Practice of Econometrics: Classic and Contemporary*, Addison-Wesley, Sydney, 1991.
6. C. Mulvey, 'Wage levels: do unions make a difference?' in J.R. Niland (ed.), *Wage Fixation in Australia*, Allen and Unwin, Sydney, 1986.

7 P. Miller and S. Rummery, 'Unionism and the structure of male wages for youth', *Journal of Industrial Relations*, vol. 31, no. 2, 1989, pp. 185-211.
8 V. Christie, 'Union wage effects and the probability of union membership', *Economic Record*, vol. 68, no. 200, 1992, pp. 43-56.
9 P. Miller and C. Mulvey, 'Trade unions and the distribution of paid overtime', *Journal of Industrial Relations*, vol. 33, no. 2, 1991, pp. 220-33.
10 P. Miller and C. Mulvey, 'Trade unions, collective voice and fringe benefits', *Economic Record*, vol. 68, no. 20, 1992, pp. 125-41.
11 R. Kornfeld: 'Australia's trade unions, wage, fringe, and job tenure effects', National Bureau of Economic Research, mimeo, 1990.
12 R.B. Freeman and J.L. Medoff, *What do Unions do?*, Basic Books, New York, 1984.
13 P. Miller and C. Mulvey, 'Australian evidence on the exit/voice model of the labour market', *Industrial and Labour Relations Review*, vol. 45, no. 1, 1991, pp. 44-57.
14 R. Drago and M. Wooden, 'Turnover downunder: trade unions and exit behaviour in Australia', *Journal of Industrial Relations*, vol. 33, no. 2, 1991, pp. 234-248.
15 G. Crockett et al, 'The impact on unions on workplace productivity in Australia', *Western Australian Labour Market Research Centre Discussion Paper*, 92/5, 1992.

CHAPTER 7

Discrimination in labour markets

7.1 Introduction

Discrimination exists when members of a group of people are denied opportunities to develop their capabilities which are available to others in the same society and are denied equal rewards for equal capabilities. The grounds for discrimination are invariably that the group affected is accorded a low status by the rest of society. To be discriminated against a group has to be readily distinguishable and, usually, to be in a minority. Aborigines meet both criteria, and women do so partially for, although women and men are usually distinguishable, women are not in a minority in the population. However, in the labour market, women are in the minority, albeit only just. In Australia, as in most societies, they are discriminated against.

Our definition suggests a distinction between two forms of discrimination, that which occurs before one enters the labour market and that which occurs within the labour market. Discrimination before the market is entered occurs where groups are discriminated against in upbringing and in schooling and other social services, particularly health. As a result, they bring to the labour market less human capital (in the broadest sense), and the range of occupations open to them is correspondingly restricted. This restriction of choice can also be of a more direct form, where workers identical except for one characteristic, say race, are afforded unequal entry into an occupation.

Discrimination within the market occurs where once individuals of a certain group are admitted into any employment, they are paid less than otherwise identical individuals and/or have less scope for advancement within that employment.

In practice, it is not always easy to make a clear distinction between these two types of discrimination and we shall see that there are interrelationships between them. Nevertheless, it will be found to be a useful conceptual division, which we shall attempt to retain. Much of the theoretical and empirical research undertaken by labour economists has concentrated, naturally enough, on discrimination within the labour market, and this will also be our main focus.

We do, however, in Section 7.2 provide some information on the forms taken by discrimination before the market. In Section 7.3 we discuss several theories of labour market discrimination and in Section 7.4 we describe labour market discrimination in Australia, placing some emphasis on discrimination against females. Some policy implications that can be drawn from the analysis of discrimination are presented in the final section.

7.2 Discrimination before the labour market

In this section we shall confine our attention to pre-labour market discrimination against Aborigines and women. It is possible that discrimination is also suffered by migrants from a non-English speaking background. The evidence on such discrimination, particularly in education, is the subject of much dispute however, and the issue will not be pursued here.[1]

Education and health

One important form of discrimination before the market is in education, with women and Aborigines possessing less human capital than men and whites respectively. Take the case of women first. We saw in Chapter 4 that a major determinant of how much education children receive is the socioeconomic background of their parents. Boys and girls are distributed equally across social classes yet until the last decade girls received less education than boys. Currently the tendency for women to receive less education than men is only observable in universities, and then only in higher degrees rather than bachelor degrees. Enrolment rates in voluntary schooling are, in fact, slightly higher for girls. From Table 7.1 it can be seen that the same is true for bachelors degrees and that it is only in enrolments for higher degrees (which are quantitatively relatively small) that women are under-represented.

This position of more or less equal distribution of enrolments in voluntary schooling and for first degrees has only recently been attained. As recently as 1971, for example, 38 per cent of males aged between fifteen and nineteen were in school, whereas for females the proportion was 33 per cent. In 1979, females accounted for only 39 per cent of enrolments

Table 7.1 University students, 1991 (%)

Enrolled	*Female*	*Male*
Bachelor degree	52.3	47.7
Masters degree	43.1	56.9
Doctorate	35.8	64.2

Source: *Selected Higher Education Statistics, 1991,* Department of Employment, Education and Training.

for first degrees. The significance of this evidence of discrimination before the market that occurred until recently is that the stock of human capital possessed by the female labour force as a whole will be less than that of the male labour force, even though at present it is only in enrolments in higher degrees that females are under-represented.

Aborigines receive, on average, substantially less education than does the population as a whole. One set of indicators of this are relative retention rates in secondary schooling which are set out in Table 7.2.

Table 7.2 Retention rates in secondary schooling, 1985

	Aborigines (%)	*Total population*
Year 9 to Year 10	79	92
Year 9 to Year 11	32	62
Year 9 to Year 12	15	40

Source: *Aboriginal statistics, 1986* (Department of Aboriginal Affairs) and *National Schools Statistics Collection, 1985* (ABS, cat. no. 4221.0).

The retention ratios show what proportion of Year 9 students stay on to subsequent years of secondary schooling and they are substantially lower for Aborigines. It follows that Aborigines will also be very under-represented in universities. Two other statistics serve to emphasise the relatively low amount of education received by Aborigines. In 1981, 12.5 per cent of the Aboriginal population had never been to school; the figure for the whole population is 3.0 per cent. Only 4 per cent of Aborigines, but 24 per cent of the whole population had post-school qualifications.

The standards of health and housing services received by Aborigines are also much lower than those of white Australians, and this compounds the effect of a low level of education. Hearing difficulties are relatively common among young Aborigines and this has an adverse effect on educational achievement. One measure of the prevalence of hearing difficulty is the incidence of a disease called otitis media. In 1983, 20 per cent of Aborigines aged between two to three years had this disease whereas only 1 per cent of white children were affected. Other indicators show that young Aborigines are more likely to suffer from poor health than whites. Poor health leads to absenteeism from schools and also has an independent effect on labour market experience as ill health is a common cause of unemployment. Overcrowded and poor quality housing also mitigates against Aboriginal children studying at home.

Segregation

The second main form of discrimination before the market is the unequal access to various occupations afforded to the discriminated group. In part this reflects unequal possessions of human capital, for if a group has little in the way of qualifications, it follows that those occupations which require higher qualifications are closed to that group. Beyond that, however, convention may restrict certain groups to a narrow range of occupations. Whatever the cause there is a high degree of segregation, by gender and by race, in the Australian labour market.

The eight occupations which quantitatively contribute most to the overall level of segregation by gender in Australia are shown in Table 7.3.

The eight occupations shown in Table 7.3 are quantitatively important, and accounted for about 45 per cent of total employment in 1984. The degree of segregation is striking. Females make up, for example, 99.1 per cent of stenographers and typists, and 92.8 per cent of nurses but 1.9 per cent of the group comprising machine workers.

Table 7.3 Occupations contributing most to segregation, 1984

	Total employment	*Percentage*	
Occupation	*('000)*	*Females*	*Males*
Bookkeepers and cashiers	164.9	81.0	19.0
Employers, workers on own account, directors etc.	430.7	15.5	84.5
Housekeepers, cooks, maids etc.	222.8	77.7	23.3
Machine toolmakers, metal machinists, mechanics etc.	430.5	1.9	98.1
Nurses	155.7	92.8	7.2
Other clerical workers	804.1	63.9	36.1
Proprietors, shopkeepers, shop assistants etc.	467.6	63.4	36.6
Stenographers and typists	200.4	99.1	0.9

Source: Karmel and Maclachlan.[2]

Table 7.4 Women in disproportionately female occupations, 1911–85

		Female labour force in these occupations (%)	
Year	*Females as % of total labour force*	*Expected*	*Observed*
1911	20	23	84
1921	20	26	83
1933	23	22	74
1947	22	33	78
1961	25	32	80
1966	30	34	80
1971	32	39	82
1975	35	28	80
1980	37	30	81
1985	38	31	82

Source: K. Mumford.[3]

Occupational segregation has existed for a long time. In Table 7.4 we show the extent of segregation over the period 1911–85.

The figures are to be interpreted as follows. A disproportionately female occupation is one in which women form a higher proportion of the workforce than they do of the total labour force. The 'expected' proportion of women reported in the third column of Table 7.4 is the percentage of the female workforce that would be found in these occupations had women been distributed was the total labour force. Thus in 1985, for example, when women accounted for 38 per cent of the workforce, 82 per cent worked in predominantly female occupations although we would expect only 31 per cent of females to be in these occupations. The table shows that despite the large proportionate increase in female employment the degree of segregation appears to have changed very little this century. However, the types of occupation in which women are concentrated change. In 1911, domestic service and the manufacture of clothing were dominant whereas now it is clerical work, typing and sales. In 1984, in fact, no less than 41 per cent of female workers were employed in the latter three occupations.

The figures in Table 7.4 represent one simple way of measuring occupational segregation. It is possible to devise more sophisticated indices of segregation. Unfortunately, different indices generate different trends and it is a matter of some dispute as to whether segregation increased or decreased between 1961 and 1981.[4]

The extent and persistence of this segregation of the labour market into male and female components is, nonetheless, striking. Its causes are complex, arising from both economic and social forces. Among major influences are the past lower level of human capital investments by women (which also reflects segregation), social influences which reduce the aspirations of women, prejudice on the part of employers and male employees, and traditional views on sex roles. Women are concentrated in areas where the work is 'derivative of housework' such as the manufacture and retailing of food and clothing, cleaning, and caring for the sick and young.

Segregation by sex, is often viewed with concern and it has been argued that it must be eliminated if women are to attain economic equality with men. The elimination of segregation would mean that the proportion of men to women would be the same in every occupation. There is no reason, however, to suppose that this would be an optimal allocation, for as long as men and women differ in unalterable characteristics, such as physical strength and manual dexterity, then welfare will be maximised if the sexes are distributed unequally across occupations according to their comparative advantages. We shall discuss the effects of segregation on earnings in Section 7.5. There we shall also see that, at least in the last twenty years, the existence of segregation has worked in favour of women in the sense that some adverse employment consequences of the raising of the pay of women relative to that of men have been avoided.

Aborigines are also concentrated in relatively few occupations. In 1986 about three-quarters of male Aborigines worked in three occupational groups—labourers and related workers, tradespersons and machine operators.[5] Similarly nearly three-quarters of Aboriginal women were in three occupational groups—clerical workers, labourers, and personal service and sales. Aborigines are under-represented in managerial and professional employment. Of Aborigines 9 per cent are in this group, whereas for all Australians the proportion is 24 per cent and 43 per cent of employed Aborigines work in the public service.

The figures above refer to Aborigines in employment. A further form of discrimination faced by Aborigines is difficulty in obtaining a job. Employment to population ratios are relatively low and unemployment rates are high. (Strictly speaking unemployment is not a form of pre-labour market discrimination as once a person is unemployed they are by definition in the labour force. It is convenient to present the figures here, however.)

The differences shown in Table 7.5 between the labour market experience of Aborigines and the total population are striking. The difference in the employment to population ratio is no less than 23.1 per cent, while unemployment rates are nearly four times greater for Aborigines. In some areas employment prospects are even bleaker for Aborigines. A survey undertaken in 1987 in non-metropolitan areas of New South Wales estimated the unemployment rates of Aboriginal males to be 76 per cent and that of females to be 65 per cent.[6]

Table 7.5 Labour force status of the population aged more than fifteen years, 1986

	Employment to population ratio (%)	*Labour force to population ratio (%)*	*Unemployment rate (%)*
Aboriginal population	31.3	48.3	35.4
Total population	54.4	60.0	9.3

Source: Junankar and Kapuscinski.[5]

7.3 Models of labour market discrimination

We now turn to discrimination within the labour market which has received the greatest theoretical analysis from economists who have tended to take the pre-market factors as given and then attempted to explain the different treatment accorded to groups once they are in employment. This form of 'pure' labour market discrimination might be defined as occurring when persons who otherwise possess the same characteristics as the majority are afforded adverse treatment solely on the basis of their race or sex (or some other characteristic).

We will briefly describe three models of discrimination. The first of these is based upon prejudice or distaste while the other two models, the statistical discrimination model and the monopsonistic discrimination model, are based on profit maximising behaviour by employers.

The distaste model

This was first developed by Becker in an attempt to explain overt discrimination in rates of pay against blacks in the United States.[7] Discrimination can be enforced by employers, employees, or consumers. Each of these groups can have a distaste for associating with the discriminated group (which we will take to be blacks).

The extent of this distaste can be measured by what is termed a 'discrimination co-efficient', d. Thus an employer with distaste, faced with black and white workers with equal marginal products and with a wage for black workers of W_b would act as if the wage rate were W_b (l+d). Therefore, that employer would employ blacks, rather than whites of equal productivity, only if the wage paid to blacks was lower. If the black wage is lower and blacks are not employed, the employer is sacrificing profits in order to avoid the disutility of associating with blacks. The employer sacrifices profits for, where the two groups have equal marginal products, profits are maximised by employing all blacks as they have the lowest wages. It has been argued that the persistence of this sort of discrimination is incompatible with competition as non-discriminators would drive the discriminators out of business, although it is possible that some entrepreneurs may settle for permanently lower profits to avoid employing blacks. Alternatively, complete segregation in employment would occur with no differences in wages.

The latter is also the likely result if the discrimination is enforced by employees. In this case white employees have a distaste for working with blacks and, offered a wage rate, W_i, in a situation where blacks are employed, act as if the wage rate were W_i (l-d). The logical outcome of this situation is, however, completely segregated establishments with no racial differences in pay for workers of equal ability. Where, as in Australia, overt discrimination in rates of pay is limited, then we would predict on this view that there would be considerable segregation (in this case by sex) and we have seen that this is the case.

The third group who may express distaste for the discriminated group is consumers. Faced with the price, P, of a good produced by blacks they act as if the price were P(l+d). As few purchasers meet the producers face-to-face, this form of distaste in general is likely to be relatively unimportant. Further, women are commonly employed in situations where they meet consumers, distribution being a good example, which suggests that this is not an important element in sex discrimination. It may be more important, however, in the case of Aborigines.

Becker used these concepts to develop a theory of discrimination in the form of an international trade model in which two groups (blacks and whites) trade, with the discrimination co-efficient representing a tariff. The relevance of this approach is to be doubted and it is difficult to extend it realistically to the male-female case.

Statistical discrimination

We have seen in Chapters 4 and 5 that employers screen applicants for jobs in various ways. Different worker characteristics are used to select individuals. Some, referred to as signals, are alterable characteristics such as education while others, such as race and sex, are unalterable and are known as indices.

Say employers, either on the basis of past experience or of prejudice, come to believe that women or Aborigines have lower productivity (in some broad sense) than men or non-Aborigines. In the case of Aborigines, sheer prejudice may cause some employers to undervalue worker capabilities or they may be seen as unreliable because of an alleged tendency to 'go walkabout'. In the case of women, employers may think that absenteeism will be higher for married females with children or that females are more likely to quit than men. If the firm has made investments in specific training of women, then the presumed higher quit rates will impose financial costs upon the firm.

Statistical discrimination then occurs when faced with two applicants, otherwise apparently similar, one of which is male and the other female, the employer simply assumes that the individual female in question will also tend to have the higher potential to quit that is thought to be possessed by all females. The employer either selects the male or pays the female a lower wage. In this case, distaste does not enter the calculation, because statistical discrimination arises from the costs of gathering information.

Monopsonistic discrimination

This explanation of discrimination is again based on profit maximising behaviour rather than distaste. Employers have monopsony power when they face an upward-sloping supply curve for a type of worker. If this is the case then, as explained on p. 130, the marginal cost of employing an extra worker is greater than the wage paid to that worker, for the higher wage paid to the marginal worker has also to be paid to those previously working at a lower wage. Thus the cost-minimising rules that we derived in Chapter 3 have to be amended. The cost-minimising condition for the employment of any pair of inputs was derived for labour and capital, but can equally be written in terms of male (M) and female (F) labour as:

$$\frac{W_M}{MRPL_M} = \frac{W_F}{MRPL_F}$$

This is appropriate when the employer is hiring in competitive labour markets where the marginal cost of each type of labour is its wage. Otherwise, it is the marginal cost that is appropriate and hence the cost-minimising employer hires up to the point where:

$$\frac{MC_M}{MRPL_M} = \frac{MC_F}{MRPL_F}$$

If males and females have different supply schedules (in Figure 7.1, S_M and S_F respectively) then this condition implies that they are paid different amounts, even where their marginal products are the same. It is plausible to argue that the elasticity of labour supply to a firm would be lower for females than for males because the former are likely to have fewer alternative employment opportunities due to inflexible working hours and smaller travel to work areas. The result is as shown in Figure 7.1 which assumes that males and female have the same marginal products, but that females have lower supply elasticities. The marginal cost of employing labour of both types (MC_{M+F}) is derived by the horizontal addition of the marginal cost schedules for males and females (MC_M and MC_F respectively), and total employment is determined by the intersection of the

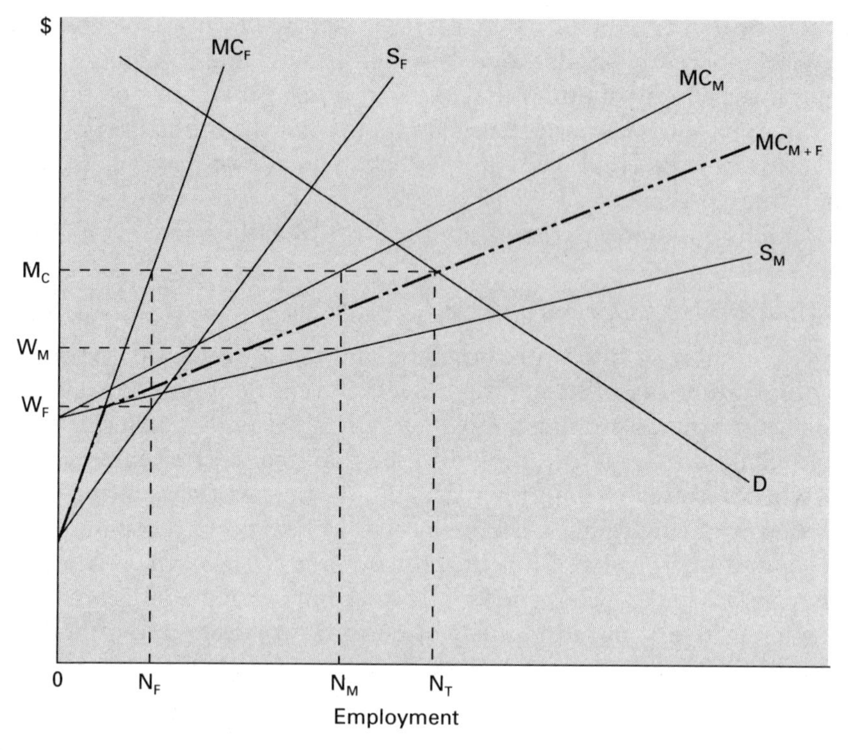

Figure 7.1 Monopsonistic discrimination

marginal product and the aggregate marginal cost schedules; hence N_T workers are employed. Males and females are each employed up to a point where their marginal cost is at this level but the difference in supply elasticities result in a wage difference. N_F females are employed, and the wage necessary to bring forth this supply is W_F; male employment is N_M at the higher wage W_M. (The reader will note that discrimination in pay here arises in the same way as does price discrimination in product markets where sellers have monopoly power. In price discrimination, products with the same cost are sold at different prices in different markets, the price being higher the less elastic is demand.)

Where discrimination is of this sort then both men and women are being exploited in the sense that they are being paid less than their marginal products. We saw in the previous chapter that trade unions tend to eliminate monopsonistic exploitation and hence this explanation has to be heavily qualified in unionised industries. It is possible that male-dominated unions may tacitly collude with employers to allow exploitation of women (but not of men). In this case, however, we are really back to distaste or low status as the real cause of the discrimination. In general, however, the lower supply elasticity of female labour may lead to some monopsonistic exploitation of women (with the caveat that this is unlikely to take the form of lower minimum rates of pay in Australia). Specific tests of this hypothesis (in the United States and Britain) have not, however, yielded conclusive results. We should finally note that for a firm to act in the way we have described it may either actually possess monopsony power or it may collude (formally or informally) with other employers to avoid bidding up the price of female labour and hence it can act as if it had monopsony power. The analogy in product markets would be where firms tacitly agree to refrain from price competition.

7.4 Discrimination within the labour market in Australia

Labour market discrimination takes two main forms. First, discrimination in rates of pay for similar work and, second, in the average level of earnings. We shall discuss each in turn. Our emphasis will be on discrimination against women, as lack of data has very much precluded analysis of the earnings of Aborigines.

As we shall see shortly, women do earn less than men and Aborigines less than non-Aborigines. It is important to be clear from the outset that it does not necessarily follow that all of the observed earnings differences reflect labour market discrimination. These groups may possess, for example, less human capital and hence would earn less if there were no discrimination. At the end of the section, we shall look at how earnings functions can be used to estimate how much of the observed male–female earnings differential is due to labour market discrimination.

Rates of pay

From the inception of the arbitration system at the turn of the century until 1969 the Australian Arbitration Commission (now called the Industrial Relations Commission) made two awards for occupational classifications in which both men and women worked, and thus overtly discriminated against women. To give some examples, in 1964 the award rate of pay for a female process worker in engineering was only 74 per cent of that for a male; for a knitter the proportion was 70 per cent, and for a bookbinder it was 62 per cent. In its decision of 1969 the commission decided that no such distinction should be drawn in future except that the change be phased in over three years and that the male adult minimum wage should not apply to women. In 1974 the adult minimum wage was also extended to women. Thus, to the extent that workers are covered by the commission's awards no discrimination in rates of pay can occur.

Most women are not, as we have seen, employed at the same work as men. There are few male typists or female miners. The Arbitration

Commission in its 1969 decision adopted the principle of 'equal pay for equal work' but this could be applied only to jobs done by men and women. Thus, at the end of the three year phasing-in of that decision it was estimated that only 28 per cent of female workers had in fact gained equal pay.

The commission in 1972 extended the principle to encompass 'equal pay for work of equal value', an approach similar to that adopted in anti-discrimination legislation in other countries. In its 1972 equal pay decision the bench stated that 'implementation ... will call for the exercise of the broad judgement which has characterised work value inquiries'. This 'broad judgement' has been easiest to apply within occupations or industries where similar work can be fairly readily identified. It has been argued, however, that the commission's reluctance to compare dissimilar work has meant that the equality principle has not been fully applied to some female dominated occupations, such as nursing.[8]

The reward for work done at award rates of pay does not, of course, comprise the whole of earnings and there remains scope for discrimination against women in the other elements of pay. In Table 7.6 we show average weekly earnings decomposed into three parts, that due to working a standard week at award rates of pay, that due to payments by results and over-award rates of pay, and that due to working overtime.

Table 7.6 Make-up of average weekly earnings: full-time non-managerial workers, 1991 (%)

	Females	*Males*
Award (or basic) pay	96.0	87.5
Payment by results and over-award pay	1.7	3.2
Overtime	2.3	9.3

Source: *Distribution and Composition of Employee Earnings*, (ABS, cat. no. 6306.0).

It is evident that the proportion of pay made up by overtime payments is substantially lower for females than for males. It has been shown that this difference does not reflect direct discrimination in the allocation of overtime opportunities but is the result of another form of segregation.[9] Which is that females are under-represented in occupations and industries in which there is a high incidence of working overtime. The lesser amount of overtime worked by women may also reflect supply conditions as many women do not wish to work overtime. The fact that men receive more of their pay in the form of over-award and piece-work payments may represent discrimination, but the extent of such discrimination is not known. It seems unlikely, though, that there can be much overt discrimination against women in terms of pay for performing the same tasks as are done by men.

Overt discrimination against Aborigines in award rates of pay no longer occurs. As in the case of women, however, the Arbitration Commission used to act in a discriminatory way. Prior to 1968, Aborigines were excluded from the provisions of the various awards covering the pastoral industry, and tended to be paid significantly less than other Australian workers. In 1968, however, the award was extended to Aborigines and the pay of most workers increased substantially. Subsequently there occurred a marked decline in the employment of Aborigines in agriculture. In 1971, 24 per cent of all Aborigines worked in agriculture but by 1986 this proportion had declined to 7 per cent. It is a matter of some dispute as to how much of this decline was due to the 1968 decision. The increase in Aboriginal wages must have led to some reduction in employment but technological changes such as the use of helicopters in mustering were also leading to job losses.

Unequal opportunities for advancement

The second form that discrimination can take within the market is through unequal opportunities for advancement within an occupation or industry. Where discrimination of women takes this form the cause is probably to be found in traditional sex relationships, that women are not placed in positions of authority over men. There are numerous examples. In education the majority of primary school teachers are female yet there are few female principals. Only two vice-chancellors are female. In the public service virtually all senior positions are held by men. In 1985, only one out of thirty-one department heads was a woman.[10] Few women occupy executive or managerial positions and those who do are in occupations which are female dominated, for example, editing women's magazines or retailing.

The result is that we would expect women to have flatter lifetime income profiles than men. This is in fact the case as can be seen from an examination of Figure 7.2 where income is plotted by age and sex for three educational levels. For each group, the female profiles are less sloped than the male, the difference increasing with educational level. These differences in lifetime earnings also arise from the fact that married women typically leave the labour force for periods of five to ten years to raise children. This may be viewed as a form of societal discrimination against women but it is not clear to what extent it constitutes discrimination within the labour market. Absence from the market would be expected to lead to flatter profiles, but this effect may be compounded by employers giving less training to all women in the knowledge that some will leave. From the available data we are unable to assign differences in earnings to each cause, but there is no doubt that some of the difference does reflect discrimination.

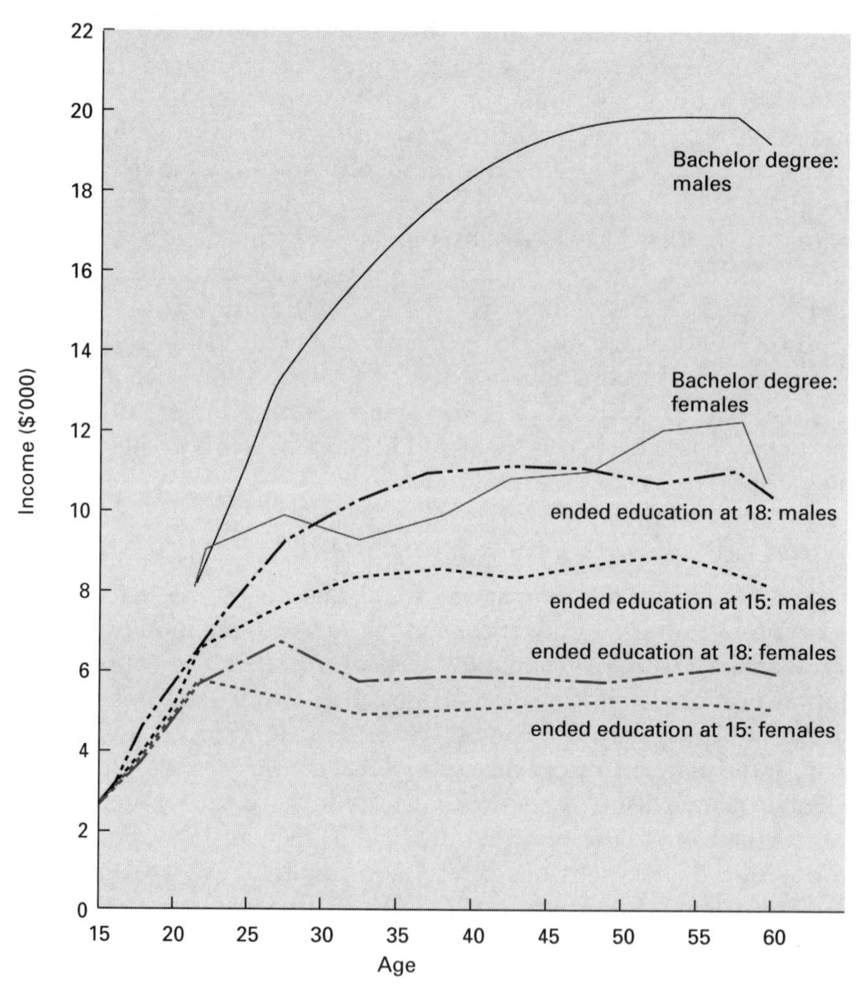

Source: Census of population and housing, 1976

Figure 7.2 Age–income profiles, males and females, 1976

Aborigines largely work in unskilled occupations in which there are few prospects for advancement. More generally it seems probable that they are denied equal opportunities for advancement within various occupations. For evidence on the earnings of Aborigines we have to rely on figures for incomes. In Table 7.7 we compare the incomes of the Aborigines and of the total population who were employed.

Male Aborigines had average incomes which were 71 per cent of those of the total population and for females the corresponding proportion was 80 per cent. As no statistical analysis of such figures has been undertaken we cannot quantify the causes of these differences but it is safe to say that they at least in part reflect discrimination within the labour market.

Table 7.7 Real average annual incomes of the employed population, 1986

	Males	*Females*
Aborigines	9 872	7 966
Total population	13 934	8 999

Source: Treadgold.[11]
Note: Figures are in 1980-81 dollars.

Statistical analysis

In comparing the pay of men and women it is preferable to use data on hourly, rather than weekly, earnings as women work fewer hours than men. In 1990, on this basis, women earned about 12 per cent less than men. To investigate how much, if any, of this difference is due to discrimination within the labour market we use statistical earnings functions. The basic methodology is as follows. For males estimate an earnings function:

$$E_m = m(X_m) \quad (1)$$

where E_m is the average hourly earnings of males and X_m is a vector of male characteristics, that is, the variables found on the right-hand side of equation (2) on p. 142 for example.

Then estimate an earnings function for females, where the subscript, *f*, denotes female:

$$E_f = f(X_f) \quad (2)$$

Thus *m* gives us the set of returns earned by males from their characteristics and *f* shows the returns gained by females from their characteristics.

The next step is to ask, what would the earnings of females be if they had the same characteristics (for example, years of schooling) as men but retained the payoffs that females gain from their actual characteristics? That is, estimate:

$$E_f^{/} = f(X_m) \quad (3)$$

Comparisons of E_m E_f and $E_f^{/}$ can then help us identify the source of differences in earnings between men and women. Thus, say we obtained the following results:

$$E_m = \$10.00,\ E_f = \$9.00,\ E_f^{/} = \$9.50$$

The observed difference in the hourly earnings of men and women is \$1.00. $(E_f^{/})$ tells us (subject to all the unavoidable estimation errors) that if females had the same characteristics as men but retained the female payoffs to those characteristics then their earnings would be $9.50. So half the difference is explained by, for example, females having less labour market experience and so on. The other half is due to them being rewarded for their characteristics at a lower rate than men. This latter half of the earnings difference is usually ascribed to employer discrimination against women.

It is usual to also estimate:

$$E_f^{II} = m(X_f) \quad (4)$$

that is, estimate how much females would earn if they retained their own characteristics but received the male payoffs to characteristics. This can similarly be used to decompose the observed differential into two parts.

Chapman and Mulvey have made such estimates using data from a survey of Australian households undertaken in 1982 by the Australian Bureau of Statistics.[12] Observed average hourly earnings, were $6.68 for men and $5.65 for women. Imputing male characteristics to females, that is estimating E_f^I in our terminology, makes very little difference to female earnings. On the other hand, E_f^{II} that is female earnings on the assumption that they retain their actual endowments but get the returns estimated from the male equation, are estimated to be $6.44, or only 5 per cent less than men. While the authors qualify this result to some extent, particularly because of measurement difficulties, it is in order to conclude that a large part of the observed earnings difference is due to females receiving a lesser reward than men to their human capital and other endowments. These lesser rewards are, in turn, taken to be due to employer discrimination.

Drago has made estimates of the extent of discrimination from a survey of twenty-three work places in 1988.[13] The methodology was different from that adopted by Chapman and Mulvey and this latter study produces rather lower estimates of discrimination. Drago suggests that women earn about 4 per cent less than men with apparently similar labour force characteristics. On this basis about one-third of the observed wage differential reflects discrimination.

We can conclude that discrimination against women does occur within the labour market, although it is not easy to estimate its precise extent. On the basis of the few Australian studies it seems that of the observed wage differential of around 12 per cent around one-half to two-thirds is explicable in terms of observable characteristics and about one-third to one half is due to discrimination within the labour market.

7.5 The equal pay decisions and affirmative action

It was shown in the previous section that up until 1969 there was open discrimination against women in the system of awards in that in most occupations the rate of pay for females was below that of men. The intention to eliminate this discrimination was announced in 1969 although its implementation was phased in over three years.

We look at two issues concerning the implementation of the equal pay decisions. First, was the change in award rates of pay reflected in earnings? For one way in which the intentions of the (then) Arbitration Commission could have been subverted would have been if there were offsetting changes in the other elements of earnings. To investigate this we show in the first two columns of Table 7.8 female award pay as a proportion of that of males, and female earnings as a proportion of male earnings. These two proportions are then expressed as a ratio in column three.

Table 7.8 Female and male rates of pay and weekly earnings

	1	2	3
	Female award rates as % of those of males	*Female earnings as % of those of males*	*Earnings ratio (col. 2) as % of rates ratio (col. 1)*
1947	60.9	52.5	86.2
1969	72.0	58.4	81.1
1972	77.4	64.3	83.1
1976	92.4	77.1	83.4
1980	91.6	(79.6)	(86.9)
1986	92.3	(82.6)	(89.5)

Source: 1947–73, Gregory and Duncan[14]; 1980–86, Mumford.[3]

Note: Figures in parentheses not strictly comparable with previous years.

Consider firstly column one. It can be seen that while female award rates of pay increased as a proportion of male rates between 1969 and 1972 the largest increase occurred subsequently. (For statistical reasons the ratio in column one cannot reach 100.0.) It is clear that the movement in the earnings indices after 1969 mirrored very closely the changes in the awards series; this is most obviously seen from column three.

The second issue is what effect did these changes have on the level of female employment? From the standard cost minimising rules we would predict that as female pay rose relative to that of men employers would decrease the number of females employed relative to the number of males. The increase in the relative pay of women occurred at a time when the rate of growth of female employment was significantly in excess of that of male employment. Nonetheless, the substantial change in relative pay did have some moderating effect on the growth of female employment. Gregory and Duncan estimated that over the period 1969–76 the wage change reduced the rate of growth of female employment by about 1.5 per cent per year.[14] Thus only a very limited amount of substitution away from women occurred, despite the substantial increase in female pay relative to that of men. In this instance segregation acted to protect female employment, for the amount of substitution which can take place when labour markets are highly segregated is very limited.

How does segregation which, as we have seen, is a form of discrimination before the labour market, affect the level of earnings of women? Is it, for example, the case that the occupations into which women are segregated are low paying and therefore that segregation depresses the average earnings of women? Rimmer has estimated what average female earnings would be if females received the pay that they do within occupations but were distributed across occupations in the same proportions as men are.[15] She finds that redistributing women in this way would serve to reduce average female earnings. That is a number of male dominated occupations are in fact low paying. On the other hand were females to receive male earnings within occupations but be distributed as they actually are then average female earnings would roughly equal those of men. This suggests that the emphasis of policies against discrimination should be on securing equal opportunities within occupations rather than equal access to occupations.

Current legislation on discrimination is contained in two Acts. The first is the Sex Discrimination Act of 1984 which enables women to seek redress where they feel they have been discriminated against in job or promotion applications. The second piece of legislation, the Affirmative Action (Equal Employment Opportunity for Women) Act, 1986, seeks to prevent discrimination occurring in the first place. The Act requires all but the smallest employers to set goals with respect to the numbers of women employed and to report on progress towards these goals.

Concepts for review

- Discrimination before the labour market
- Discrimination within the labour market
- Segregation
- Disproportionately female occupation
- Statistical discrimination
- Equal pay for equal work
- Equal pay for work of equal value

Questions

1 Is it possible to believe that human capital theory can contribute towards an understanding of the average male–female wage differential and that in Australia the differential is determined by the national wage setting institution? (Australian National University)
2 Suppose you wished to improve women's labour market opportunities and outcomes. What policies would you advocate? (University of Adelaide)
3 Distinguish between 'pre-market' and 'market' discrimination against women. What effect does such discrimination have on the wages and employment of women? (Curtin University of Technology)
4 A senior policy analyst argued that equal opportunity for Australian workers would be unfair to men. Was he correct? (La Trobe University)
5 To what extent are the lower earnings of Australian women, relative to men, the result of discrimination? Which theory of discrimination (if any) best explains the differential? (La Trobe University)

References

1 R. Holton, 'Social aspects of education' in M. Wooden, et al. (eds), *Australian Immigration*, AGPS, Canberra, 1990, pp. 158-226.
2 T. Karmel and M. Maclachlan, 'Occupational sex segregation—increasing or decreasing?', *Economic Record*, vol. 64, no. 186, 1988, pp. 187-95.
3 K. Mumford, *Women Working*, Allen & Unwin, Sydney, 1989.
4 See reference no. 2.
5 P.N. Junakar and C.A. Kapuscinski, 'Aboriginal employment and unemployment: an overview', *Economic Papers*, vol. 10, no. 4, 1991, pp. 30-43.
6 R.T. Ross, 'The labour market position of Aboriginal people in non-metropolitan New South Wales', *Australian Bulletin of Labour*, vol. 15, no. 1, 1988, pp. 29-56.
7 G.S. Becker, *The Economics of Discrimination*, University of Chicago Press, Chicago, 1971.
8 C. Short, 'Equal pay—what happened', *Journal of Industrial Relations*, vol. 28, no. 3, 1986, pp. 315-36.
9 D. Brereton, 'Gender differences in overtime', *Journal of Industrial Relations*, vol. 32, no. 3, 1990, pp. 370-85.
10 See reference no. 3.
11 M. Treadgold, 'Intercensal change in Aboriginal incomes, 1976-86', *Australian Bulletin of Labour*, vol. 14, no. 4, 1988, pp. 592-609.
12 B.J. Chapman and C. Mulvey, 'An analysis of the origins of sex differences in Australian wages', *Journal of Industrial Relations*, vol. 28, no. 4, 1986.
13 R. Drago, 'The extent of wage discrimination in Australia', *Australian Bulletin of Labour*, vol. 15, no. 4, 1989, pp. 313-25.
14 R.G. Gregory and R.C. Duncan, 'Segmented labour market theories and the Australian experience of equal pay for women', *Journal of Post Keynesian Economics*, vol. 3, no. 3, 1981, pp. 403-29.
15 S. Rimmer, 'Occupational segregation, earnings differentials and status among Australian workers', *Economic Record*, vol. 67, no. 198, 1991, pp. 205-16.

CHAPTER 8

Models of the labour market

8.1 Introduction

In this chapter we describe four models of the labour market which have been developed over the last twenty years or so. While in some respects they are distinct, there are also links between them. The recent reawakening of interest in the dual labour market hypothesis, for example, may be in part due to the theoretical basis that can be provided by the theory of efficiency wages.

In Section 8.2 we describe the 'job competition model' of the labour market which was put forward in the 1970s by Thurow. This stresses competition between people, partly on the basis of their training costs, for jobs. The wages attached to the jobs are given, as occurs in internal labour markets, and are not subject to competition. In Section 8.3 we discuss the 'dual labour market hypothesis' which was developed by Doeringer and Piore and which was an extension of their work on internal labour markets. The hypothesis is a special case of a broader view that the labour market comprises distinct segments between which mobility is very limited. As the name suggests, dual labour market theory sees the labour market as being divided into just two sectors. These are termed the 'primary' and 'secondary' sectors and the characteristics of jobs are held to differ considerably between the two sectors.

The last two sections are devoted to two theoretical models which, through their rationalisation of some observed patterns of labour-market behaviour, have important macroeconomic implications arising from the downward rigidity of money wages. In Section 8.4 we will discuss the 'theory of implicit contracts' which sees employers and workers as entering into implicit contracts over the cyclical variability of wages and employment. Finally in Section 8.5, we discuss what has, perhaps, proved to be the most influential of these four models, the 'theory of efficiency wages'. Starting with an old idea, that paying 'high' wages can be efficient if it secures 'good' workers, efficiency wage theory develops a series of propositions which seem to be in accord with observed behaviour in labour markets. We write 'seem to be' because efficiency wage theories, have not proved easy to test empirically.

8.2 The job competition model of the labour market

The term 'job competition' is used to distinguish the model from the traditional wage competition model of the labour market.[1] In the latter, Thurow argues, people enter the labour market with a set of skills and then compete with one another on the basis of the wages they would accept. In Thurow's model people compete for jobs on the basis of the costs of training them for the jobs, for it is central to this model that most skills are acquired on the job rather than in formal education. Education does play a role in this model but it is one consistent with the screening hypothesis rather than with human capital theory (see Chapter 4). An alternative rationalisation of the title is that instead of people competing for jobs, there are jobs looking for people to fill them. We shall see that, as well as drawing upon the analyses of on-the-job training and of signalling that we have already looked at, this view of the labour market rests upon the existence of manorial internal labour markets.

There are two main elements in the job competition theory. First there exists a 'distribution of job opportunities' (in a firm or in the economy), each job having a wage associated with it. Employers then select people from what is termed the 'labour queue' to fill these jobs, the basis of selection being that the best (highest paid) jobs are given to workers who have the most desired characteristics, where the latter are held to determine the costs of training people to perform their jobs adequately. We now consider the labour queue and the job distribution in more detail and then show how they interact.

Workers queue for the best jobs and employers choose those from the head of the queue to fill them. The workers' positions in the queue are determined by their background characteristics for it is these that affect their training costs. Background characteristics include such attributes as education, age, race, sex, socioeconomic background, and natural ability.

These characteristics, to repeat, do not give workers skills to perform any particular job but do influence training costs, or at least employers' perceptions of these costs. Thus employers, not knowing the training costs for each individual, simply rank workers on the basis of background characteristics.

We should note three points here. First, if the vector of background characteristics is replaced by, or can be approximated by, education alone then we get back to the screening hypothesis that we discussed in Chapter 4. In this model, however, education by developing certain skills does reduce training costs and hence provides something employers value, where the (extreme) screening hypothesis holds that education produces no work benefits. As far as employer behaviour is concerned, however, the result is the same. Second, not all employers assign the same weights to the various worker characteristics. Hence workers with the same characteristics may receive different wages in different firms; we shall see in Section 9.3 of Chapter 9 that such wage differences are commonly observed. Third, employer discrimination may determine the place of certain groups in the labour queue.

In terms of the wage competition model, or of our analysis in Chapters 4 and 5, the tendency of employers to attempt to minimise training costs implies that the training is specific and that they bear the costs. For if the training, and the resulting skills, were general then employers would be unconcerned with training costs as they would not be bearing them. Yet Thurow believes that 'very few skills are technically specific to one and only one firm'. So how can this concern with training costs be rationalised? In this model, as we shall see when we look at the job distribution, wage differentials are inflexible and cannot fluctuate to compensate for variations in worker quality. The employer tries to find workers whose training costs (appropriately amortised) are less than the gap between the marginal product of the job and its associated wage. Thus the observed tendency of employers to attempt to recruit the best workers in a world where skills are general is seen as evidence of the existence of job, rather than wage, competition.

Workers wish to move up the labour queue as this is the only way they can gain access to jobs with the best training ladders and so improve their earnings prospects. Many of their characteristics are unalterable (they are indices in the terminology introduced in Chapter 4) but some, particularly qualifications, can be changed. Thus education is a main method of signalling ability to employers and of advancing in the labour queue. It ultimately becomes a defensive measure. It is a 'good investment, not because it would raise an individual's income above what it would have been if no others had increased their education but because it raises his income above what it will be if others acquire an education and he does not.'

The second part of the model is the job distribution, which is a frequency distribution of the jobs available where the dimension assigned to a job is the wage that it carries. Diagrammatically the national job distribution might be as shown by the outer line in Figure 8.1 and within it there would be the job distributions of individual employers, one of which is shown. The job distribution fixes the shape of the distribution of earnings, for the only role of the labour queue is to determine who gets which jobs. The shape of the job distribution curve is influenced by three factors—technology, the sociology of wage determination, and the distribution of training costs.

The nature of the jobs available, for example, the amount of capital equipment per worker and the skill requirement of jobs, is held to be determined by technology. The nature of technological change, in turn, is largely exogenous to the model although the possibility is allowed that changes in the labour queue may induce technological change of a particular sort.

If technology determines the jobs then the wage attached to each job is determined largely by convention. The idea that wages are 'attached' to jobs has been mentioned several times in this discussion and reflects Thurow's view that productivity is an attribute of jobs not of people. Thus the job carries the wage which is earned, of course, by its occupant. How these relative wages are determined is not discussed in much detail, but the point is made that once a set of wage relativities has become established it is perpetuated by the forces of fairness and the use of comparisons in wage bargaining. We have seen that internal wage structures tend to be fairly rigid and in the next chapter we shall see that there is a high degree of stability in the pay differences between industries and between occupations.

The third determinant of the shape of the job distribution curve is training costs. Assuming that training costs are borne by the employer, then if, for example, there is an expansion in the supply of graduates whose training costs (to the firm) are lower than, say, year 12 high school leavers, graduates would be used to fill jobs that would otherwise have been occupied by the latter. Firms make this change because, on the assumption that the wages tied to the various jobs do not change, profits increase as workers with lower training costs are recruited.

One of Thurow's objectives in formulating this view of the labour market was to explain the inequality of incomes and the relation between education and inequality. Say a large extension of university education occurs so that a higher proportion of new entrants to the labour market each year are graduates and a smaller proportion have reached year 12

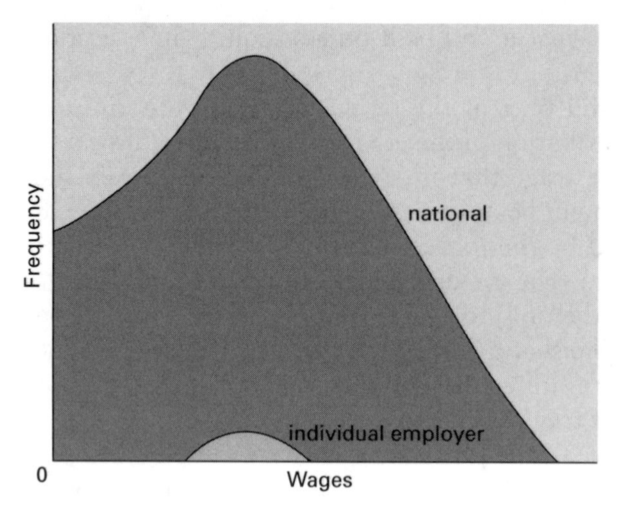

Figure 8.1 The job distribution

high school as their highest qualification. The composition of the labour queue is thus altered. Employers recruit graduates to fill the best of the jobs that were previously occupied by workers with year 12 qualifications. As a result, the average earnings of both groups of workers fall relative to the national average, for graduates now extend further down the job distribution and workers with year 12 qualifications have lost their highest paying jobs. It is not possible to predict unambiguously what would happen to the earnings relativity between the two groups.

Thurow shows that the actual changes which occurred in the United States income distribution between 1949 and 1972 were consistent with the job competition model. This is not surprising, for Thurow started with the facts and worked backward—'the job competition model was constructed in the light of the actual changes in the distribution of earnings'. The facts are, however, also consistent with a neoclassical or human capital view of the world. In the simple example in the preceding paragraph a neoclassical prediction would be that, if the demand curves for different types of a labour remained the same, then the change in relative supplies would reduce the earnings of graduates relative to those of Higher School Certificate workers. There is no reason to suppose that the demands for different sorts of worker have remained unaltered, however, and hence shifts in demand, together with our postulated shifts in supply, could be used to rationalise any change in relative earnings.

The moral of this is that we are not likely to be able to choose between the models on the basis of predictions, nor using statistical techniques. In any event, in reality labour markets have elements of both job competition and wage competition, and it really becomes a matter of judgement as to which model one believes gives the best description of actual behaviour.

As it stands, the job competition model is consistent with seniority provisions, job ladders, inflexible internal wage structures, the apparent failure of wages to adjust downwards under conditions of excess supply and other features of the labour market.

The major objection raised against the model is its technological and sociological determinism, which insulates the job distribution from the influence of supply and demand. Thus, it is argued, if marginal products are tied to jobs rather than to people, what forces firms to pay marginal products? Further, if there are people queuing for the best jobs, why doesn't competition force down the wages for such jobs? Thurow's response to such arguments would presumably be, first, that people do not receive marginal products and, second, that wages are not much influenced by supply and demand. Which really brings us back to the same place— that one finds the model, or at least elements in it, persuasive or one does not. Parts of it can be usefully integrated into dual labour market theory, but before we move on to consider that let us just note one further implication of the job competition model. We saw that education is used as a screening device by employers and is used by individuals to protect their place in the labour queue. As in the screening hypothesis, it follows that measures of the social rate of return to education are incorrectly based and would be too high. The analogy has been drawn between individuals acquiring more education to improve job prospects and a crowd at a football game all standing on tiptoe to improve their view. Energy is expended yet everyone ends up in the same relative position as before; as others stand on tiptoe, however, there is a return to the effort made by any one individual. Thus, the sum of returns to the group is positive yet everybody would be better off standing flat on their feet.

8.3 The dual labour market hypothesis

For a long time it has been argued that the labour market is divided into various segments, there being little movement between the segments, and hence the workers in any one are not in competition with those in others. One of the earliest statements of this view was provided over 100 years ago by Cairnes:

> What we find, in effect, is, not a whole population competing indiscriminately for all occupations, but a series of industrial layers, superimposed on one another, within each of which the various candidates for employment possess a real and effective power of selection, while those occupying the several strata are, for all purposes of effective competition, practically isolated from each other...We are thus compelled to recognise the existence of non-competing industrial groups as a feature of our social economy.[2]

The crucial point about the different segments of the labour market is that people with similar characteristics, such as their human capital, get treated or rewarded differently in different segments. The reader will see, therefore, that the concepts of segmentation and discrimination have very similar definitions. In the case of discrimination, however, the different treatment is based upon a visible characteristic whereas this need not be the case in segmented markets. It should also be noted that the segregation of the Australian labour market by gender can be seen as a form of labour market segmentation.

As anticipated in the introduction to this chapter we shall discuss one theory of segmentation, that of the dual labour market, in which there are two segments. This originally evolved as a time-specific hypothesis to explain conditions in urban labour markets in the United States in the 1970s. Despite this restricted focus it has proved influential in the analysis of labour markets although the extent to which we can generalise the theory to other countries is not yet clear. We may anticipate subsequent discussion by stating that duality in labour markets in advanced economies in general is less marked elsewhere than it is in American urban areas. However, much discussion of low-paid workers, of poverty more generally, and of unemployment among certain groups now incorporates some aspects of the hypothesis.

Dual labour market theory consists, in fact, of three related hypotheses: first, that there are two sectors in the national labour market, a primary sector which contains 'good' well-paid jobs and a secondary sector which contains 'bad' low-paid jobs; second, that entry mechanisms and wage determination processes are different in the two sectors; and third, that there is limited mobility between the sectors so that workers become trapped in the secondary sector.

The theory was developed by, among others, Doeringer and Piore and follows their analysis of internal labour markets.[3] Employment in the primary sector typically occurs in relatively closed manorial labour markets while in the secondary sector, labour markets are unstructured or open. Bearing this in mind, we can briefly sketch the main characteristics of the jobs in each sector.

Jobs in the primary sector tend to offer stable employment patterns and carry, relative to the secondary sector, high wages. Being located in fairly closed internal labour markets they require the development of task-specific skills and are characterised by on-the-job training and well-defined advancement ladders with most jobs being filled by internal promotion. There are set procedures for the settling of grievances and a well-established system of seniority rights for the allocation of overtime, lucrative piece-rate jobs, layoffs, and so on. Most workers in the primary sector are unionised and the firms in the sector tend to enjoy some degree of monopoly power in their product markets. Thus primary employment is found in oligopolistic enterprises in manufacturing, banking, and transport, for example, and also throughout the public sector.

The characteristics of the secondary market, and of the jobs in it, can be summarised as the inverse of those in the primary sector. Wages tend to be low and tasks require little in the way of general or specific skills. Thus there is little training or scope for advancement and, in general, internal labour markets are undeveloped. Unions are typically absent or weak, and job allocation and firing decisions are at the whim of the boss or manager. Working conditions are often poor and unpleasant. Neither worker nor employer has any great interest in developing permanent employment relationships, and high labour turnover results. It is thus instability of employment that, perhaps above all, characterises secondary employment. Not surprisingly, workers in this sector are referred to as 'disadvantaged'. However, workers who place a low value on permanent work relationships may actually prefer secondary employment. Some working mothers fall into this category as do some young people, and moonlighters.

In some variants of the hypothesis, the primary sector is subdivided into an upper and lower tier. In the upper tier are professional and managerial jobs. The main reason for drawing the distinction is that in the upper tier, as in the secondary sector, job changing may be quite frequent, but in the primary sector it is done for personal advancement.

Many writers have disputed that such a polarisation of labour markets exists but before discussing this and other criticisms of dual theory let us look at the second and third parts of the hypothesis. The second point is that wages are determined differently in each sector; this, together with recruitment policies, is held to lead to different payoffs to human capital in each sector. Clearly, most people would prefer to work in the primary sector and hence there would be a Thurow-type labour queue, with workers ranked in terms of their training costs and their ability to fill satisfactorily the available jobs. Following Thurow, schooling is held to be a widely-used screening device, but so may be race and sex. Thus discrimination may operate at this point to deny equal access to certain groups, and hence women and racial minorities may be over-represented in secondary employment. Once in the primary sector, the worker may be expected to acquire skills on the job and as a result would have an upward sloping lifetime earnings profile. As workers are selected for the primary jobs (and within the primary sector for places on the 'best' promotion ladders) largely on the basis of education, it follows that there are positive returns to investment in human capital.

In the secondary sector where, as we have seen, most jobs are unskilled and where there is little training, employers have small incentive to adopt detailed recruitment procedures. There may be internal labour markets in the secondary sector but they would have many ports of entry with short advancement paths. As employers are more or less indifferent between workers, and do not fully, if at all, utilise any skills that workers may possess, it follows that the return to the workers' human capital is likely to be significantly lower in the secondary sector. This prediction (which forms the basis of a test of the hypothesis) arises from a feature of the theory shared with the job competition model, that productivity is a function of the job rather than the worker.

The relatively high turnover of labour which occurs in secondary sector employment leads us to the third part of the dual hypothesis which is that mobility between the two sectors is low, because workers in secondary sectors get caught in a vicious circle. Denied entry to primary employment they move into secondary employment where they are likely to change jobs quite frequently. One of the worker characteristics that employers in the primary sector value is employment stability, however, so that the longer a worker is in the secondary sector the lower become the chances of moving out.

It is worth noting at this point that this may be an explanation of the existence of unemployment. Some workers who are unable to gain admittance to the primary sector may prefer to join a queue and remain unemployed rather than to seek employment in the secondary sector. They fear that if they take up secondary employment they may get stuck with it.[4]

A hypothesis which rests upon the division of a national labour market into just two parts must be a heroic simplification and should be interpreted accordingly. It has been subject to some criticism and we shall discuss the main points that have been made and summarise the rather inconclusive results of some tests of the hypothesis.

The most fundamental doubt is whether there is a dichotomy between good jobs and bad jobs or whether there is a continuum of jobs varying from the good through the indifferent to the bad. Further, the theory does not offer much guidance as to which jobs belong to which sector. In a general sense technology is held to determine the range of available jobs but the theory lacks any specific criteria for allocating jobs to each sector.

Thus a crucial first stage in testing the dual labour market hypothesis is to identify which jobs belong to the primary sector and which to the secondary sector. As we have seen, primary and secondary jobs vary in their characteristics. Some work uses one characteristic of a job such as the level of wages or its position on some scale of occupational prestige—while other authors use some combination of characteristics to place jobs in each sector. Flatau and Lewis have shown that, in Australia, the correlations between the various job characteristics are not very high.[5] For fifty-two occupations they derived ten job characteristics such as earnings, education, job durations, and unemployment rates. Occupations which rated highly on some factors rated poorly on others and thus methods of assigning jobs on the basis of a few factors are inappropriate.

Once the primary and secondary sectors have been identified the hypothesis can be tested in several ways. One method is to ask if it is true that the rate of return to human capital is lower in the secondary sector? The American evidence on this (no Australian work has followed this line) tends to find that it is, thus apparently confirming duality. It has been widely pointed out, however, that if wages are one of the criteria used for allocating workers to the secondary sector then the effect of education on earnings in that sector is inevitably understated. The reason is that the low-wage sector inevitably contains those with little education, but also those with education who have in some other sense failed. Putting these two groups together yields low estimates of the rate of return to education. The alternative human capital explanation of low-income employment would be, of course, that workers in secondary markets are worse than those in primary sectors. They earn less because they have less human capital, but there is no reason to suppose that their rates of return to education are any different from those of primary sector workers. Some work based on earnings functions has managed to avoid this problem associated with preselecting workers to the two different sectors. Dickens and Lang analysed a sample of male heads of household, in the United States, and found a different wage equation for each sector and some statistical evidence of a queue of workers for primary sector jobs.[6]

Another possibility is to test the third aspect of the hypothesis which is that mobility between sectors is limited. Although we should note that there is no obvious method of defining the critical level of mobility for acceptance or rejection, the weight of the evidence suggests that mobility in the United States is greater than could plausibly be argued to be consistent with the dual hypothesis. Young people seem able to move out of secondary employment easily but, in general, blacks do not, suggesting, again, a relation between discrimination and duality.

A further dimension of duality may be the division between casual and permanent employment, for casual employment bears all the characteristics of secondary employment. Casual workers can usually be dismissed at an hour's notice and they are not entitled to benefits such as sick leave or paid annual leave. In 1989, 13.1 per cent of males and 29.1 per cent of females were employed on a casual basis. Casual employment has increased significantly in the last decade. As a proportion of all employees casual employment has increased from 13.3 per cent in 1982 to 20 per cent in 1989.[7]

While casual employment may be described as secondary employment it is not clear whether its existence is supportive of dual labour market theory in any but a descriptive sense. For example, is it true that there is low mobility between casual and permanent employment and that workers are trapped in casual employment? Many casual workers are teenage students working, for example, one evening and on Saturdays in the retail trade. They will subsequently move into full-time permanent employment. On the other hand, in 1986, 42 per cent of casual workers indicated in response to a survey that they would prefer permanent employment, implying low mobility between the two sorts of employment.

While the various empirical tests for duality have not proved conclusive a consensus appears to be emerging that is able to explain some features of the labour market in the United States that are not in conformity with standard theory.[8] There is little formal evidence on duality in Australia.

To sum up, the dual labour market hypothesis lays stress on the discontinuities that exist; that there is a clearly defined break between the two sectors; that the rate of return to qualifications is different; and that mobility between the sectors is very low. It is more than a description of a situation where there are some good jobs and some bad jobs.

The main policy implication it carries is that to reduce the number of people in secondary employment it is necessary to expand the number of primary jobs. What is emphatically denied is that expanding education would have any effect, for this would simply alter the composition of the labour queue. Many people in secondary employment are underemployed at present anyway, it is argued, in the sense that full use is not being made of their human capital.

8.4 Implicit contract theory

One task facing macroeconomic theorists is to explain wage stickiness and unemployment. That is, to explain why, in the face of an excess supply of labour, wages do not fall so as to clear the labour market and thus why involuntary unemployment occurs. We shall look at this issue in more detail in Chapter 10, but it is convenient here to look at a rationalisation offered by implicit contract theory.

The implicit contracts are between workers and firms. There are in fact several variants of implicit contract theory and here we shall describe what has probably been the most influential version which is based upon the assertion that workers and firms have different attitudes towards risk. The basic idea is that workers are risk averse and firms are risk neutral (or less risk averse than workers).

Before proceeding let us explain what these terms mean. One is described as 'risk averse' if one declines a fair bet. For example, the actuarial outcome, or expected value, of tossing a coin and either winning (say) \$10 if one wins or losing \$10 if one calls incorrectly is \$0. For one has an evens chance of both winning and losing. Thus the expected value of the bet is the same as not taking part in the bet at all. If one prefers not to take part one is risk averse. A risk neutral person would be indifferent between taking part and not taking part in the bet.

The risks in question here are those of unemployment and of variations over time in wages. Workers cannot expect firms to guarantee both stability of employment and of wages. The assumption made is that workers opt for wage stability. Take the following simple example. Workers in a firm can expect wages of $500 in a good year and of $400 in a bad year. Good and bad years occur with equal frequency so that the average expected wage over years will be $450. Workers are risk averse, remember, so they would prefer a certain wage of $450. Firms are risk neutral so are willing to guarantee an annual wage of $450. (In fact workers may be willing to pay an insurance premium for this guarantee and accept a certain wage of something slightly less than $450.) The argument then goes that workers and firms enter an implicit contract. Firms offer fixed wages and workers undertake not to leave the firm in search of higher wages in good years. The firm is unable, of course, to guarantee both stable employment and stable wages and the corollary is that in bad years layoffs have to occur. It is a further feature of the implicit contract that when, at a later stage of the economic cycle, the firms demand for labour expands, the jobs are first offered to those workers previously laid off. This is in accord with experience in the United States where studies have shown that up to 75 per cent of laid off workers are subsequently re-hired by their employers.

The assumption that workers prefer wage stability to employment stability may appear to be counterintuitive. One rationalisation is that the risks of unemployment may not be as great as they appear. Seniority rights usually apply in the form of last-in first-out layoff rules and hence after a few years employment with a firm the risk of being laid off is very low. Further, in a fixed wage-variable employment contract some of the costs of unemployment are met by the government through the payment of unemployment benefits. In a fixed employment-variable wage contract, however, there is no system through which the government would offer compensation for lower wages in bad years.

Implicit contract theory is, by definition, untestable. It does offer a theoretical explanation of some empirical observations. These are also, however, explained by the existence of firm specific human capital and the operation of internal labour markets. Further, the system of layoffs and re-hires that plays quite an important role in the risk aversion variant of the theory does not appear to operate in Australia. Those wishing to explore these theories further, however, are referred to the non-technical survey by Sloan and Wooden.[9]

8.5 Efficiency wage theories

Efficiency wage models, like the implicit contract theories that we discussed above, were stimulated by a need to explain wage rigidity and involuntary unemployment. At the same time they seem also to be able to explain discrimination, duality, and, otherwise not readily explicable, differences in wages between industries.

The essential notion is that wages and worker productivity are positively related. This is not a particularly new idea—it can be found, for example, in Marshall's *Principles of Economics*. In modern economics, however, until the last couple of decades little was made of it outside the development economics literature where links between wages, calorific intake, health and productivity were described. We shall restrict our attention to models of industrial economies.

To show the basic idea underlying the efficiency wage hypothesis consider a profit maximising firm in the short run, that is the period during which the capital stock is fixed. The production function relates output not just to labour input, but also to the effort with which labour works. Worker effort is, in turn, assumed to be higher the higher is the real wage. The firm now has to choose both the real wage it will pay, and the level of labour inputs, in a way as to maximise profits.

It can be shown that the solution to this problem is that the firm will set the real wage at a level which satisfies the condition that the elasticity of effort with respect to the real wage is unity. This wage, which minimises wage costs per efficiency unit is called the 'efficiency wage'. The firm pays this efficiency wage and hires labour up to the point where the marginal (physical) product of labour is equal to the efficiency wage.

What happens when there is a decline in demand for goods and services leading to an excess supply of labour? The efficiency wage does not alter and firms simply employ fewer workers. These workers may be willing to work for a lower wage, but it is not efficient for the firm to reduce wages. Thus involuntary employment emerges.

There are several possible reasons for expecting a relation between the real wage and worker productivity and, by this stage of the book, we have come across all of them in one form or another. First, as we saw in Chapter 1, in the vast majority of work situations workers control the amount of effort (in the broadest sense) they expend on their jobs. One way to minimise shirking is to pay wages greater than the supply price of labour. As workers thus earn more than they could in other firms they have less incentive to shirk because of the costs of being fired. Efficiency wage models that explore these relations are, not surprisingly, collectively known as shirking models.

One objective that has been raised to shirking models is that there appear to be cheaper alternative methods to reduce shirking. One would be for employers to require workers to post bonds (pay a deposit) when gaining employment. They would lose the bond or deposit if caught shirking. While formal bonding systems of this sort are virtually unknown, informal arrangements, such as job ladders and a system of seniority rights, which can serve the same function are, of course, very common.

A second cause of the real wage–productivity link, and one we have described in some detail, arises from the costs of turnover, which will be relatively high where firm specific skills are important.

Third it is likely that the higher the wage offered by a firm the higher the average quality of job applicants it attracts. Thus lacking precise information about worker quality firms simply raise the wage to increase their chances of hiring labour of high quality. As we have seen, there are other ways of ascertaining worker quality, for example, by looking at educational qualifications.

Fourth, there are what may be termed sociological explanations for the payment of wages above their market clearing levels. Especially in work situations where teamwork is important the payment of high wages is argued to improve worker morale and hence worker productivity.

Efficiency wage models can, then, explain the rigidity of real wages and the existence of involuntary unemployment. They can also explain labour market duality. It seems plausible to assume that the relationship between wages and productivity is stronger in some industries and occupations than in others. Where it is of importance we will observe relatively high wages and job rationing as queues of workers attempt to obtain these jobs; this is the primary sector. In other occupations where the wage-productivity link is weak or absent the market operates in a way similar to that described by competitive theory; these comprise the secondary sector.

Efficiency wage models can also help us understand the quite significant differences in pay received by apparently similar people who work in different industries. We return to this in the next chapter but the explanation is, again, based on the probability that the wage productivity relation differs across industries.

It is difficult to formally test efficiency wage models. One direct test, admittedly on data of some antiquity, has been undertaken on the effects of the $5 a day minimum pay rate introduced by Henry Ford into his car plants in 1914.[10] This had the effect of doubling the pay of most workers. There is no doubt that the wage was set way above the competitive level and long queues of workers formed. Productivity and profits rose. Why? Not as Raff and Summers argue because of the dramatic fall in turnover which followed, because training costs were not very high for the semi-skilled work. Nor were more skilled workers attracted to Ford as no attempt was made to replace existing ones. The authors argue that a decrease in shirking and an improvement in morale provide the most convincing explanations.

Less formally, efficiency wage models are consistent with many features that we observe in labour markets. The basic ideas are quite straightforward although much of the work is presented in a formal theoretical way. Useful surveys of efficiency wage models have been provided by Akerlof and Yellen and by Katz.[11]

Concepts for review

- Labour queue
- Job distribution
- Primary sector
- Secondary sector
- Dual labour market
- Risk aversion
- Implicit contracts
- Efficiency wage
- Shirking
- Bonding

Questions

1 Discuss the relationship between wages and work effort and its implications for labour markets. (Curtin University)
2 Evaluate the dual labour market hypothesis. Is the concept of dualism of any value from the point of view of policy makers? (University of Western Australia)
3 Compare and contrast theories of wage determination which seek to explain wage 'stickiness'. (Australian National University)
4 'Sticky wages can be explained by models of efficiency wages, or implicit contracts, or trade union bargaining.' Explain briefly. Evaluate these models of wage determination in terms of their ability to explain macroeconomic wage rigidity during economic recessions. (Australian National University)
5 Discuss, in the Australian context, the evidence for and against the dual labour market hypothesis. What are the implications for labour market policy? (University of New England)
6 Discuss the similarities and differences between the theory of internal labour markets, implicit contract theory and efficiency wage theory. (Curtin University)

References

1 L.C. Thurow, *Generating Inequality*, Macmillan, Melbourne, 1975.
2 J. Cairnes, *Some Leading Principles of Political Economy Newly Expounded*, Macmillan, London, 1874.
3 P.B. Doeringer and M.J. Piore, *Internal Labour Markets and Manpower Analysis*, D.C. Heath & Co., Lexington, 1971, Ch. 8.
4 I.M. McDonald and R.M. Solow, 'Wages and employment in a segmented labor market', *Journal of Political Economy*, vol. 100, 1985, pp. 1115-41.
5 P. Flatau and P.E.T. Lewis, 'Segmented labour markets in Australia', *Murdoch University Economics Programme Working Paper No. 56, 1991.*
6 W.T. Dickens and K. Lang, 'A test of dual labour market theory', *American Economic Review*, vol. 75, no. 4, 1985, pp. 792-805.
7 P. Dawkins and K. Norris, 'Casual employment in Australia', *Australian Bulletin of Labour*, vol. 16, no. 3, 1990, pp. 156-73.
8 W.T. Dickens and K. Lang, 'The re-emergence of segmented labour market theory', *American Economic Review*, vol. 78, no. 2, 1988, pp. 129-34.
9 J. Sloan and M. Wooden, 'Labour markets from the micro-economic perspective: implicit contract theory', *Australian Economic Review*, no. 67, 1984, pp. 120-9.
10 D.M.G. Raff and L.H. Summers, 'Did Henry Ford pay efficiency wages?', *Journal of Labor Economics*, vol. 5, no. 4, Part II, 1987, pp. S57-S86.
11 G.A. Akerlof and J.L. Yellen, *Efficiency Wage Models of the Labor Market*, Cambridge University Press, Sydney, 1986. L. Katz, 'Efficiency Wage theories: a partial evaluation' in S. Fischer (ed.), *NBER Macroeconomics Annual*, MIT Press, Cambridge, 1986.

CHAPTER 9

Pay relativities

9.1 Introduction

At many points in the book so far we have analysed differences in pay. In Chapter 4 we looked at how pay relates to education and training and we began Chapter 5 with a very simple model of wage determination. Later in Chapter 5 we discussed pay differences within firms and between firms in local labour markets. Chapter 6 was concerned with the effects of trade unions on earnings and Chapter 7 was devoted to an analysis of discrimination.

This chapter concludes our discussion of pay relativities. It is concerned with three matters: pay relativities between occupations, industries and persons. It will be evident to the reader that the major determinant of differences in pay between occupations is the amount of education and training needed to enter it and to that extent we have nothing to add to our earlier analysis. We present data on occupational pay differences and examine secondary influences on occupational relativities, notably non-pecuniary aspects of employment. Finally, we shall look at movements in occupational pay relativities over time.

Section 9.3 is concerned with differences in average earnings between industries. It is clear that even after standardising for differences in the occupational composition of the workforce in each industry there exist industrial differences in pay. The existence of these differences has long puzzled labour economists and we shall look at some possible explanations, notably that provided by the theories of efficiency wages that were discussed in the previous chapter. Section 9.3 concludes with a discussion of secular changes in industrial relativities.

In Section 9.4 we look at the effect that the Australian system of wage determination has had on the structure of wages. It is sometimes hard for

Australian students to come to grips with the fact that in all other industrial countries wages are negotiated directly between workers and employers without the constant intervention of a body such as the Industrial Relations Commission. There is a clear trend towards a weakening (or abandonment) of the role played by the commission and we will discuss the reasons for this.

The final section of this chapter is devoted to an analysis of the interpersonal distribution of earnings. We shall see that the shape of this distribution is remarkably similar across countries and through time. Thus it is tempting to look for a common explanation of its form, and we shall analyse a statistical theory of distribution.

9.2 Occupational pay relativities

Relativities in Australia

To give an impression of magnitudes we present in Table 9.1 the ten highest and lowest paying occupations for men.

The figures relating to average hourly earnings are, of course, averages within occupations. Further, the earnings in occupations where many people work on their own account are likely to be understated due to the prevalence of schemes to minimise tax liabilities. The list of high paying

Table 9.1 Highest and lowest paying occupations: average hourly earnings, males 1991

Occupation	*$*	*Occupation*	*$*
Air transport operating support workers	28.7	Handpackers	10.9
Specialist medical practitioners	27.8	Garment tradespersons	10.7
Mining engineers	26.7	Jewellery and precious metalware tradespersons	10.5
Clerical engineers	26.3	Other filing, sorting and copying clerks	10.5
General medical practitioners	25.0	Nursery and garden labourers	10 4
Lawyers	24.0	Nurserymen	10.3
Radiographers	22.1	Laundry workers	9.6
Metallurgists and materials scientists	22.0	Upholsterers and bedding tradespersons	9.5
Dental practitioners	21.8	Other leather and canvas tradespersons	9.5
Journalists	21.8	Craftworkers	9.1

Note: Occupations where the standard errors of earnings are relatively high have been excluded.
Source: Distribution and Composition of Employee Earnings and Hours, (ABS, cat. no. 6306.0).

occupations comprises occupations which demand qualifications which can only be obtained after a considerable number of years training and is thus in conformity with our analysis of education and training. This is only partially true of the low paying list. While this consists of some unskilled occupations it also contains four trades occupations, that is occupations which require apprenticeship training. While it is not our purpose here to analyse individual occupations this is something of a puzzle.

Leaving this aside we know that the acquisition of skills imposes costs, mainly in the form of foregone earnings. Thus the earnings of (say) general medical practitioners have to be higher, over their working life, than those of workers in occupations requiring no formal training. If we imagined a world in which the only characteristic which affected earnings was education (or qualifications more generally) and that wages were determined by supply and demand then we would expect the net present value of earnings in all occupations to be equal. Of course, as we know, there are many other influences on earnings, but nonetheless, in terms of Table 9.1 we would expect that once we allowed for the long training periods of the occupations in the high paying list the apparent differences in lifetime earnings would be reduced, or even disappear.

Table 9.2 Occupational earnings: top ten occupations listed in order of net present value of lifetime earnings at various discount rates, 1976

	0 per cent	*10 per cent*	*20 per cent*
1	Medical practitioners, dentists	Members of armed services	Members of armed services
2	Air pilots, navigators	Miners, quarry workers, etc.	Tobacco preparers, etc.
3	Law professionals	Tobacco preparers, etc.	Chemical, sugar workers, etc.
4	Chemists, physicists, etc.	Stenographers, typists	Miners, quarryworkers, etc.
5	Architects, engineers, etc.	Chemical, sugar workers, etc.	Potters, kilnworkers, etc.
6	Biologists, veterinarians, etc.	Electricians, etc.	Electricians, etc.
7	Teachers	Other clerical workers	Deck, engineer room hands, etc.
8	Other professionals	Deck, engineer room hands, etc.	Bricklayers, plasterers
9	Professional medical workers	Bricklayers, plasterers	Mineral treaters
10	Administrative, executive (government, not elsewhere specified)	Watchmakers, jewellers, etc.	Carpenters, etc.

Source: Richardson and Hancock.[1]

An analysis of this sort was undertaken for a more broadly defined set of occupations using the 1976 census by Richardson and Hancock,[1] who discounted lifetime earnings back to the age of fifteen. No allowance could be made for the direct costs of education and training (such as fees, books) or for the fact that many students are able to partially offset the income foregone during education by working part-time or by the receipt of tertiary education allowances. The rank order of occupations in terms of the present value of lifetime earnings obviously depends upon the rate of discount used. To illustrate the effect we show in Table 9.2 the top ten occupations at various discount rates. In the first column we see that if no discount rate is applied (that is we simply add up lifetime earnings in each occupation) the list comprises professional and highly qualified workers. At discount rates of 10 and 20 per cent, however, these disappear from the top ten and are replaced mainly by manual workers.

The authors' calculations cover seventy-one occupations and they show that the differences in present values are lowest when a discount rate of about 10 per cent is applied, although there are still some marked differences between occupations. In general, the results of this study confirm the view that one major cause of occupational earnings differences is differences in qualifications and skills.

Compensating differentials

Occupations (or, more generally, jobs) differ in their non-wage characteristics such as the physical conditions of work, security of employment, and the provision of fringe benefits. Compensating differentials in pay are those that are necessary to compensate for differences in the non-wage conditions of employment.

Before considering the implications of compensating pay differentials let us look more closely at the non-wage characteristics of jobs. First, jobs vary in the number and extent of fringe benefits they offer. Fringe benefits include employer contributions to superannuation funds, workers' compensation, subsidised canteen and sport facilities, private use of company or government cars, housing and so on. While the provision of fringe benefits is widespread simple economic theory suggests that it is not a very efficient way of remunerating people. A person will always prefer $100 after tax to a fringe benefit worth $100. For if they wanted to purchase the benefit, they could. But alternatively they could buy another good or service costing $100 which yields greater utility. Thus they either prefer $100 to a benefit worth $100 or they are indifferent between them. There are no circumstances under which the benefit could be preferred to $100.

The argument above was couched in terms of after tax dollars. If the tax system either exempts fringe benefits from tax, or taxes them at a lower average rate than income then it will be efficient for some remuneration to be in the form of fringe benefits. The reaction to the introduction of Fringe Benefits Tax in 1986 reinforces these arguments. Previously, many benefits were exempt from tax; subsequently they have been taxed at a rate now roughly equivalent to the top marginal income tax rate. As a result, many employees opted to exchange benefits for higher earnings. While fringe benefits may lead to compensating differentials between occupations, within occupations fringe benefits are positively related to earnings. The higher a person's place in the earnings hierarchy the greater, on average, the value of the fringe benefits they receive.

Differences in job security may give rise to compensating wage differentials. Occupations where employment varies markedly over the economic cycle may have to pay, for similar workers, higher than average wage rates. Finally, by way of example, jobs vary in their innate characteristics. Some are monotonous, others varied, some are carried out in dirty, unpleasant conditions, others in air-conditioned carpeted offices, some are dangerous, most are safe. The idea of compensating wage differentials would suggest that those jobs with bad characteristics would have to offer more pay. We have to be a little careful here, however, for what may appear to be favourable to one person may be unfavourable to others. Working in an office was cited above as a possibly favourable characteristic. But large numbers of people could not tolerate working in an office, preferring to work out of doors.

The idea of compensating wage differentials was put forward over 200 years ago by Adam Smith and may explain some differences in pay between some occupations demanding similar levels of education and training. On the other hand many boring, dead-end jobs carried out in apparently unpleasant conditions also happen to be low paid. This is, of course, one aspect of the dual labour market hypothesis that we discussed in the previous chapter. Jobs in the primary sector are good ones in most respects, jobs in the secondary sector are bad in most respects.

Trends in occupational pay relativities

For trends over long periods of time we have to rely upon studies of the rates of pay of unskilled workers compared to those of skilled workers. In Australia this century there has been a long-term increase in the pay of unskilled workers relative to that of skilled workers, although there has been considerable fluctuation around the long-run trend. Skill relativities in Britain and in the United States have followed in the same trend. In the United States, for example, in 1899 the average pay for clerical and administrative workers in manufacturing was two-and-a-half times those of production workers; by 1980 it was one-and-a-half times as great.

Two broad explanations can be offered for the narrowing of skill relativities. First, the great increase in both compulsory and voluntary education that has occurred has altered the supply of skilled workers relative to unskilled. As long as the demand curves for each group of worker has not changed in a compensating way these changes in relative supplies would bring about the observed outcome. Second, and this is particularly important in the last half of the century, skill relativities have been reduced by immigration. One aspect of immigration policy has been to encourage migrants with skills in scarce supply in Australia.

The long run narrowing of skill relativities has at certain times been reversed in the short run. Between 1954 and 1968, for example, the ratio of the pay of unskilled workers to skilled workers declined from about 85 per cent to about 77 per cent. Data on earnings seem to suggest, as we shall see in Section 9.5, that a similar widening may have occurred in the last decade.

9.3 Industrial pay relativities

The pay differences that exist between industries are shown in Table 9.3. The industrial classification that has to be used is rather a broad one and a finer classification would show a greater variation in earnings. As they stand the data show that, mining apart, earnings do not vary greatly between industries; in the case of both males and females earnings in the

Table 9.3 Pay by industry as a percentage of average industrial pay; average weekly earnings of full-time workers, 1991

	$	
Industry	*Male*	*Female*
Mining	148	120
Manufacturing	93	91
Electricity, gas and water	103	100
Construction	105	85
Wholesale and retail trade	85	85
Transport and storage	101	104
Communication	98	100
Finance, property business services	115	96
Public administration and defence	97	108
Community services	112	115
Recreation personal and other services	81	81
All industries	100	100

Source: *Distribution and Composition of Employee Earnings and Hours,* (ABS, cat. no. 6306.0).

lowest paying industry are 81 per cent of the average while in the highest paying they are 15 per cent greater than average.

These are earnings averaged across all workers in each industry and as such will be in part caused by differences in the education, and training and other attributes of workers in the industry. Thus these observed relativities must be distinguished from what may be termed 'true' industrial relativities—differences in pay between industries for otherwise similar workers.

There is no doubt, however, that true industrial relativities exist. That is, that a worker in a well-defined occupation—driving a 3 tonne truck for example—will be paid different wages in different industries. The evidence on this for Australia comes from estimates of earnings functions. We saw on p. 142 that dummy variables can be included in earnings functions to capture the effect of unions. Similarly, they can be used to estimate the effect of the industry in which a person works; the dummy variable takes on a value of 1 if a person works in a certain industry and a value of 0 if they do not. Invariably, we find that industry dummy variables are significant.

Causes of industrial pay relativities

What are the causes of differences in earnings between industries? It has to be said that there is no completely satisfactory explanation. All we can do is to offer a few partial explanations which are conceptually plausible and which are supported by some empirical work.

We have seen that where firms possess some monopoly power they are likely to earn economic rents. Unions, directly or indirectly, then bring about some sharing of these rents between the managers and owners of firms and workers. The direct effect occurs through negotiation in cases where firms are unionised. In non-union firms the threat of unionisation may also bring about rent sharing. In either case we would expect wages to be higher where product market imperfections give firms monopoly power.

To test this relation we need measures of monopoly power, such as industrial concentration (as measured, for example, by the proportion of output accounted for by the largest four firms in an industry). In general lack of data has precluded empirical work of this form in Australia. In Britain and the United States, although the results of empirical work are by no means clear-cut, the balance of the evidence suggests that wages are higher in industries where there is monopoly power.[2] In both of these countries there is also some evidence that wages are higher in industries where the average size of establishment is relatively high. This may arise to compensate workers for the (alleged) disutility of working in a large establishment or because large establishments are easier to unionise.

Finally, the efficiency wage hypothesis may provide part of the answer. The basic idea, it will be recalled from the previous chapter, is that firms (industries) which pay relatively high wages reap labour productivity gains and minimise wage costs per unit of output. If the link between wages and productivity is stronger in some industries than in others we would expect wages to vary between industries for this reason. It is not clear, however, why this should be true for all types of worker in an industry. For what the evidence shows is that in industries where pay is relatively high, all types of worker, from managers to cleaners, get remunerated favourably.

Changes in industrial pay relativities

The usual method of showing the extent of changes over time in industrial pay relativities is to derive the rankings, by pay, of industries in different years. Spearman rank correlation co-efficients are then calculated between the rankings in the two years. These rank correlation co-efficients can be interpreted in the same way as the more familiar product moment correlation co-efficients. Thus if two rankings remained unaltered the co-efficient would be unity; if they were precisely inverted the co-efficient would be minus unity; if they were unrelated it would be zero, and so on.

The degree of stability in a ranking will tend to be greater the higher the degree of aggregation and this should be borne in mind when interpreting results. For the period 1953–67, it is possible to derive average earnings of male production workers in 140 secondary industries. We have calculated the rank correlation co-efficient between earnings in 1953 and 1967 to be 0.71. For later periods earnings, data are only available at a much higher level of aggregation. Watts and Mitchell have calculated rank correlation co-efficients between various years for adult male non-managerial workers for the fifteen industries shown in Table 9.3; between 1966 and 1988 the co-efficient is 0.86.[3] These results are similar to those obtained for other countries. Everywhere, it seems, changes in pay by industry occur very slowly. This is probably due to the widespread use of comparability in negotiations over wages, whether these are played out in front of a body, like the Industrial Relations Commission, or bargained between unions and employers. It is usually seen as fair by both sides if workers maintain their proportionate wage relativity with some perceived reference group, or in a more general sense their place in the pay ranking. To the extent that each group succeeds in this attempt then of course there will be little change in overall relativities.

9.4 The operations of the Industrial Relations Commission

We described in Chapter 1 the evolution of the Australian system of wage determination. In this section we do two things. First we examine the evidence on the effect that the Industrial Relations Commission (or its predecessors) has had upon the structure of wages. Second, we discuss some criticisms that have been made of the commission and the arguments that have been put forward for moving to a less centralised system of wage determination where the focus would be placed upon bargaining at the level of the enterprise.

What effect has the Australian system had upon the set of wage relativities? The definitive answer to this will never be known as we do not know the counter-factual, what would have happened otherwise? One method that has been used is to compare the wage structure in Australia with those in other countries. The most common comparison is with Britain, on the grounds that the industrial ethos and the extent and structure of unions are fairly similar in the two countries. About ten years ago quite a bit of empirical work followed this methodology although this topic seems to have fallen out of fashion.

The results of this work can be summarised as follows.[4] First, with one exception, the set of wage relativities in Australia and Britain are very similar; this is true whether the basis of comparison is by industry, or by occupation, or between individuals. Second, wherever there are differences they are all in the same direction, that the spread of pay is rather narrower in Australia. Third, and this is the exception referred to, differences in pay between men and women are very much less in Australia. In 1981, when average female earnings were 88 per cent those of males in Australia, the corresponding proportion in Britain was 73 per cent. Fourth, the union markup seems to be about the same in both countries. Finally, the overall distribution of earnings between individuals is rather more equal in Australia. This is particularly so at the bottom end of the earnings distribution. Lower paid workers stand rather closer to the central level of earnings in Australia than in Britain.

Thus, perhaps surprisingly, two different institutional settings produce broadly similar outcomes, although differences in pay tend to be slightly less in Australia. Despite this, the alleged shortcomings of the Australian system of wage determination have been a subject of widespread debate in the last decade. One issue is the extent to which the arbitration system has rendered the Australian labour market inflexible and has thus reduced its efficiency.

The Hancock report

The operation of the whole system was reviewed in 1985 by the Hancock committee of inquiry into industrial relations.[5] While the report recommended numerous changes (which are outside the province of this book) to institutions, procedures, and to the law, it proposed no fundamental change to the system of centralised wage fixation.

The main criticisms of the arbitral system that are made by those who argue for deregulation of the labour market centre on the wage signalling function of the labour market. It is argued that the arbitration system impedes this function in at least two ways. First, it imposes a uniform set of wages and employment conditions across all firms in an industry, irrespective of whether they are profitable or unprofitable, growing or declining. Second, that the system has made wage relativities more rigid than they would be in the absence of regulation. The first contention is correct with respect to award rates of pay but, at least in an upward direction, firms can vary the other elements of pay. Collective bargaining, which we have argued is the likely alternative to arbitration, also imposes a similar uniformity.

Essentially the issue is how important is the wage signalling function of the labour market. The view taken by the Hancock committee was that it is not very important: 'The allocation of labour is insensitive to changes in relativities between the wage levels of major categories of labour.'

So how does labour get reallocated? The answer is through variations in vacancies. In firms and industries seeking to expand employment there will exist vacancies, and employers may relax normal hiring standards to fill them. Where employment is declining or static there will be fewer, or no, vacancies. These differences can bring about changes in labour allocation because of the large numbers of new workers who present themselves at the labour market each month looking for jobs.

We shall explain in more detail in the following chapter the flows that take place in the labour market each month. Here we can note that between February and March 1992 the following numbers of people entered employment: 140 000 people who were previously unemployed and 144 000 people who were previously not members of the labour force. Grossed up to annual terms these movements are very large.

Thus, the labour market is able to adjust even if relative wages are fairly rigid, although obviously the process might be facilitated if appropriate changes in relative pay occurred at the same time. The reader will also recall from Section 5.4 of Chapter 5 that long job durations are typical for those in employment at any one time. We can thus see how this is made consistent with a considerable amount of labour reallocation.

Enterprise bargaining

Following the Hancock report the debate about labour market deregulation continued unabated. Several large employer groups, the Liberal party, and ultimately the government and unions through the Accord, supported a move towards enterprise bargaining. At the time this book is being written it is therefore clear that some decentralisation of the system of wage determination is going to occur but the precise framework is not known, as the various parties hold different positions on the role of the Industrial Relations Commission in a system of enterprise bargaining. There is little point in speculating about the outcome, so here we shall outline the broad issues.

Under enterprise bargaining, wages and other conditions of work are negotiated between an employer and the workforce in an enterprise. What is an enterprise?

> An enterprise is a unit with a set of definable human, technological and financial resources. Enterprises come in all shapes and sizes. They may be independent units, such as single businesses. They may be in one location or multiple locations. Enterprises can be private or public ...[6]

Several arguments have been put forward in favour of bargaining at the enterprise level. First, and most fundamentally, it is argued that it enables individual workers to identify with the enterprise and its performance. Workers have a self-interest in bringing about more efficient work practices and hence in increasing labour productivity because this will lead, it is argued, to increased pay. Thus some proponents of enterprise bargaining talk of 'employee relations' rather than 'industrial relations'. To use an old cliché, the former is apparently concerned with increasing the size of the cake as well as with its division.

Second, the set of wages and work conditions that emerge will be appropriate to technological and market conditions at the particular enterprise. Under a centralised system, of course, the same minimum structure of award rates, penalty rates and so on are imposed on all enterprises in a given industry, whatever the circumstances of that enterprise. Third, as the circumstances of the enterprise change so too can the terms of the bargain between workers and employers.

Fourth, it is argued that enterprise bargaining will encourage dispute resolution at the work place. In the existing system, arbitration is always in the background and this has discouraged the development of industrial relations at the work place, as parties believe that ultimately the issue will be arbitrated. Fifth, it is believed that enterprise bargaining will lead to more flexible wages and to a more flexible labour market that will adjust more easily to changing conditions.

There are several difficulties that may be encountered with enterprise bargaining. The incidence and importance of these will depend upon the role (if any) assumed by the Industrial Relations Commission in the system. At the extreme, of course, we can envisage a case where legislation is enacted to abolish the commission. This may seem rather radical but we should remind the reader that virtually every other industrial country in the world gets by without such a regulatory body. At the other extreme is a system where the commission sets guidelines, for example the maximum rate of increase in wages, within which the parties bargain at the work place. This is roughly what happened in 1992, but is not really what the proponents of enterprise bargaining have in mind.

One problem is that unions are organised along craft and industrial lines, and hence an employer at any one work place would have to negotiate with several, or even many, unions. Enterprise bargaining is most effective when workers in an enterprise all belong to one union or have some other arrangement where they can collectively negotiate with employers. Thus in the long term, to reap the benefits claimed, enterprise bargaining would have to be accompanied by changes in union structure.

Equity problems may arise. We have seen that there is evidence to suggest that centralised wage determination has led to a more equitable distribution of earnings and has raised the relative position of the low paid. A move to enterprise bargaining will then disadvantage low paid workers. The extent to which this occurs will, again, depend upon the role of the commission. Decentralised enterprise bargaining would also make a national wages policy, such as the Accord, impossible. Whether or not this would be a undesirable outcome depends, of course, on the advantages and disadvantages of wages policies; these will be discussed in Chapter 11.

9.5 The personal distribution of earnings

Here we are concerned with the distribution of individual earnings. We have seen throughout this and the previous five chapters that there are a large number of influences on the earnings of individual workers. Some of those influences tend to raise the relative earnings of any worker, others to lower them. We get a picture of the net outcome from surveys of earnings undertaken annually by the ABS. We begin by describing the shape of the distribution in 1991 and then proceed to attempt an explanation of it. Finally, we look at how the distribution has changed over time.

The distribution in 1991

The ABS divides workers into two groups: managerial and non-managerial. Workers are included in the former group if they are described as managerial, executive, professional, or higher supervisory staff. The form of the distribution of personal earnings differs according to which group of workers is included and in most of this section we shall confine attention to full-time, adult non-managerial workers. It is preferable to confine attention to full-time workers in order to minimise the effect of variations in hours of work. In the 1991 survey, non-managerial workers accounted for 86 per cent of full-time workers.

In Figure 9.1 we plot the distribution of earnings in the form of a frequency distribution. The horizontal axis shows the ranges of earnings used in the survey and the vertical axis shows the percentage of workers falling into each range (the small percentage of workers earning more than $1000 a week is excluded).

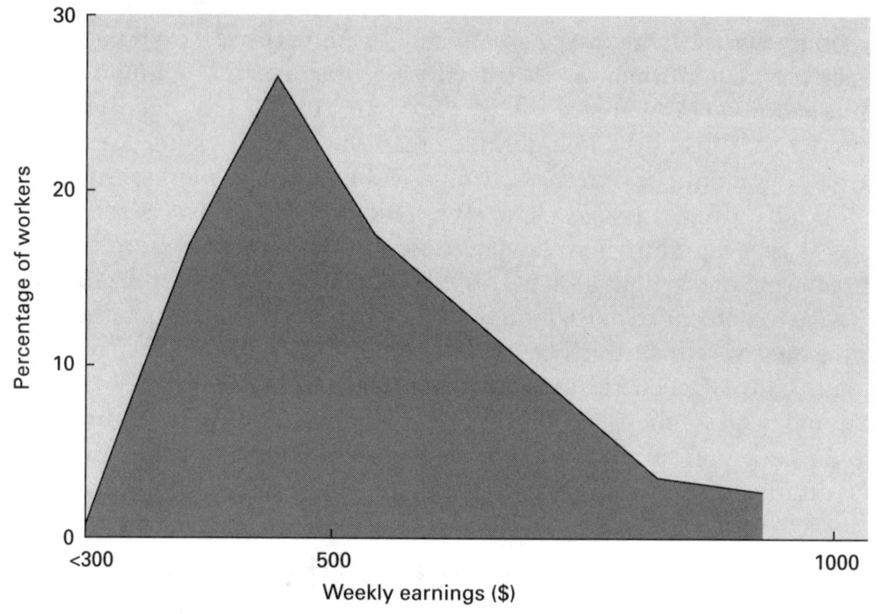

Note: Figures refer to full-time adult non-managerial workers.

Source: Drawn from data in Distribution and Composition of Employee Earnings and Hours, (ABS, cat. no. 6306.0).

Figure 9.1 The distribution of earnings (natural scale)

It can be seen that the earnings distribution is not normal. It is positively skewed, the upper part of the distribution being more elongated than the lower. We can gain a numerical impression of this by comparing median earnings with mean earnings. Median earnings are those of the person who occupies the middle place in the ranking of earnings: thus half of all workers earn less than median earnings and half earn more. Mean earnings are more commonly referred to as average earnings—the total earnings of the group divided by the number of people in the group. In a normal distribution median and mean earnings are the same. In 1991 median earnings of full-time adult non-managerial male workers were $550 and mean earnings, were $596.

In Figure 9.2 we show the same set of data in a different way. In this graph earnings are plotted on a logarithmic scale, that is an equal distance on the horizontal axis is given to the same proportionate, rather than absolute, differences in earnings. Thus, for example, the distance between $300 a week and $600 is the same as the distance between $600 and $1200. Plotted on this scale the shape of the frequency distribution is nearly symmetrical. In other words, the distribution is approximately normal in the logarithm of earnings. We can therefore describe the distribution of the earnings of non-managerial workers as 'lognormal'.

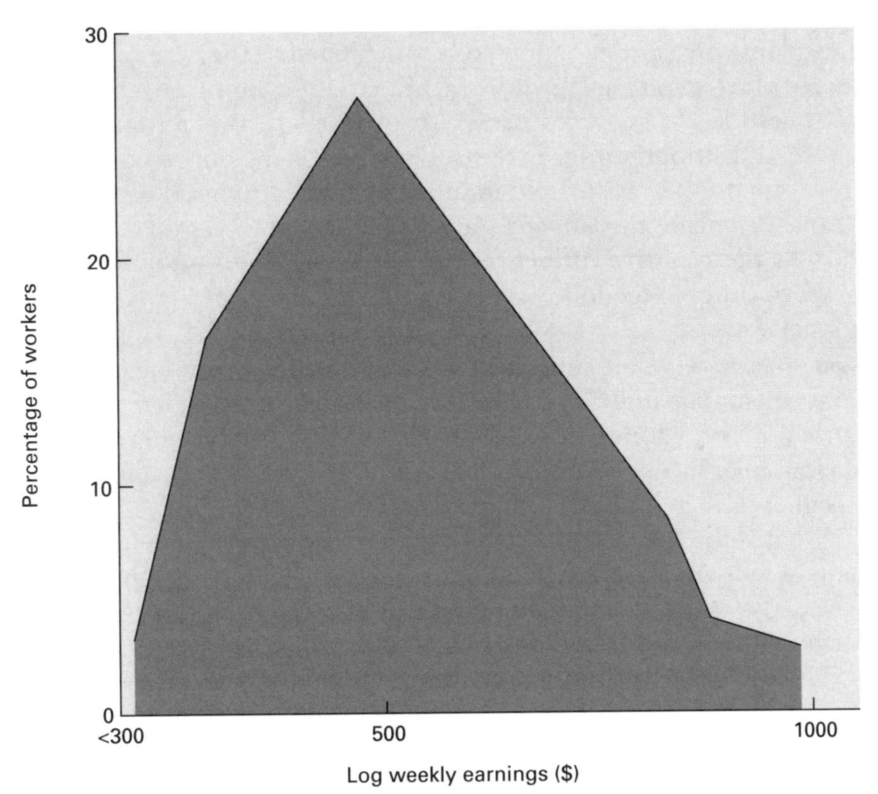

Note and source: as for Figure 9.1.

Figure 9.2 The distribution of earnings (logarithmic scale)

The significance of this is that when we examine the distribution of the earnings of similar groups of workers in other countries we invariably find that they too are lognormal. (When both managerial and non-managerial workers are included the distribution is lognormal for approximately the bottom 90 per cent of workers but above that level of earnings the upper tail is thicker than the lognormal.) This observation was made in a range of different societies as long ago as the 1890s by Pareto and has persisted since. Lydall, for example, studied earnings in thirty countries and found this general pattern was almost uniform.[7] For non-managerial workers alone, the distribution in Australia has been virtually lognormal since 1965, the first year for which we have information for that group. In Britain the distribution is also lognormal as, remarkably, it was in 1886.

The generation of lognormal earnings distribution

As the shape of the distribution is the same across a range of different societies and in most modern societies the same way as in the nineteenth century, it must surely be the outcome of the same process. We can provide an intuitive, rather than a formal, explanation of a statistical process which can explain why earnings come to be distributed as they are.

We start by showing how earnings might come to be normally distributed, as it becomes easier to proceed to the actual case of a lognormal distribution once we see the sense of the normal distribution. Let us suppose that there are ten influences on earnings. These are listed in Table 9.4 where the left side shows positive influences on earnings and the right the negative influences. Let us now suppose that the labour market operates in the following way. All workers receive, to start with, a notional wage of $200 a week but for every factor that works in their favour they receive an extra $20 a week, and for every factor working against them they lose $20 a week. Further assume that there is an evens chance (or a probability of 0.5) of each circumstance being favourable or unfavourable. In our example there is nothing in between the extremes; you either have good health (plus $20) or poor health (minus $20).

What is the shape of the resulting earning distribution among a large group of workers? We show in Figure 9.3 a diagrammatic representation of the early stages of the final outcome of the process which generates the distribution.

Workers start with their assumed notional earnings of $200. If they have positive characteristic A they move to the right, earning $220, if negative they go to the left, earning $180. Characteristic B now adds or

Table 9.4 Influences on earnings: hypothetical example

	Favourable	*Unfavourable*
A	English native tongue	Native tongue not English
B	IQ over 100	IQ under 100
C	Good health	Poor health
D	Above-average strength	Below-average strength
E	Middle-class parents	Working-class parents
F	Tertiary education	Secondary education
G	Industrial training	No industrial training
H	Closed internal labour market	Open internal labour market
I	Union member	Non-union member
J	Concentrated industry	Competitive industry

subtracts $20 to or from earnings. Thus to take the left-hand side where A operated unfavourably reducing earnings to $180, the effect of B is to either increase earnings to $200 or reduce them to $160. This process continues and we show it working through four characteristics. By the time characteristic D has had its effect there are five possible earnings and underneath each is shown the relative frequency with which it would appear. In terms of the diagram the frequencies show how many possible 'paths' there are from A to each earnings level. The reader should be able to trace the effect of the next six influences (it would take too much space here) and confirm that the net outcome of all ten, and the relative frequencies with which each would occur, are as shown in the lower two rows of the figure. Earnings would be distributed normally around a central value of $200 a week (the mode, median, and mean are all $200) and range from $0 to $400.

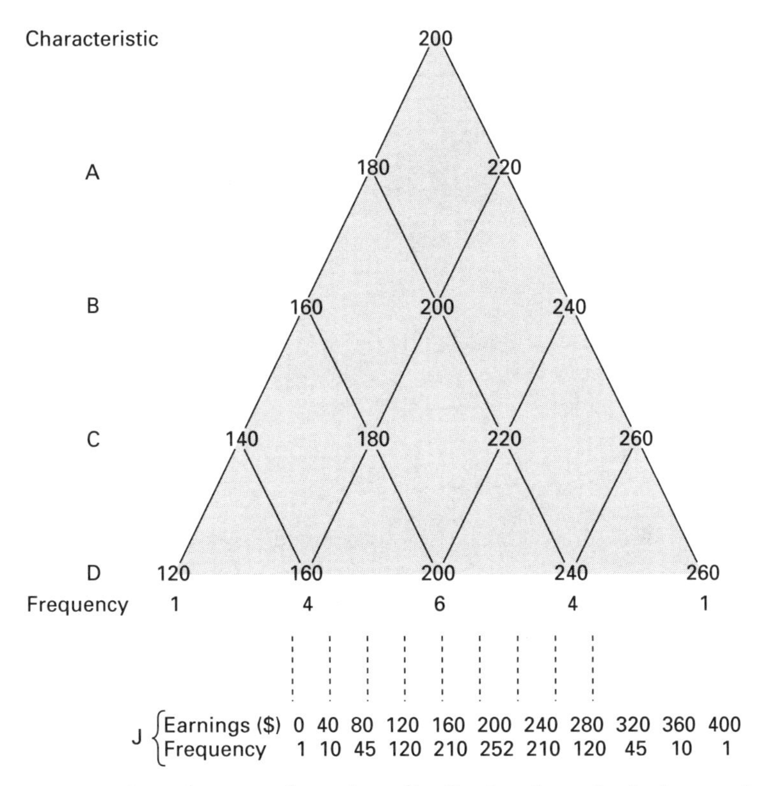

Figure 9.3 Generation of a normal earnings distribution: hypothetical example

Thus normal earnings distributions are generated if the labour market operates in such a way that rewards for certain attributes are additive, and the characteristics themselves are randomly distributed. We have seen, however, that earnings distributions are not normal.

We can explain how lognormal distributions are generated by making just one change to the hypothetical example of ten characteristics affecting earnings. We now assume that if an influence works favourably it adds a certain percentage to earnings and if unfavourably it decreases earnings by the same percentage. In the previous example it will be remembered that each characteristic affected earnings by the same absolute amount; here the effect is proportionate.

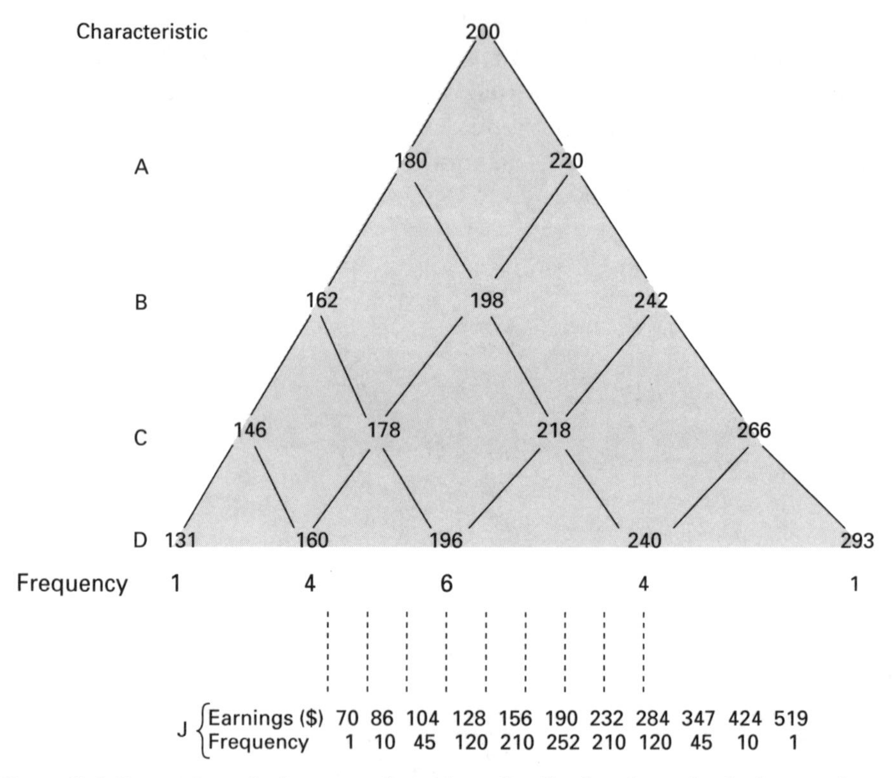

Figure 9.4 Generation of a lognormal earnings distribution: hypothetical example

The early stages, and the final outcome, of this process are shown in Figure 9.4, in which each influence is assumed to raise or lower earnings by 10 per cent. Characteristic A increases initial earnings to $220 or lowers them to $180, and the effect of adding or deducting 10 per cent to these is to generate four possible outcomes, one of $162, two of $198, and one of $242. We again show the working of the process through the first four stages. From the levels of earnings and their relative frequency at the fourth stage we already see that the distribution is not normal. The mode is $196, but the upper tail is more elongated than the lower (highest earnings are $93 above the mode, but lowest earnings are only $65 below the mode).

The bottom two rows of Figure 9.4 show the levels of earnings, and their relative frequency, generated by the interaction of all ten influences. It is not symmetric around the mode of $190 (the mean is $208) and compared with the normal distribution in Figure 9.3 has a truncated lower tail but a longer upper tail. Thus compare the frequency with which each level of earnings occurs in Figures 9.3 and 9.4. In the normal case fifty-six workers earn $80 or less; in the lognormal distribution only eleven workers earn $86 or less. More workers are, however, found in the upper earnings ranges in the lognormal distribution. In the normal distribution example the highest level of earnings is $400; in the lognormal case ten workers earn $424 and one earns $519. The comparatively long upper tail is caused by the same percentage change being added to increasingly larger numbers, with the opposite effect working at the lower end of the distribution.

We thus obtain the prediction that if an individual's earnings are determined by the effect of numerous random and equal influences and if these influences interact in a multiplicative way, that is, each raising or lowering earnings by the same proportion, then earnings would be distributed lognormally among a large group of individuals. The question now arises: Is this a plausible description of how earnings are determined in practice?

We would argue that in a broad sense the answer to this question is 'yes'. We have seen throughout this book that the amount people earn depends on a variety of factors starting with genetic endowments, moving through to family background and education, and to influences within the labour market. It also does seem likely that these factors have a proportionate, rather than an equal absolute, effect on earnings. To take an obvious example, if a worker is absent through ill health for one-fifth of the year, the loss of earnings would be greater if the person is a highly-paid oil-rig worker than if he or she was a labourer. Again, if the union markup is 10 per cent then clearly the absolute effect would vary according to the level of earnings upon which it is exerted.

Is it true, however, that the influences are independent of one another? This was assumed in our example, where the chances of a characteristic operating favourably or unfavourably were independent of the effects of other characteristics. In practice some influences seem to be correlated with each other. For example, the chances of a young person going to university are not independent of genetic endowment or of upbringing. In general those who start life in favourable circumstances seem to have a better chance of success in latter stages and vice versa. Let us first note that although some influences are correlated in this way it cannot be true for all. If it were, then the resulting earnings distribution would be U-shaped and this is not the case. Further, we have so far been dealing with non-managerial workers only and these cumulative influences are more likely to be operative for highly-paid professional and managerial workers. This again is in accord with the evidence, for we reported earlier that when distributions for all workers are plotted the upper tail is thicker (contains more individuals) than it is in the lognormal distribution. In general it seems that there are enough independent influences to offset the effects of correlated influences. Finally, in our hypothetical example every characteristic had the same proportionate effect. This clearly is not the case in practice, but the generation of such distributions does not depend upon this assumption. It is the task of research to identify the magnitude of these various influences.

We saw in Chapter 6 that the variables included in statistical earnings functions such as education, experience, and union membership, typically explain about 40 per cent of the variance in earnings. A further 10 per cent is likely to be transitory; this arises from the fact that earnings surveys are usually undertaken in a given week of the year and there are many reasons why a person's earnings in one week are not a fair reflection of annual or long-term earnings. This leaves about one-half of the variance of earnings unexplained. All that can be done is to suggest what might cause this. First, we all know that if we take two individuals whose measurable characteristics are the same they are not likely to achieve equally, either in education or in work. They would differ in personality, energy, ambition, willingness to work hard, and so on. Lydall has coined this group of abilities the 'D-factor' (where D stands for drive, dynamism, doggedness, and determination).[8] Second, remembering we are now talking of all male workers, the special rewards for responsibility would influence the upper earnings ranges. Finally, the importance of luck should not be underestimated.

The fact that the earnings of non-managerial workers are approximately lognormally distributed does not imply that the spread of earnings is always the same, or the same in all countries. There are several ways of measuring the extent of dispersion in an earnings distribution. The method

Table 9.5 The dispersion of earnings: full-time adult non-managerial male employees, 1965-91

Percentile point	*1965*	*1971*	*1975*	*1980*	*1986*	*1991*
10	75.3	71.2	76.0	75.2	71.5	69.5
25	84.8	82.6	85.6	84.3	82.4	80.6
75	122.5	125.0	121.0	122.4	127.4	126.8
85	137.4	141.7	135.9	137.1	149.1	143.5

Note: Earnings at each percentile point are expressed as percentages of median earnings.

Sources: 1965, 1971, 1975, from Norris;[9] 1980, 1986 and 1991 estimated from *Distribution and Composition of Employee Earnings and Hours*, (ABS, cat. no. 6306.0).

used here is to select various percentile points of the distribution and to express these as a percentage of the median of the distribution. For example, to gain an impression of how far away from the median low paid workers are, we first estimate earnings at the tenth percentile. These are the earnings of the worker who, if earnings are ranked in order, occupies a place 10 per cent from the bottom of the earnings ranking. This worker's earnings are then expressed as a percentage of median earnings, which are the earnings of the person occupying the middle rank. Similar ratios can be calculated at other points in the distribution.

In Table 9.5 we show the results of such an exercise for various years since 1965, the first year that such data were collected.

Below the median the lower the percentage figures the greater the dispersion of earnings around the median; while above the median the converse holds. An inspection of Table 9.5 reveals that the dispersion of earnings widened quite considerably between 1965 and 1971, narrowed up until 1980 and subsequently widened again between 1980 and 1986. Between 1986 and 1991 lower paid workers lost ground relative to median earnings, but above the median the spread of earnings narrowed slightly although remaining greater than in the rest of the period.

Thus the dispersion of earnings in Australia is significantly greater now than in 1975. Similar changes have taken place in Britain and in the United States. A corollary of such changes is that if low wage workers are defined, not in absolute terms, but relative to the median, then more people will be found low wage employment. In Table 9.6 low wage workers are defined as those who earn less than 75 per cent of the median, and high wage workers are those who earn more than 175 per cent of the median. Those earning between 75 and 175 per cent of the median are termed medium-wage workers.

It is evident that there has been a marked polarisation of employment with many more men and women to be found in either high or low wage employment and many fewer in median wage employment. Not surprisingly the authors refer to this as the 'law of the shrinking middle'. The figures refer to both full-time and part-time workers and the authors suggest that the major, but not the only, cause of the change has been the growth of part-time employment that we have discussed earlier. In the case of full-time workers, the polarisation will have been less marked. Nonetheless it has undoubtedly occurred and will have reinforced any dualism that exists in the Australian labour market (see Section 8.3 of Chapter 8).

The interesting question is whether it will be reversed in future for there has been a clear tendency for periods of narrowing in the distribution to be followed by periods of widening and so on. It can in fact be argued on the basis of the earnings surveys referred to and of the variance of award rates of pay for earlier periods that the distribution of the earnings of non-managerial workers is much the same as it was in 1914. When we think of the profound changes that have taken place in the economy and in society in general in this period this stability is at first sight surprising, and lends further credence to the ideas we have sketched out in this section. The factors that influence earnings may change over the years but they interact in such a way as to generate the same sort of earnings distribution.

Table 9.6 Shares of low, medium and high wage employment; men and women, 1975-89 (%)

		1975	*1983*	*1989*
Men	Low	17.4	20.0	24.7
	Medium	75.8	72.1	66.6
	High	6.8	7.9	8.7
Women	Low	25.5	31.9	33.3
	Medium	70.8	61.4	57.6
	High	3.7	6.7	9.1

Source: King, Rimmer and Rimmer.[10]

Concepts for review

- Non-pecuniary characteristics of employment
- Compensating pay differentials
- Skill relativities
- Observed and true industrial relativities
- Enterprise bargaining
- Lognormal distribution

Questions

1 Discuss the case for and against the deregulation of the Australian labour market. (La Trobe University).

2 Discuss the main reasons why some people get paid more than others, that is, why we do not observe all wages to be equal. (University of Adelaide)

3 Is the concept of compensating wage differentials useful in understanding the structure and distribution of earnings? (University of Western Australia)

4 What have been the notable features of the structure of pay across occupations and industries? How would you explain these features? (Curtin University)

5 Norris has made an intuitive attempt through the use of a statistical process to explain why the shape of the distribution of earnings is the same between countries and in different periods of time. Describe the process and the forces at work. (Macquarie University)

References

1 S. Richardson and K. Hancock, 'Discount rates and the distribution of lifetime earnings in Australia', *Journal of Human Resources*, vol. 20, no. 3, 1985, pp. 346-60.

2 L. Katz, 'Efficiency wage theories; a partial evaluation', in S. Fischer (ed.), *NBER Macroeconomics Annual*, MIT Press, Cambridge, 1986.

3 M.J. Watts and W.J. Mitchell, 'The impact of incomes policy on the male inter-industry wage structure', *Journal of Industrial Relations*, vol. 32, no. 3, 1990, pp. 353-69.

4 K. Norris, 'The wages structure: does arbitration make a difference?', in J.R. Niland (ed.), *Wage Fixation in Australia*, Allen & Unwin, Sydney, 1986, pp. 183-201.

5 *Australian Industrial Relations Law and Systems*, Report of the Committee of Review, AGPS, Canberra, 1985. The detailed discussion of labour market flexibility is to be found in vol. 3.

6 *Enterprise-Based Bargaining Units*, Business Council of Australia, Melbourne, 1989, pp. 2-3.

7 H.F. Lydall, *The Structure of Earnings*, Oxford University Press, Oxford, 1968.

8 H.F. Lydall, 'Theories of the distribution of earnings', in A.B. Atkinson (ed.), *The Personal Distribution of Incomes*, Allen & Unwin, London, 1976.

9 K. Norris, 'The dispersion of earnings in Australia', *Economic Record*, vol. 53, no. 144, 1977, p. 483.

10 J.E. King, R.J. Rimmer and S.M. Rimmer, 'The law of the shrinking middle: inequality of earnings in Australia, 1975-89', *Scottish Journal of Political Economy*, 1992.

CHAPTER 10

Unemployment

10.1 Introduction

To be unemployed is for the vast majority of people an extremely unwelcome prospect. It invariably involves a reduction in income and often leads to a sense of failure, to a feeling that the individual is to blame for his or her unemployment. Unfortunately, periods of relatively high unemployment occur from time to time and the average level of unemployment has been significantly higher in the last decade than previously.

We begin this chapter by explaining how unemployment is measured in Australia and look at reasons why in some circumstances the published statistics tend to understate the extent of unemployment. In Section 10.3 we introduce two distinctions which are essential to any understanding of unemployment. The first is between labour market stocks and flows, and the second is between the incidence and the duration of unemployment. As we shall see, some unemployment is inevitable and even desirable to enable the labour market to perform its allocative function and in Section 10.4 the notion of the full employment rate of unemployment (at which the overall labour market is, in some sense, in balance) is examined. In some years, and the early 1990s would be an example, the actual unemployment rate comes to exceed the full employment rate. How this comes about is the subject matter of Section 10.5. The concluding section discusses the unemployment rates of various groups, particularly those of young people.

10.2 The measurement of unemployment

The major source of data on unemployment is the Labour Force Survey which is undertaken each month by the Australian Bureau of Statistics

(ABS). (The other series on unemployment is published by the Department of Social Security and refers to the number of people receiving unemployment benefit.) Each month the ABS surveys a sample of private dwellings which contain about three-fifths of 1 per cent of the population.

To be classified as unemployed, a person must respond to three questions in the following way. 'No' I have not undertaken any paid work in the week of the survey; 'Yes' I have actively sought work in the month preceding the survey; and, 'Yes' I am available to start work. The purpose of the second question is to distinguish between the unemployed and those who do not wish to work and who are 'not in the labour force'. As we shall see shortly, people may respond to this question in a way to understate the extent of unemployment.

The absolute numbers of unemployed can be more conveniently expressed as a percentage of the labour force, that is the total of the employed and the unemployed: this is known as the unemployment rate. Unemployment rates since 1965 are shown in Table 10.1.

It can be seen that experience since 1975, and, even more so since 1980 has been totally different from the previous decade. (The period between 1950–65 was also one of low unemployment, with rates averaging around 1.5 per cent.) The unemployment rate increased in two large steps, from 1.8 per cent in 1973 to 5.5 per cent in 1977, and from 5.6 per cent in 1981 to 8.9 per cent in 1983.

The published unemployment rates tend to understate unemployment rates at particular stages of the economic cycle. In cyclical downturns the supply of labour tends to be understated leading to a phenomenon known as 'hidden unemployment'. Further, particularly in the early stages of downturns, the demand for labour tends to be artificially inflated leading to unemployment being understated; the activity which leads to this effect is known as 'labour hoarding'.

Hidden unemployment

As we have seen, to be counted as unemployed a person is required to have actively sought work in the month prior to the survey. Actively seeking work includes such things as responding to job advertisements, approaching employers and so on. Such activity involves the direct costs of correspondence, travel and so forth, and the opportunity costs of time. Given the costs involved, in periods of relatively high unemployment many people cease, given the costs involved, seeking work because they believe the prospects of obtaining it to be very low. Yet they would like to work and they would seek work in more favourable conditions. Such persons are referred to as discouraged workers. This type of unemployment, which is not reflected in published statistics of unemployment, is known as hidden unemployment.

Table 10.1 Unemployment rates, 1965–91

Year	*Percentage*
1965-69 (average)	1.5
1970-74 (")	2.2
1975-79 (")	5.0
1980-84 (")	7.2
1985-89 (")	7.2
1990	8.2
1991	10.5
1992	10.5

Note: Figures are for November each year (except 1992 which is for March), seasonally adjusted.
Source: *The Labour Force, Australia*, (ABS, cat. no. 6203.0).

One straightforward method of estimating the extent of hidden unemployment is as follows. It will be recalled from Chapter 2 that the labour force participation rate for any group in the population is measured by:

$$\frac{\text{number in employment + number actively seeking work}}{\text{number in population as a whole}} \times 100$$

The overall participation rate tends to fall as unemployment rises and to rise as unemployment falls. Now say the observed participation rate changes over time as shown in Figure 10.1. It is assumed that the observed

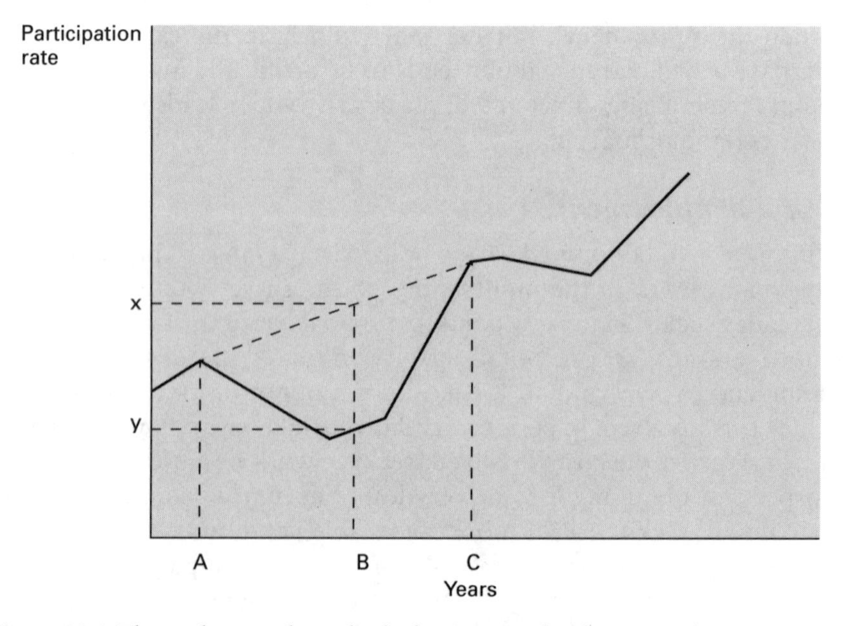

Figure 10.1 The peak-to-peak method of estimating hidden unemployment

and true participation rates coincide at peaks in the series, for example in years A and C. To estimate hidden unemployment in year B it is assumed that the 'true' participation rate is x, obtained by linear interpolation between A and C. The difference x–y between the true and observed participation rates is then applied to the relevant population and an estimate of hidden unemployment for this group is obtained. This method also has its weaknesses. The most important is the assumption that all peaks are true ones, that is that they are of equal strength. If in the diagram A was the peak of a weak cyclical upswing, whereas C represented a strong peak, then the trend line between the low peaks would be incorrectly sloped.

Estimates of hidden unemployment using this method have been made by Chapman.[1] The assumption made is that 1966 and 1989 were years in which the true and observed participation rates coincided and in which there was no hidden unemployment. The resulting estimates for the 1980s are presented in Table 10.2.

Table 10.2 Measured and estimated unemployment (%)

Year	*Measured unemployment rate*	*Estimated total unemployment rate*	*Hidden unemployment rate*
1980	5.9	9.4	3.5
1981	5.6	9.7	4.1
1982	6.7	11.9	5.2
1983	10.0	15.8	5.8
1984	8.6	14.4	5.8
1985	7.9	13.0	5.1
1986	8.0	11.3	3.3
1987	7.8	10.6	2.8
1988	7.1	8.9	1.8
1989	5.9	5.9	0

Source: Chapman.[1]

In Table 10.2 hidden unemployment is the difference between the author's estimated total unemployment rate and the measured (ABS) rate. It is evident that in years when measured unemployment is relatively high a considerable amount of hidden unemployment emerges. Thus in 1983 when unemployment peaked at 10 per cent, there was an estimated additional hidden unemployment of 5.8 per cent.

One corollary of the cyclical movement of hidden unemployment is that as employment expands as the economy moves out of recession part of the effect is taken up by an increase in the participation rate, and hence a decline in hidden unemployment, rather than a fall in measured unemployment.

Labour hoarding

Labour hoarding basically arises because labour is, as we saw in Chapter 5, a quasi-fixed factor of production and because, partly as a result, large sections of the labour force are employed in fairly closed internal labour markets. We saw in Chapter 5 that if a firm experiences a downturn in the demand for its product it does not follow that labour is laid off immediately. The reason for this is the existence of fixed costs of employing labour, which provides a rental element in the costs of labour. Labour is only laid off when its marginal product falls below its variable costs of employment. The protection thus afforded workers is greater the greater is the rental element, which is largest in the case of skilled workers. There are other reasons for expecting employment to adjust more slowly than output to downturns in economic activity. There are usually legal constraints in the sense that due notice of the termination of employment contracts has to be given, and the desire to maintain good industrial relations tends to slow down adjustment. In the case of skilled workers an additional reason for not reducing employment may be that, whatever the fixed costs of such labour, firms may fear that in any subsequent recovery they will simply find it difficult to recruit skilled labour.

Thus employment adjusts more slowly than output to changes in demand and hence firms may employ, at least temporarily, more labour than is required to produce current levels of output. In other words they hoard labour. It is evident that labour hoarding is likely to be more pronounced in cyclical downswings that are perceived to be short lived rather than extended, and more pronounced in the early stages of a downswing than in the later stages.

The fact that employment tends to fall more slowly than output provides a way to measure labour hoarding, for the corollary is that output per worker would tend to fall, at least in the early stages of recessions. Therefore, the difference between actual output per worker and 'potential' output per worker can be used as a measure of labour hoarding. Formally, if Q denotes actual (or measured) output per worker, and Q^* denotes potential output per worker, the rate of labour hoarding is:

$$(1 - \frac{Q}{Q^*}) \times 100$$

One difficulty in estimating hoarding is the identification of potential output per worker. One method is to assume that observed productivity equals potential at cyclical peaks and then to use a peak-to-peak method, similar to that described in the estimation of hidden unemployment, shown in Figure 10.1 to derive estimates for intervening years. All the difficulties discussed in that case are relevant here. There is an additional problem, already alluded to, which is that labour hoarding is also likely to be negligible in sustained downswings as firms attempt to pare down labour to minimum levels. In such circumstances the short-run assumptions that have to be made become less appropriate.

Mangan has made estimates of the extent of labour hoarding in Australia between 1944 and 1977. The unweighted average of hoarding rates in manufacturing industries was found to be, for example, 7.6 per cent in the period from 1968 to 1977. The trend within the period was roughly in conformity with expectations. As unemployment rose in early 1975 and 1976 so did hoarding, but as the recession continued hoarding declined. In the context of the fairly low measured unemployment rates around this period these rates of labour hoarding were surprisingly large.

The figures for hoarding at the industry level show that hoarding is usually at higher-than-average levels in concentrated, capital-intensive industries which employ a high proportion of relatively skilled, highly paid labour, which in turn has a low tendency to quit.[2] These are, of course, the characteristics which our analysis of Chapter 5 would lead us to expect.

Labour hoarding does not seem to have been eliminated in the subsequent years of relatively high unemployment. Using slightly different methods from those employed by Mangan, it has been found by Bosworth and Westaway that labour hoarding in 1982 was at about the same level as in 1977.[3]

10.3 The dynamics of unemployment

Stocks and flows

Unemployment is a stock and its magnitude is determined by the size of two flows, those moving into and those moving out of unemployment, and by the period of time which, on average, elapses between these two movements, that is the average duration of unemployment. There are various reasons why people move into unemployment. People move from employment into unemployment either voluntarily, that is they want to change jobs, or involuntarily, because they are laid off. Others move from outside the labour market into unemployment; examples are young workers entering the labour market for the first time or returning after raising children. Similarly, those who leave the unemployment pool either move to employment or leave the labour force (some retire, some become discouraged, women leave to raise children). To see more clearly the relations between flows, duration and the stock of unemployment let us imagine a labour force which is constant so that the only flows are from and to employment.

Say the labour force is 100 and the numbers unemployed are counted every Thursday. In the first instance, 10 persons become unemployed each Monday and remain unemployed for a week. The following Monday they re-enter employment and are replaced in the unemployment pool by another ten, and so on. Hence, when the unemployed are counted every Thursday they number ten and the unemployment rate is 10 per cent. The numbers unemployed would increase either if the flows increased or if duration increased, or both. Thus, say now twenty persons become unemployed each Monday, the duration of unemployment remaining at one week; twenty persons are unemployed each Thursday and the unemployment rate is 20 per cent. The same rate of unemployment would be observed if, as in the first case, ten persons became unemployed each Monday and remained unemployed for two weeks: each Thursday twenty persons would be unemployed, being the ten who joined the Monday of that week plus the ten who became unemployed the previous Monday.

Thus we have the result that, given the static labour force of the sort described, the unemployment rate, U, is as follows:

$$U = \frac{I}{L} \times D \qquad (1)$$

where I represents the inflows to unemployment, L is the number of persons in the labour force, and D is the average duration of unemployment, both I and D being measured in the same units of time. In our example in the first case:

$$U = \frac{10}{100} \times 1 = 10 \text{ per cent}$$

and in the second case U rose to 20 per cent either if I became 20 or if D became 2.

Once the labour force is allowed to vary, things get rather more complicated but the essence of the result remains, that is that unemployment increases if either the flow into unemployment or the average duration of unemployment increases, or if some combination of the two occurs. We begin by describing more generally the flows that take place within the labour market and then move on to look more closely at flows into unemployment and at the duration of unemployment.

Flows within the Australian labour market

As we briefly indicated in the previous section we can place any individual in one of three 'states' with respect to the labour market. The first is that one is in employment and the second is that one is unemployed as defined and measured in Section 10.2. The third possibility is that one is not in the labour force. That is, that one did not work in the week of the Labour Force Survey and that one did not actively seek work in the month preceding the survey.

Each month the Labour Force Survey provides data not only on the number of people in each state, but also on the number of people who have moved from one labour market state to another in the preceding month. The stocks in March 1992 and the flows that occurred between February and March of that year are shown in Figure 10.2.

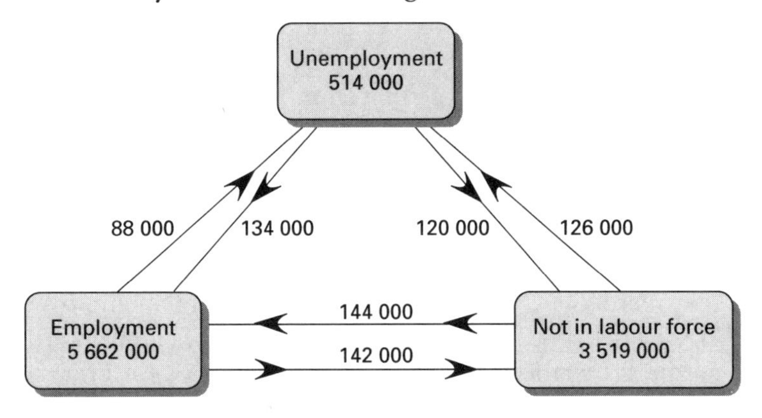

Figure 10.2 Stocks and flows, March 1990

It is apparent that these movements through the labour market are substantial, bearing in mind that the figures in Figure 10.2 refer to movements per month. Consider the movements in and out of employment. The flows out of employment in the month were equivalent to no less than 49 per cent of the number of people unemployed on the March survey date, while the flows into unemployment were equivalent to 42 per cent of the stock of unemployed. The flows to and from the other stocks are similar in absolute magnitude but are, of course, much smaller in proportionate terms because the number of people who are in employment or not in the labour force are much greater than the number who are unemployed.

Table 10.3 Stocks, flows and unemployment durations

	March 1989	*March 1992*	*Percentage increase*
Unemployment rate (%)	6.2	10.5	69
Flows into unemployment (000)	142	214	50
Flows out of unemployment (000)	199	254	28
Median interrupted duration of unemployment (weeks)	13	23	77

Source: *The Labour Force, Australia*, (ABS, cat. no. 6203.0).

The various flows through the labour force market vary with economic conditions. Consider the flows into and out of unemployment that took place in March 1989 and in March 1992. (Because there is considerable seasonal variability in the flows it is important to compare the same months.) The relevant data are assembled in Table 10.3.

In this period there was a 69 per cent increase in the unemployment rate. Table 10.3 explains how this came about. First, there was a 50 per cent increase in the number of people entering unemployment. Second, at the same time there was an increase in the number of people leaving unemployment each month but this increase was significantly less, being 28 per cent. Thus as the number of people entering unemployment increased by much more than the number leaving unemployment the number of unemployed rose. Finally, once a person became unemployed in 1992 they were likely to spend a longer time being unemployed than in 1989; this is evident from the final row which shows a dramatic increase in the median number of weeks the unemployed had remained unemployed.

Thus to return to equation (1), experience shows that as unemployment increases, part of the explanation is an increase in the flows into unemployment and part is a result of increases in the average duration of unemployment. Quantitatively, however, the increase in unemployment durations is the most important.

The duration of unemployment

Unemployment is unevenly distributed among the unemployed in the sense that while many people remain unemployed for short periods of time some suffer long-term unemployment. The distribution of unemployment by duration is shown in Table 10.4.

It can be seen that while around one-half of the unemployed had been unemployed for less than twenty-six weeks, a significant proportion of

Table 10.4 Distribution of unemployment by duration, 1992

	Percentage	
	Males	*Females*
Less than 4 weeks	10.6	16.4
4 and under 13 weeks	19.2	24.5
13 and under 26 weeks	17.3	17.8
26 and under 52 weeks	17.6	12.9
52 and under 104 weeks	20.9	16.8
Over 104 weeks	14.4	11.7
Median duration	26 weeks	16 weeks
Average duration	53 weeks	40 weeks

Source: *The Labour Force, Australia*, (ABS, cat. no. 6203.0).

both males and females had been unemployed for over two years. The distribution of unemployment by duration is strongly positively skewed. One indication of this is given by the relation of the medians of the durations to the means—the mean being more than twice the median for both genders. The table also shows that unemployment durations are shorter for women than for men.

On p. 110 we discussed the duration of jobs and analogous to the concepts of the length of a job there are two measures of the length of a spell of unemployment. First, there is the average duration of unemployment for those currently unemployed. The figures in Tables 10.3 and 10.4 refer to interrupted spells of unemployment. Some people who were unemployed on the survey date will have just become unemployed, others will be coming near to the end of their spell of unemployment and so on. The average person will, however, be halfway through his or her spell of unemployment. Thus, to estimate the average completed spell of unemployment of those unemployed on the survey date we simply double the length of the average interrupted spell of unemployment. Readers can do this themselves for the figures for 1992 in Table 10.4. Here we report the average completed spell in 1981, which was seventy weeks.

The second measure of an unemployment spell is to estimate how long someone becoming unemployed in any given week can expect to remain unemployed. This measure of an unemployment spell produces much lower results, about sixteen weeks in 1981.[4] The reader will recall that these two measures of unemployment duration differ in the same way as did measures of job duration. In Table 5.1 we found that those currently employed could expect very long job durations while those jobs that started in any given week had a relatively short expected duration.

How, in the case of unemployment durations, can we explain the difference? First, we note that the corollary is that the longer a person is unemployed the longer they can expect to remain unemployed. Table 10.5 shows how the expected future duration of an unemployment spell varies with its length to date.

The table shows that someone starting an unemployment spell could, in 1981, expect sixteen weeks of unemployment. At the other extreme people who had already been unemployed for sixty-five weeks could

Table 10.5 Duration of unemployment, persons, 1981

Weeks unemployed so far	*Weeks of unemployment to go*	*Total spell of unemployment*
0	16	16
26	32	58
65	86	151

Source: Foster and Gregory[4]

expect a further eighty-six weeks unemployment, making their total completed spell 151 weeks.

Why is it that the longer one is unemployed the longer one can expect to remain unemployed? There are two influences at work. First, different people have different probabilities of leaving unemployment. For example, skilled workers have a high probability of leaving, older unskilled workers have a low probability. As time proceeds, those with good chances get jobs and those left are increasingly those with a poor chance of leaving unemployment. Second, the probabilities themselves change, as employers use duration of unemployment as a screening device. They assume that there must be 'something wrong' with a person who has been unemployed for a long time. Also psychological effects may work against the long-term unemployed. They become dispirited and hence search for work less effectively.

10.4 The full employment level of unemployment

It is well known that in any advanced industrial economy some unemployment always exists due to job changing and to imbalances between the skills and location of the unemployed and those of the jobs offered by firms seeking to employ additional labour. In this section, we analyse more formally the notion that when in some sense the labour market in aggregate is in equilibrium, there will exist some amount of unemployment. Various labels can be attached to this rate of unemployment, for example the 'full employment rate' of unemployment, the 'natural rate' of unemployment, the 'equilibrium rate' of unemployment or 'the non-accelerating inflation rate of unemployment'. While not suggesting that these concepts are completely interchangeable they are all based on the essential fact that some unemployment will exist when the overall labour market is in equilibrium. Thus, for our purposes it is a matter of choice as to which to use and here we will use the term the 'full employment rate of unemployment'.

As a first approach to defining the state at which the labour market as a whole is in equilibrium, let us argue that this equilibrium (full employment) would exist if the aggregate supply of labour is equal to the aggregate demand for labour. As demand consists of those in employment, N, plus the number of unfilled vacancies, V, and the supply consists of those in employment, N, plus those actively seeking work, U, this condition of equilibrium is that:

$$N + V = N + U \tag{2}$$

or

$$V = U$$

The question now arises as to what the level (or rate) of unemployment would be when the number of unfilled vacancies equals the number unemployed. The basic point is that the level is not known, a priori, but depends upon the characteristics of the national labour market. To investigate this issue we first look at an extreme case where U = V at a zero level of unemployment and vacancies. This would be the case if all jobs required just one skill and all workers possessed that one skill. Jobs would be identical in all other respects and all would carry the same wage. Further all jobs and all the workers would be located in the same place and information about job vacancies would be instantaneously transmitted to workers at no cost. In this situation, once a vacancy occurred it would be immediately filled if any worker were without a job. Vacancies and unemployment could not co-exist although of course there could be positive unemployment and no vacancies, or positive vacancies and zero unemployment.

But the world is not like this. There is a myriad of skills, and jobs differ enormously in their skill requirements, wage, and many other respects, while workers and jobs are spread throughout the country. Also, and this is the point we will investigate first, workers have imperfect knowledge of job opportunities and similarly firms are not fully aware of the characteristics of workers seeking jobs. Thus both unemployed workers and firms have to engage in search activity (some employed workers would also be searching for new jobs but we will concentrate here on the behaviour of the unemployed). In Section 5.5 we described the information networks that may be used by workers searching for jobs and saw that an unemployed worker might be expected to search until the expected marginal returns from search activity came to equal the marginal costs of search. We can see that, among other things, the average duration (and hence the average stock) of search unemployment is greater the less efficiently is information about job vacancies made available and the higher is the marginal cost of search. A major part of the costs of searching is the income foregone through not accepting available jobs (in the hope that a more highly paid or more desirable job will be found). It follows that if the government provides financial benefit to the unemployed the marginal costs of search are reduced, and further that any changes in the level of benefit are likely to affect the duration, and level, of search unemployment.

When examining the effect of unemployment benefit on the behaviour of unemployed it is the ratio of income when out of work to income in work that is relevant. These ratios, which vary for different groups, are

Table 10.6 Replacement ratios, 1989–90

	Percentage
Single adult	29.6
Couple, no children	50.7
Couple, two children	65.0
Couple, four children	72.0

Note: Based on average weekly earnings.
Source: Bradbury, Ross, and Doyle.[5]

known as 'replacement ratios'. Replacement ratios for four hypothetical household types are shown in Table 10.6.

It can be seen that replacement ratios are higher for couples than for single persons and, in turn, are higher for couples with children. Replacement ratios have not changed significantly in the last decade. There was a substantial increase, however, in the early 1970s and, as we would predict from our analysis of search, this led to a small increase in the level of unemployment (other influences on unemployment being held constant).

It should be emphasised that because the level of unemployment is positively associated with the level of benefits relative to earnings it does not follow that such benefits (or increases in them) are undesirable. For the vast majority of people unemployment is an unwelcome prospect and the state sees sound social reasons for offsetting some of the financial cost. Further, there are real allocative economic gains from people finding the jobs to which they are best suited and hence, again, the government sees fit to meet some of the costs of search. There are, of course, some people who are induced to become voluntarily unemployed by high replacement ratios and who do not seek work very actively.

The other main determinant of the level of unemployment at which vacancies equal unemployment is how closely the skills and locations of the unemployed match those of job vacancies. This unemployment emerges because the structure of the demand for labour changes over time due, for example, to changes in technology. Where these changes are large it becomes impossible for the composition of the labour force to change at the same pace and hence unemployment emerges. Thus in recent years the employment of relatively unskilled workers in the textile industry, largely located in Victoria and New South Wales, has declined. These workers are unable, at least without retraining, to fill vacancies for skilled data processors. The unemployed may also reside in areas where there are few job vacancies whereas numerous vacancies exist elsewhere.

We can use our discussion above to classify unemployment into three types and this classification enables us to express full employment in another way. Unemployment that arises because those who are moving between jobs or who are entering, or re-entering, the labour force have imperfect information and thus have to spend time searching for jobs is termed 'frictional' unemployment. Normally, such unemployment will last for relatively short periods of time.

The term 'structural' unemployment is used to describe that which arises because of imbalances between the type of labour sought by employers and the type of labour seeking work. The final type of unemployment, which will be discussed in the next section, arises not because of labour market frictions or because of imbalances but because there is a deficiency of demand relative to supply for all labour. This last sort of unemployment is termed 'demand deficient' unemployment. Full employment is then said to exist when there is no demand-deficient unemployment.

The unemployment-vacancy relation

We have argued that the labour market is in equilibrium in an aggregate sense when the number of unemployed approximates the number of unfilled vacancies. (It must be emphasised that this is only true if both vacancies and unemployment are correctly measured. It has already been shown that published figures for unemployment do not always correspond to true unemployment and there are also severe weaknesses in the ABS vacancy series.) When aggregate unemployment and vacancies (correctly measured) are equal, the implication is that disequilibrium rules in various submarkets, so that in some there is an excess supply of labour, in others an excess demand. What we have done is to examine some of the major factors that determine the extent of this disequilibrium. When unemployment and vacancies do not correspond, then the aggregate market is in disequilibrium. In slack conditions, unemployment tends to rise and the number of vacancies to fall, and when output is close to its potential, unemployment is low relative to the number of vacancies. Hence there is an inverse relation between unemployment and vacancies, as represented by the UV curves in Figure 10.3. The more 'efficient' is the labour market in matching the unemployed with vacancies the closer to the origin is the UV curve. Thus in the situation depicted, overall equilibrium holds at any point on the 45 degree line, but clearly the equilibrium unemployment rate, U^{**}, is greater if we are at point B on UV_1 than if we are at A on UV_0 where the equilibrium, or full employment, rate is U^*.

What is the full employment rate of unemployment in Australia? Unfortunately, it is not possible to answer this question with any great degree of accuracy. One approach is to estimate the rate of unemployment at which unemployment equals vacancies. However, the vacancy series is very unreliable. An alternative is to attempt to decompose total unemployment into types, but this also is not easy. Another method is to estimate the non-accelerating inflation rate of unemployment (NAIRU). This is an

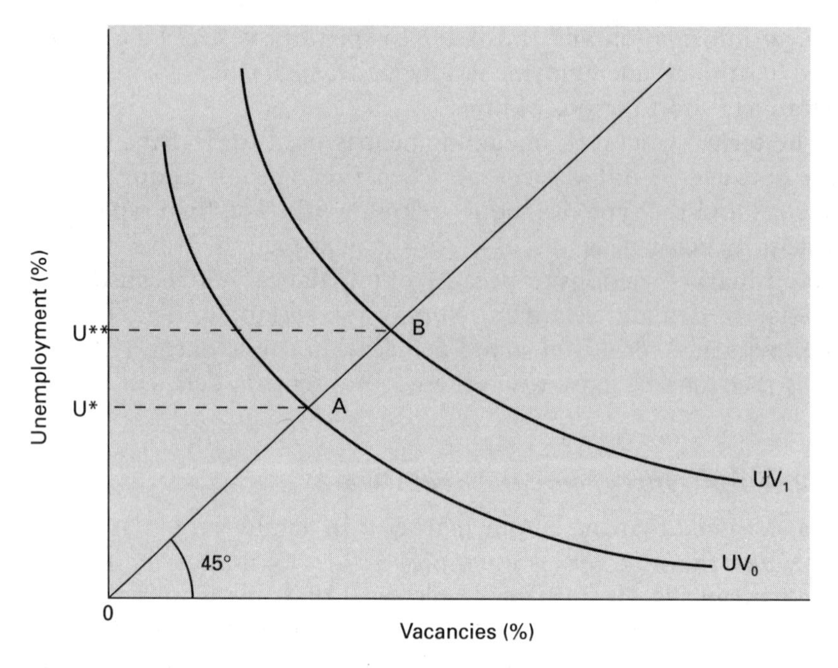

Figure 10.3 The unemployment-vacancy relation

analogous concept to the full employment rate of unemployment. Put simply the idea is as follows. At 'high' rates of unemployment there will be a tendency for the rate of inflation to fall in the face of excess supplies in labour markets. Conversely at 'low' rates of unemployment, excess demand for labour will tend to lead to the rate of inflation accelerating. It thus follows that there will be an unemployment rate at which the inflation rate is constant. This is the NAIRU.

It is not surprising that different investigators using different methods have come up with different estimates of the full employment rate of unemployment. We can draw three broad conclusions. First, it is widely agreed that it was rather less than 2 per cent in the post-war years up until around 1970, and that it has increased since then. Second, the consensus view of the current full employment rate of unemployment is that it is around 5 per cent.[6] Third, there is agreement that the full employment rate has increased at the same time as the 'actual' unemployment rate. There thus arises the possibility that the full employment rate tracks the actual rate.

This tendency is known as the 'hysteresis' or lagging effect; the full employment rate tracks the actual rate. The effect may arise in various ways. One plausible argument is that as the actual rate of unemployment rises increasing numbers of people are unemployed for relatively long periods of time. While unemployed their work skills decay, they become less and less employable and thus the mismatch between vacancies and job seekers increases and so does structural unemployment. Thus the full employment rate rises.

Policy issues

Whether an hysteresis effect exists or not is a very important policy question, for without such an effect the conventional view is that the full employment rate of unemployment cannot be reduced through monetary or fiscal policy. As we shall see in the next chapter, any attempt to reduce unemployment below its full employment level can only be successful in the short run. The inflation rate will accelerate and, as expectations and behaviour adjust to the higher inflation rate, unemployment returns to its original level. This is not to say that the full employment rate cannot be reduced, simply that it cannot be reduced through aggregate demand policies. Microeconomic policies are needed. Thus, for example, the level of frictional unemployment could be reduced by improving information flows in the labour market. This could be done by improving the operations of the Commonwealth Employment Service (CES) or perhaps, as some cynics have suggested, by abolishing the CES and leaving the task to the private sector. Similarly, structural unemployment would be reduced by policies that were successful in retraining unemployed workers in the skills demanded by employers.

Table 10.7 Trends in long-term unemployment, 1974–89

	Unemployment rate %	*Long-term unemployment as a proportion of total unemployment* %
1967–73 (average)	2.0	2.8
1974	2.7	1.3
1975	5.0	4.4
1976	5.1	8.6
1977	6.0	12.7
1978	6.5	15.7
1979	6.1	18.2
1980	6.1	19.9
1981	5.9	20.9
1982	7.0	18.8
1983	10.2	27.6
1984	8.8	31.2
1985	8.1	31.0
1986	8.2	27.5
1987	8.0	28.6
1988	7.0	28.4
1989	5.9	22.8

Source: Flatau, Lewis and Rushton.[7]

Were an hysteresis effect to operate, however, conventional macro-economic policies would reduce the full employment rate, for as the level of economic activity rose, and actual unemployment rates fell the full employment rate would follow it downwards as training activity, skill acquisition, and an increasing socialisation of young people into work, took place.

There is evidence that an hysteresis effect has been operating in Australia. One argument centres on the substantial increase in long-term unemployment—defined as those unemployed for more than one year—as shown in Table 10.7.

In the earlier part of the period, unemployment was below 3 per cent and the long-term unemployed accounted for a very small proportion of total unemployment. In the mid 1970s unemployment increased significantly and so too, after a lag, did the long-term unemployment ratio, reaching 20 per cent by the end of the decade. A further shift upwards in both series occurred in the early 1980s; in 1984 over 30 per cent of unemployed people had been unemployed for over a year. As we saw in Section 10.3, the chances of escaping unemployment decline drastically with the length of unemployment. Thus it seems highly probable that the increase in the long-term unemployment ratio has in turn increased the full employment rate of unemployment.

10.5 Unemployment above the full employment rate

If unemployment comes to exist on a scale greater than that which would exist at full employment, there are two ways in which the excess of unemployment over the full employment level could be measured. To show this point we make use of a diagram representing the aggregate demand for, and supply of, labour (Figure 10.4). The demand curve is drawn upon the assumption of a given capital stock and technology; it is derived (in the way described for an individual firm in Chapter 3) from a production function, and its negative slope reflects the assumed tendency of the marginal physical product of labour to decline with employment. The supply curve is drawn with a positive slope. An increase in the real wage increases the participation rate; this offsets (reinforces) any possible negative (positive) effect on the hours supplied by existing workers. Noting that the horizontal scale would be more correctly denominated in worker hours, it is simpler for our purposes to assume it to be in terms of numbers of workers.

In Figure 10.4 the labour market is in equilibrium at a real wage of $(W/P)_E$ with N_E workers employed. Corresponding to this level of employ-

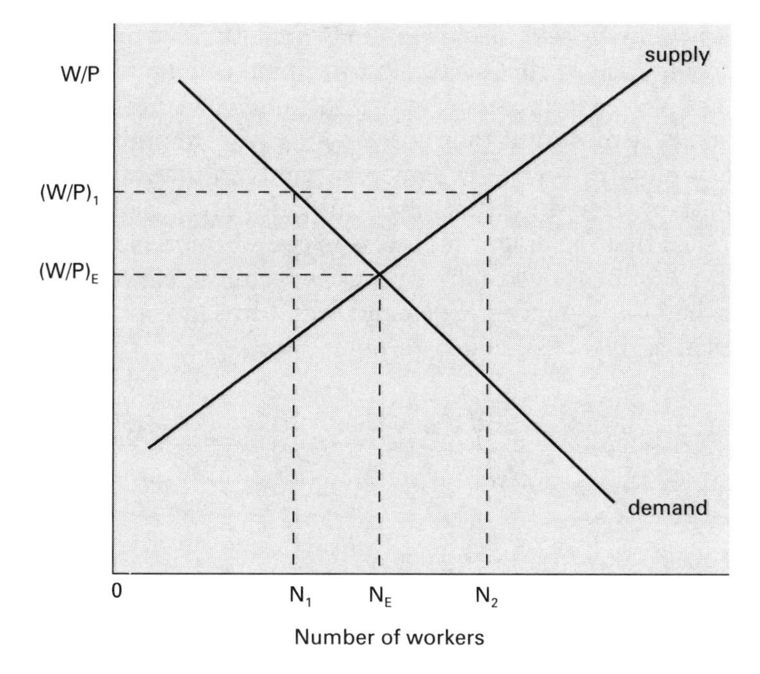

Figure 10.4 Two measures of excess unemployment

ment there is a level of unemployment whose scale cannot be deduced from the diagram as it depends upon imbalances in the multitude of submarkets and upon the other factors discussed in Section 10.4. Although the numbers unemployed at N_E are not known we can identify situations where the actual numbers unemployed are higher than at N_E. Say the real wage is $(W/P)_1$; the numbers of people employed are N_1, and hence, from Figure 10.4, unemployment is higher than at N_E. What is the scale of the excess unemployment at $(W/P)_1$? In one sense it is represented by the shortfall of employment below its equilibrium level N_E, that is it is given by the distance N_E–N_1. At the wage of $(W/P)_1$ however, the supply of labour is N_2; thus the shortfall of employment below the level necessary to absorb all those who supply labour at that real wage is N_2–N_1. It is this second concept of unemployment that is implicit in the Labour Market Survey measures of unemployment in which people are asked whether they are actively seeking work, for their answer to that question presumably depends on their view of the prevailing level of wages. Thus the scale of excess unemployment varies according to whether we compare the actual demand with the supply forthcoming at the actual real wage, or at the equilibrium real wage. Neither measure is unambiguously superior to the other, the appropriateness of each depends upon the purpose to which it is put.

We can identify two situations in which there would be excess unemployment. Assume first an economy in macroeconomic equilibrium such that the aggregate demand for goods and services is sufficient to generate the level of output that corresponds with the full employment level of unemployment. The real wage is 'right' so that, in Figure 10.5, point B is attained, and interest rates, the price level, and the stock of money are such that the money market is in equilibrium. Now say there is a decline in investment due to increasingly pessimistic expectations being held about the future. Aggregate demand falls, firms face an accumulation of inventories, and tend to reduce output.

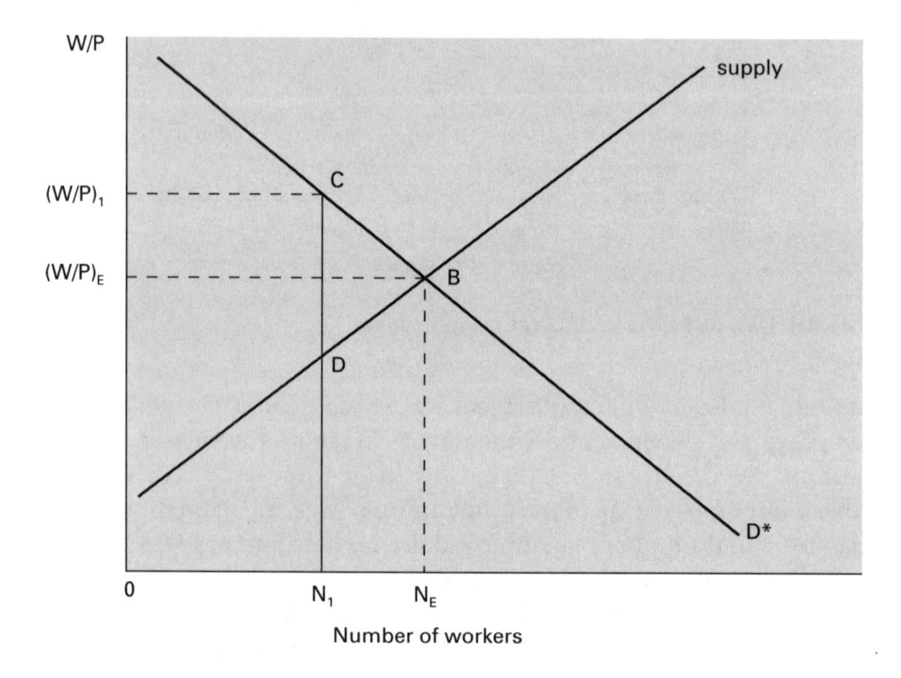

Figure 10.5 Keynesian and classical unemployment

Firms cannot sell all the goods they would like, they are constrained in the goods market. The demand curve, D*, ceases to be relevant in these conditions for it is derived from the assumption that the individual firms (whose demands for labour are added to obtain D*) are able to sell all they want to at the going price. (The reader who is unsure of this point should check the analysis of Section 3.3 of Chapter 3.) If the constraint on sales reduces employment to N_1, the effective demand curve for labour becomes vertical at all real wage levels below $(W/P)_1$. Unemployment is higher than the full employment rate, as employment, N_1, is below its equilibrium level. If wages and prices were flexible then the excess supply of labour and of goods would tend to reduce both money wages and prices. However, the level of the real wage is indeterminate. At N_1 the real wage can be anywhere between the levels represented by points C and D; the real wage may therefore be above, below, or at its equilibrium level. Unemployment of this sort has become known as 'Keynesian unemployment': it is caused by a deficiency of effective demand. It could be reduced by a decline in the level of money wages and prices; this would increase the real net wealth of the private sector, as the real value of wealth held in the form of government debt (money or bonds) rises as the price level falls. Such a decline reduces the propensity to save out of any income and leads to an increase in consumption and hence in aggregate demand. The decline in the price level would also increase the real stock of money, reducing interest rates and, perhaps, stimulating investment.

'Classical unemployment', on the other hand, is caused by the real wage becoming too high. How can this occur? The real wage, important though it is, is not actually determined in any market. It is a ratio of two money variables: the money wage and the price level. Thus we can get a situation where the money wage increases, due perhaps to a decision of the Industrial Relations Commission, but prices increase by some smaller proportion. The reasons for this lesser adjustment of prices are various. One example would be where domestic firms were facing intense foreign competition, perhaps due to an overvalued exchange rate. Say the real wage rises to $(W/P)_1$; in Figure 10.5 the demand curve D^* remains relevant and the reaction of firms is to reduce employment, and we move from B to C. What is needed in this case is a reduction in the real wage. How can this come about? If the higher money wage level, once established, is not flexible downwards then the only remedy is for the price level to rise. An expansion of aggregate demand would help if it raised the price level relative to money wages, but not if money wages rose with prices. The real wage has to fall for employment to rise and unemployment to fall.

Wage rigidities

In both cases one cause of the persistence of unemployment above its full employment level is that prices and wages are not fully flexible, they are 'sticky'. Because prices and wages do not move quickly to the levels required to clear markets, it follows that they give the wrong signals to market participants. Additionally, if adjustments to market changes cannot take place fully through price changes, then the adjustment has to occur through quantities, such as the level of output and employment. Markets can be out of equilibrium for long periods of time. In the last fifteen years or so considerable effort has gone into the theoretical analysis of disequilibrium in markets and, particularly, of how unemployment arises as a result. Much of this analysis comes up with results that are not far removed from those of Keynes, but it obtains them using a micro-economic general equilibrium (or disequilibrium) approach rather than the conventional tools of macroeconomics.

The notion that stickiness of wages may prevent markets from moving towards equilibrium has led to renewed interest in the reasons for this inflexibility. If large-scale unemployment arises why does not wage cutting occur? There are several possible reasons. One was suggested by Keynes. Workers are much concerned, as we have seen, with their money wages 'relative' to other groups of workers. If wages, as they were in Britain in the 1930s (and largely still are), are bargained on an industry basis, for example, although workers might be willing to accept a uniform wage cut applied across all industries they would resist any attempt to reduce wages in their own particular industry because they fear that such a reduction would not be applied in every industry. In other words, a wage cut in their industry, they fear, would be a relative wage reduction. Workers may resist such reductions but why do not employers attempt to enforce them? It may well be that they feel that anyone who does so would gain a reputation as a bad employer who would, as a consequence, find it difficult to attract (or retain) good quality labour in more buoyant labour market conditions.

Our analysis of Chapter 8 provides three other reasons for wage rigidity and its associated involuntary unemployment. The dual labour market hypothesis suggests that workers unable to find primary unemployment may choose to queue for work in that sector rather than work in the secondary sector where wages are relatively flexible. We saw in Section 8.5 that the efficiency wage does not change if there is a decrease in product demand; firms simply hire fewer workers at that wage. Finally the theory of implicit contracts offered another rationalisation of wage rigidities as arising from worker preferences in favour of implicit employment contracts that offer fixed wages and variable employment. The operation of internal labour markets also offer a convincing explanation of wage rigidities in the face of variations in the demand for labour (see Chapter 5).

Returning to the main theme, unemployment of a Keynesian sort exists when deficient aggregate demand constrains employers to be off their demand curve. As we saw, in these conditions the real wage may be above or below its equilibrium level. Classical unemployment is caused by the real wage being too high.

The real wage overhang

We have seen that the unemployment rate increased significantly in the mid-1970s and the early 1980s. At that time there was considerable debate as to whether this and the ensuing high unemployment were largely Keynesian or classical in nature. It now seems there were grounds for believing that, at least in some periods, the real wage was above its equilibrium level and that some unemployment was classical in nature. The terminology used at the time was that there was a 'real-wage overhang' and we conclude this section with a discussion of this issue.

The static framework used in the foregoing discussion has to be amended, although the results of the basic analysis do not. In practice, if productivity increases the demand curve for labour shifts to the right; when we speak of the real wage having become too high we mean that it has increased relative to the change in labour productivity. To make such statements we have to adopt some period in which the relation of real wages to productivity was 'right'; in the figures that follow it is assumed, following the Treasury, that the average relation over the period 1966–73 was the appropriate one.

There are three basic steps in the calculation of the overhang. The first step is to calculate the growth of real labour costs; these are real wages plus the payroll taxes and the compulsory workers' compensation insurance premiums that have to be met by employers. The second step is to calculate the growth of average labour productivity. The reader will note that ideally it is the growth of marginal labour productivity that would be calculated; however, this is difficult to measure. The final step is to calculate real unit labour costs by expressing the growth of real labour costs as a percentage of the growth of productivity. If the former grow faster than the latter (compared to their values in 1966–73) a real wage overhang is said to exist. An index of real unit labour costs for various years is shown in Table 10.8.

Table 10.8 Real unit labour costs: non-farm sector, 1966–73 = 100

1974–75	111
1979–80	104
1982–83	107
1985–86	102
1989–90	99

Source: *Economic Round-Up*, AGPS (various issues).

It is evident that by 1974–75 an overhang of 11 per cent had emerged, it was reduced in the following five years but increased in the wage explosion that followed the ending of wage indexation. In the early years of the Accord real wages were held more or less constant and hence the annual growth in labour productivity progressively reduced real unit labour costs so that the overhang had all but disappeared in 1985–86. Thus, it is plausible to argue that the increases in unemployment in 1974–75 and 1982–83 were, at least in part, due to the significant increases in real unit labour costs. As the latter are now below their level in 1966–73 it was difficult for anyone to argue with any conviction that the high unemployment of 1991–92 was due to labour costs being too high.

We should note that the presence of payroll and income taxes means that the real wage received by the worker does not correspond to the real costs of labour to the employer. If wages rise and effective income tax rates also increase (say due to a failure to fully index tax thresholds) then we can have a situation where employers argue that real wages are too high (relative to productivity) and employees are faced with reductions in real take-home pay and press for higher money wages. There is thus scope for what are termed tax-wage tradeoffs where the government agrees to reduce income tax rates in return to union commitment to wage moderation. Such tax-wage bargains were struck on several occasions during the Accord.

The rise in unemployment

We saw from Table 10.1 that there has been a substantial rise in the average rate of unemployment in the last twenty years. In the period from the end of the Second World War until the early 1970s unemployment rates averaged less than 2 per cent. In the 1980s the unemployment rate averaged over 7 per cent and in the recession of the early 1990s it was over 10 per cent.

We have identified three potential causes of the increase in unemployment. First, the full employment rate of unemployment has increased, probably from around 1–2 per cent to around 5 per cent. Various factors have contributed to this. The increase in the ratio of unemployment benefits to average earnings that occurred in the early 1970s had a small effect and it is likely that the level of structural unemployment has increased as the average amount of protection given to manufacturing industry has been lowered. Further, there is a hysteresis effect at work such that as the actual rate of unemployment has increased so too has the full employment rate of unemployment.

For most of the 1980s and early 1990s, however, the unemployment rate exceeded the full employment rate. For some of this period, the early 1980s for example, some unemployment was classical in nature, in the sense that it was caused by the real wage being too high, relative to the level of productivity. At the same time Keynesian unemployment, caused by a deficiency of aggregate demand, has occurred. There has been some dispute as to the relative importance of these two causes—too high a real wage, too low a level of aggregate demand—in various years. The high unemployment of the early 1990s, however, was caused by a reduction in the aggregate demand for goods and services brought about by restrictive monetary policy.

10.6 The incidence of unemployment

Unemployment affects different parts of the labour force unequally and, in general, these inequalities tend to increase as total unemployment rises. In this section we look at the incidence of unemployment among various groups, paying particular attention to youth unemployment.

Table 10.9 Unemployment rates by age, 1992 (%)

Age group	*Males*	*Females*
15–19	25.6	25.3
20–24	18.1	14.7
25–34	11.1	9.8
35–44	7.4	7.5
45–54	7.0	6.2
55–59	9.8	3.7
60–64	13.0	2.5
Total	11.5	10.5

Source: *The Labour Force, Australia*, (ABS, cat. no. 6203.0).

For females unemployment rates decline continuously with age; in the case of males unemployment rates decline until ages between forty-five and fifty-four years of age and then rise. In both cases, however, there are dramatic differences between the unemployment rates of young people and those of older age groups.

High unemployment rates among young people have been a cause of considerable concern. We shall take the term 'youth' in this context to refer to the fifteen to nineteen-year-old age range. To gain an impression of the differential unemployment experience of youths we need a comparative group and here we shall use unemployment rates among the prime age groups (thirty-five to forty-four) as the basis of the comparison. In Table 10.10 the unemployment rates of the two age groups are compared (for males and females separately) in two different ways, by showing the absolute difference in unemployment rates and by expressing youth unemployment rates as a ratio of the unemployment rate for thirty-five to forty-four-year-olds.

Two main points emerge from Table 10.10. First the unemployment rates of young people are always considerably higher than those of adults, by a factor of three to four-and-a-half times. Second, the extent of the difference is greater the higher the overall level of unemployment, which is shown in the first column.

We now explain these two facts. We have assembled enough analysis at various stages of this book to answer the first easily enough. When young people enter the labour force they do not possess very accurate or extensive information about opportunities in various jobs and hence tend

Table 10.10 Youth unemployment rates, U_Y, compared with adult (aged 35–44) unemployment rates, U_A

	Overall unemployment rate (%)	*Males*		*Females*	
		U_Y-U_A	$\frac{U_Y}{U_A}$	U_Y-U_A	$\frac{U_Y}{U_A}$
1983	10.3	18.2	4.0	16.8	2.8
1986	7.6	15.3	4.6	14.6	3.0
1989	6.0	8.1	3.4	11.8	3.4
1992	10.5	18.2	3.5	17.8	3.4

Source: *The Labour Force, Australia*, (ABS, cat. no. 6203.0).

to try different jobs to acquire information. At the same time they have not developed many specific or general skills and hence there is little incentive for employers to attempt to prevent high turnover. There is further the general point that it is a characteristic of the young that they value stability rather less than do older people. Thus, labour turnover among the young is high and, to the extent that there are periods of time spent between jobs, the analysis presented earlier in this chapter would lead us to expect them to have relatively high unemployment rates. To analyse this more closely recall equation (1) of this chapter:

$$U = \frac{I}{L} \times D$$

This states that the unemployment rate for any group is equal to the number of inflows into unemployment as a proportion of the labour force multiplied by the average duration of unemployment. The inflows of young people into unemployment are, proportionately, higher than those of adults but their average duration of unemployment is lower than that of adults. The average completed durations of unemployment of those unemployed in March 1992 are shown in Table 10.11 where it can be seen that unemployment durations increase continuously with age.

Table 10.11 Estimated completed durations of unemployment of those unemployed in March 1992

Age	*Weeks*
15–19	52.6
20–24	78.0
25–34	95.8
35–54	110.6
Total	95.0

Source: *The Labour Force, Australia*, (ABS, cat. no. 6203.0).

We now turn to an explanation of the second fact, that as the overall unemployment rate rises the inequality between youth and adult unemployment rates also increases. The explanation is simple and obvious. We have seen that in virtually all labour markets there is a distinction made between those already in employment and those out of employment, with the former enjoying considerable rights. In a recession, the volume of employment increases at a slower rate than does labour supply. Hence those seeking to enter employment are in a disadvantaged position relative to those in employment, for the latter have job rights. If employment actually declines these same job rights operate against the young with even greater effect, for if a firm is trying to reduce employment the easiest procedure is simply not to replace those who leave. The young therefore find it difficult to enter employment.

Finally, we note that a similar widening of inequalities occurs during recessions for other groups who tend to have relatively high unemployment rates, such as Aborigines, and migrants from non-English speaking backgrounds.

Concepts for review

- Unemployment
- Hidden unemployment
- Labour hoarding
- Three measures of the duration of unemployment
- Frictional unemployment
- Structural unemployment
- Demand deficient unemployment
- Full employment rate of unemployment
- UV relationship
- Replacement ratios
- Hysteresis
- Keynesian unemployment
- Classical unemployment
- Real unit labour costs
- Real wage overhang
- Tax-wage tradeoff

Questions

1 Discuss the trends in unemployment over the last twenty years. What alternative explanations exist for these trends? (Curtin University).

2 Distinguish between the main types of unemployment. Which economic theories of the labour market predict that wages do not adjust to eliminate unemployment? (University of Melbourne)
3 Why might it be difficult to estimate the true extent of unemployment? What evidence would be needed to assess the relevance of competing theories for the rise of unemployment in Australia? (La Trobe University)
4 'The rate of unemployment is a stock concept and any understanding of the processes causing changes in this stock requires a detailed analysis of the flows into and out of it.' (K. Whitfield) If we follow this advice what sort of things do we learn? Does an analysis of stocks and flows help us to understand the processes causing changes in the stock? (Australian National University)
5 It seems to be true that the average unemployed male receiving unemployment benefits in Australia will be unemployed for about two-and-a-half years. It also seems to be true that one-half of those who begin to receive unemployment benefits have left unemployment within three months. Can these facts be reconciled? What interesting research and policy questions are raised by the reconciliation? (Australian National University)
6 What is the difference between Keynesian and classical unemployment? Describe the policies which could be used for each policy type. (La Trobe University)

References

1 B. Chapman, 'The labour market', *The Australian Macro-economy in the 1980s*, Reserve Bank of Australia, 1990.
2 J. Mangan, 'Labour hoarding in Australian manufacturing: an inter-industry analysis', *Australian Bureau of Labour*, vol. 7, part 4, 1981, pp. 219-35.
3 D. Bosworth and T. Westaway, 'Labour hoarding, discouraged workers and recorded unemployment: an international comparison', *Australian Bulletin of Labour*, vol. 13, no. 3, 1987, pp. 143-62.
4 W.F. Foster and R.G. Gregory, 'A flow analysis of the labour market in Australia', in R. Blandy and O. Covick (eds), *Understanding Labour Markets*, Allen & Unwin, Sydney, 1984.
5 B. Bradbury, R. Ross and J. Doyle, 'Unemployment benefit replacement rates', *Social Security*, Policy Research Paper no. 60, Canberra, 1991.
6 W.F. Mitchell, 'What is the full employment-unemployment rate? Some empirical evidence of structural unemployment in Australia, 1966 to 1986', *Australian Bulletin of Labour*, vol. 14, no. 1, 1987, pp. 321-37. R.M. Simes and C.J. Richardson, 'Wage determination in Australia', *Economic Record*, vol. 63, no. 181, 1987, pp. 144-55.
7 P. Flatau, P.E.T. Lewis and A. Rushton, 'The macroeconomic consequences of long-term unemployment', *Australian Economic Review*, 1991, no. 4, pp. 48-55.

CHAPTER 11

Wage inflation

11.1 Introduction

In this final chapter we look at the part played by the labour market in the process of wage inflation and hence of price inflation. By wage inflation we mean the annual rate of growth of weekly earnings. Wage inflation since 1980 is shown in Table 11.1.

It can be seen from column (1) that there has been considerable variation in the rate of wage inflation. The annual rate has ranged from about 2 per cent to nearly 16 per cent during the twelve-year period

Table 11.1 Wage inflation, 1980-91 (%)

	(1) Annual rate of growth of weekly earnings	*(2) Annual rate of growth of award rates*	*(3) Earnings drift*
1980	10.9	7.6	3.3
1981	14.4	13.6	0.8
1982	15.8	15.1	0.7
1983	8.1	4.0	4.1
1984	10.9	9.2	1.7
1985	4.8	2.6	2.2
1986	7.0	3.9	3.1
1987	5.6	4.1	1.5
1988	7.0	7.0	0
1989	6.3	4.5	1.8
1990	7.3	4.7	2.6
1991	2.2	2.9	–0.7

Sources: *Average Weekly Earnings, States and Australia*, (ABS cat. no.6302.0) and *Award Rates of Pay Indexes*, (ABS cat. no. 6312.0).

shown. In most years the rate of growth of weekly earnings (column (1)) exceeded the rate of growth of award rates of pay (column (2)) as set down by the Industrial Relations Commission. The difference between these two rates of growth is known as earnings drift, which is shown in column (3) of the table.

Earnings drift arises from several causes, but essentially of course arises from the other components of earnings, such as overtime, over-award payments, and incentive bonuses, increasing faster than award rates of pay. Earnings drift is also caused by people being upgraded. That is, even if the level of award rates of pay remain unaltered, earnings will increase if, on average, people are promoted to higher pay scales.

In Section 11.2 and 11.3 we will look at two explanations of wage inflation. In Section 11.2 we describe what is termed the expectations-augmented Phillips curve. In 1958 Phillips, in a famous article, presented evidence that showed that there was an inverse relationship between the rate of wage inflation and the rate of unemployment. About a decade later it was demonstrated that this relation could only exist in the short run, not the long run, and that the short-run relation depended on expectations about the rate of price inflation. These short-run relationships are known as expectations-augmented Phillips curves.

In this model trade unions do not have much of a role. Our analysis of Chapter 6 found that unions have an effect on relative pay so in Section 11.3 we explore the possibility that unions might influence the rate of growth of pay.

The final two sections are devoted to a discussion of wages policies. Section 11.4 discusses wages policies in general and the case for and against such policies. Section 11.5 discusses one particular wages policy, the Prices and Incomes Accord which has operated in various forms from 1983 to the time of writing.

11.2 The expectations-augmented Phillips curve

Much empirical analysis of wage inflation in Australia and elsewhere has centred around what is termed the expectations-augmented Phillips curve. Before embarking on an explanation of this analysis it is helpful to describe the curve as first proposed by its originator, A.W. Phillips.[1] When the Phillips curve made its appearance in 1958 it seemed to fill a gap in the Keynesian analysis of the economy. Crudely paraphrased, the Keynesian theory of inflation was that if at, or above, the level of full employment the level of aggregate monetary demand came to exceed the value of output, at current prices, which the economy could produce there would emerge an inflationary gap. This excess monetary demand would then 'pull up' prices so that the money value of output came to equal aggregate monetary demand. The mechanism by which prices were pulled up was not clearly specified and the behaviour of firms, particularly large firms, suggested that they did not necessarily put up prices in the face of excess demand. That is, they set prices by adding a mark-up to average variable costs; in the face of excess demand which did not immediately alter costs they preferred to lengthen order books or to adjust in other ways than through raising prices. The Phillips curve, which related changes in wages to the excess demand for labour, provided the explanation of how prices increased, for wages are the largest element of costs. Thus at low levels of unemployment, wages would rise, so would costs and hence so would prices.

The original Phillips curve

The Phillips curve was derived, not from any explicit or well-developed model of the labour market, but from a statistical investigation. Phillips' starting point was figures on the rate of change of money wage rates and the percentage unemployment rate for the fifty-two years between 1861 and 1913 in Britain. The relationship between these two series was estimated using an averaging device. It was noticed that the relation between the two variables differed according to whether unemployment was rising or falling. To get rid of this effect, Phillips divided his fifty-two observations into six groups, each group corresponding to a range of unemployment. All observations within each group were then averaged so that six average figures emerged which when plotted lay approximately along a curve of the form shown in Figure 11.1.

Phillips then discovered a surprising fact. When plotted on a scatter diagram the observations for both the periods 1913–48 and 1948–57 lay along the curve derived from the years 1861–1913. Because of the averaging devices used it is not possible to report statistical measures of association, but if one examines the diagrams in Phillips' article it can be seen that the relationship was a fairly close one.

Four things should be noted about the curve derived by Phillips. First, the relation is non-linear, the sensitivity of wage changes to unemployment being greater at low levels of unemployment. Second, wage stability was secured when unemployment was around 5.5 per cent. Third, the curve flattened out at a rate of wage inflation of about minus 1 per cent. Thus any increases in unemployment above 5.5 per cent appeared to have a negligible effect on the rate of wage inflation.

The final point to make on the basic Phillips relation is that it appeared to offer policy makers a very useful tool. To the extent that the relationship holds, governments are presented with a trade-off between

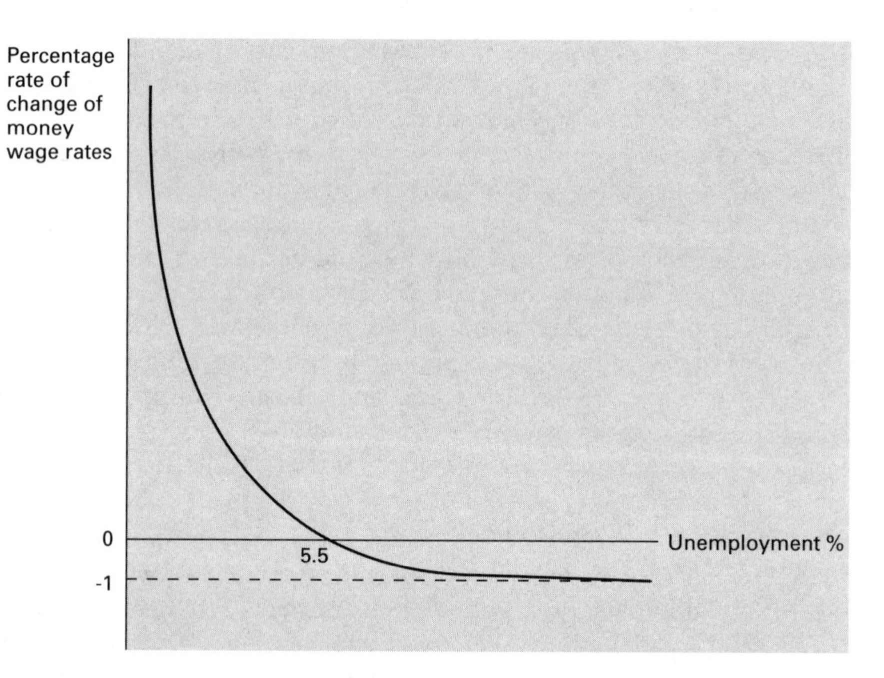

Figure 11.1 The original, short-run, Phillips curve

wage (and price) inflation and unemployment. It seemed that, starting from some initial level of these two variables, a government could choose a rather lower level of unemployment if it were prepared to tolerate a rather higher rate of inflation. The precise terms of the trade-off would depend upon the slope of the Phillips curve at the prevailing level of unemployment. There seems little doubt that in Australia, and in many other industrial countries, governments showed, and still show, by their actions that they believe in a trade-off relation between inflation and unemployment, at least in the short run. This was despite the fact that the statistical association between the unemployment rate and wage inflation was never, in any country, very close.[2]

In any case events soon demonstrated that this choice between inflation and employment may be illusory, or at least short-lived for in the 1970s and 1980s rates of unemployment and of wage inflation increased simultaneously.

One of the first to anticipate the apparent absence of a long-run relation was Friedman and we now discuss his 'fooling model' and the expectations-augmented Phillips curve.[3]

Friedman's fooling model

We saw in Section 10.4 that there exist various terms (or concepts) used to describe a situation where the overall labour market is in equilibrium.

Friedman in fact employed the concept of the natural rate of unemployment but it is convenient here to employ the non-accelerating inflation rate of unemployment (NAIRU). It will be recalled from the previous chapter that where unemployment is at this rate, probably around 5 per cent in Australia at present, the rate of price inflation will tend to be more or less constant. At lower rates of unemployment the rate of price inflation will tend to accelerate and vice versa.

We need to explain one more relation, which is that the rate of price inflation will approximately equal the rate of wage inflation less the rate of growth of productivity. To see the sense of this say wage inflation is 5 per cent and productivity growth is 2 per cent. To maintain profit margins constant prices will tend to rise by 3 per cent as although workers are being paid 5 per cent more each year, each worker is producing 2 per cent more.

We now proceed to the expectations-augmented Phillips curve. In Figure 11.2 assume the economy is in the state represented by point A. Assume the rate of price inflation is zero and has been so for some time so that people expect zero inflation in the future. The Phillips curve on which A is positioned is thus labelled $\dot{P}^e_0$ the expected rate of inflation is zero. Assume also that the unemployment level is the NAIRU (labelled U_N) and that productivity growth is 2 per cent per year. Thus, from the analysis

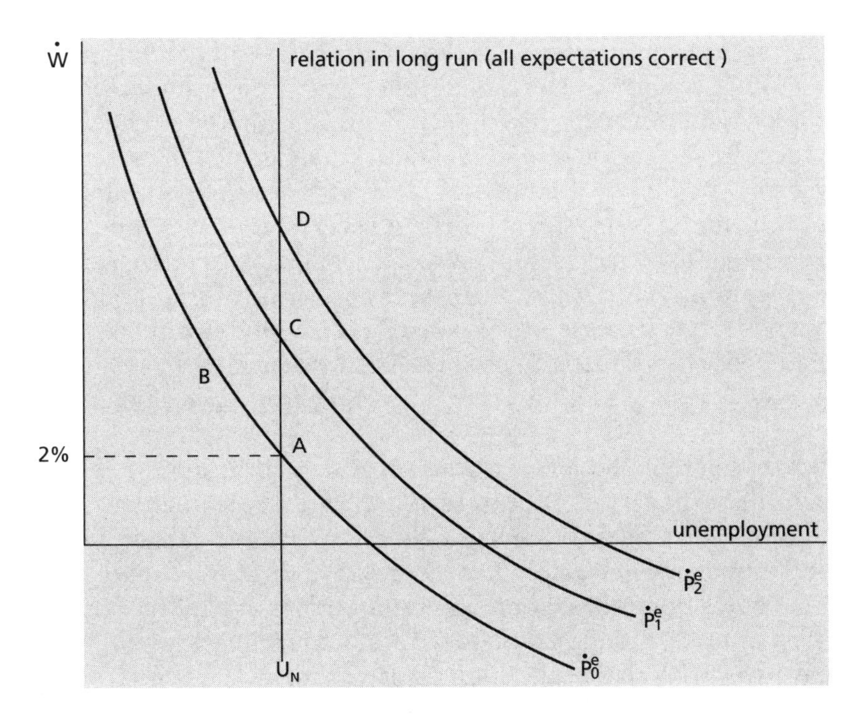

Figure 11.2 Short-run and long-run Phillips curves

above we would expect money wages to rise by 2 per cent a year as this would, given the rate of productivity growth, be consistent with a zero rate of price inflation.

Now say the government wishes to reduce the level of unemployment and to this end an expansion of aggregate monetary demand is brought about through monetary policy. We know from our analysis of Chapter 3 that with a given capital stock and a given technology, the demand for labour will increase only if the real wage falls. Equally to bring about an increase in the aggregate supply of labour an increase in the real wage is necessary. This effect comes about through an increase in participation rates (Chapter 2) and through a reduction in the time individuals spend between jobs (Chapter 10).

Thus, for the quantity of labour demanded to increase, the real wage is required to fall, whereas, for the supply to increase, the real wage is required to rise. How can these things happen simultaneously, which is necessary if employment is to increase? In the original model, as put forward by Friedman, the simultaneous rise and fall in real wages occurs because firms and workers evaluate money wages bargains differently in terms of real wages. The expansion of monetary demand leads to money wages increasing at a rate above the original 2 per cent. Employers, however, are willing to employ additional workers if they can recoup the additional costs by increasing prices by an amount such that the real wage falls. Because firms fix the prices they can bring this about either by marking up prices immediately, or by planning to do so over the average duration of wage contracts, say a year. Thus, to employers, the expected real wage falls and the quantity of labour demanded increases.

The next step in the argument is to assert that workers (unionised or not) do not immediately revise their expectations of the rate of price inflation. In our example, they assume zero inflation to continue and hence their evaluation of the increase in the rate of wage inflation is that it corresponds to an increase in real wages over and above the 2 per cent brought about by productivity growth. The workers are fooled and thus, in Figure 11.2 we move up the curve labelled $\dot{P}^e_0$ from A to a point such as B.

As time goes on, however, workers realise their mistake, adjust their expectations of the rate of price inflation upwards, seek an increase in the growth of money wages, and eventually the actual and expected rates of price inflation coincide again. Once that occurs the labour market clears with the same amount of labour employed but at a higher rate of money wage (and of price) inflation. Labour drawn into the market on the wrong inference that the real wage had risen withdraws when it becomes apparent that it has not. Similarly as workers obtain the additional increase in money wages, the real wage to employers increases and they move back along their demand curve for labour. The increased employment was only temporary and was brought about by workers incorrectly estimating the real wage. In Figure 11.2 we end up at point C, where the expected rate of price inflation is $\dot{P}^e_1$ at C this is also the actual rate of price inflation. Point C may be the ultimate position but if the authorities undertook a further expansion of demand the process would be repeated taking the economy through another clockwise loop to a point such as D.

Thus, the trade-off between unemployment and wage inflation only exists in the period during which the actual and expected rates of inflation differ, that is, while the rate of inflation is not correctly anticipated. In the long run, inflation rates come to be perfectly anticipated and the trade-off disappears. The Phillips curve becomes a vertical line, positioned at the NAIRU. At points to the left of the vertical line the rate of inflation increases, at points to the right it decreases. The curves showing the short-run trade-offs are termed expectations-augmented Phillips curves, as they can only be defined in terms of a given expectation of the future rate of price inflation.

Price expectations

A crucial role is played in the above model by people's expectations of the inflation rate. So how do people form their price expectations? One hypothesis is that they adjust their expectations in the light of past errors in their expectations. This is known as the adaptive expectations hypothesis. Formally this can be expressed as:

$$\dot{P}^e_t = \dot{P}^e_{t-1} + \lambda(\dot{P}_{t-1} - \dot{P}^e_{t-1}) \qquad (1)$$

Here $\dot{P}_{t-1}$ is the actual rate of inflation last period while $\dot{P}^e_{t-1}$ is last period's expected inflation rate and $\dot{P}^e_t$ is this period's expected inflation rate. l is a weight showing by how much people revise their expectations when they make an error.

To see the sense of all this take the case where l is 0.5, the expected inflation rate last period ($\dot{P}^e_{t-1}$) was 2 per cent but the actual rate ($\dot{P}_{t-1}$) was 6 per cent. The equation tells us that this period's expected inflation rate will be 4 per cent: people adjust their expectation upward by half the error they made in the previous period.

The adaptive expectations hypothesis suffers from a serious flaw. That is, that if inflation is on an upward trend the future of inflation will always be underestimated, and will be overestimated if inflation is on a downward trend. As inflation does seem to move in fairly smooth trends quarter by quarter rather than being randomly distributed, it follows that those who form their expectations in this way are usually wrong. Thus, it is argued, it cannot be a rational basis of behaviour.

One alternative is to argue that people do, in fact, form their expectations in a rational way. In its extreme form this hypothesis is that individuals form their expectations in line with some economic theory. For instance, suppose the Friedman argument described earlier was believed fully and it was further believed that changes in the rate of growth of the money stock were the main determinant of the future inflation rate. If the growth of the money stock were expanded then expectations of the inflation rate would be revised accordingly. Further, if people incorporated their expectations fully into their behaviour, immediate adjustments in wages and prices would follow, which would absorb the whole of the increase in aggregate monetary demand leaving output and employment unchanged. In terms of Figure 11.2, where we started at point A, people would be aware that the ultimate situation would be represented by point C and would very quickly adjust their price expectations accordingly and no decrease in unemployment would occur, even in the short run. The rational expectations hypothesis in a general sense thus has far-reaching implications for the conduct of economic policy, but to pursue these would be to stray outside the scope of this book.

In a looser sense the rational expectations hypothesis states that economic agents use all available information in forecasting future rates of inflation. Past rates will have some influence but so too will, for example, changes in monetary policy and in the exchange rate, the incidence of strikes, decisions in national wage cases, and so on. People are also likely to be strongly influenced by forecasts of inflation published in the financial press (although this begs the question of how those are made).

To sum up so far, the ability of governments to 'move' the economy along short Phillips curves depends on how quickly and efficiently people form their price expectations. If their adjustment is sluggish it may be possible for the authorities to reduce unemployment through varying aggregate demand for significant periods of time, albeit at the cost of increased inflation. If, however, price expectations are formed quickly and efficiently, the analysis suggests that the short run will be brief in calendar time.

Wage rigidities

However, there is another part of the story. In terms of Figure 11.2 the movement from A to B to C may take some time even if expectations are efficiently formed if the actual adjustment of wages and prices (not of price expectations) is sluggish. One explanation of wage rigidity is based on the operation of internal labour markets that we discussed at some length in Chapter 5. Most workers are employed in internal labour markets where a clear distinction is drawn between the 'ins' (those currently working for the firm) and the 'outs'. We saw that the 'ins' are never under any competition for their jobs from the 'outs', even if the 'outs' were willing to work for a lower wage. It then follows that conditions in the external labour market, such as the level of unemployment, will not have direct effect on the growth of money wages. Instead we would expect that the utilisation of labour within the internal labour market would influence the rate of growth of money wages in each firm.

To test this proposition we need a measure of labour utilisation within firms. One possibility is to use some measure of hours of work and several studies have followed this line, estimating equations of the following sort:

$$\dot{W}_t = b + cH + a\dot{P}_t^e \qquad (2)$$

where H represents labour utilisation within the firm and the other symbols have their usual meaning. Gregory estimated such an equation for the period 1966–82 using average weekly hours of overtime as variable to reflect labour utilisation within firms.[4] Overtime was found to be an important influence on wage growth and, importantly, performed far better than the alternatives of unemployment or vacancies as a measure of demand. (The co-efficient a was reported to be 0.60.) Dawkins and Wooden preferred to use deviations from the trend in average weekly hours of work as a measure of H in equation (2).[5] Over the period 1967–83 they, too, find that their measure of utilisation provides a better explanation of money wage growth than do more conventional variables. Like Gregory, they find the co-efficient on the price expectation terms to be rather low, around 0.55.

We can thus see why the rate of wage adjustment may be slow. Sluggish price adjustments may also occur in product markets, as there are costs involved in making price changes. Since demand factors take time to work through institutional market arrangements the monetary authorities can influence output and employment even if expectations are formed rationally. Thus although in some long-run sense, perhaps defined as a steady-state equilibrium when all expectations are correct, there may be no trade-off between inflation and unemployment, the short run may be long enough to be of interest to policy makers.

11.3 Trade unions and wage inflation

In the explanation of wage inflation discussed in the previous section the role played by trade unions was unimportant. In the short run the rate of wage inflation was influenced by the excess demand/supply of labour and by worker expectations of the rate of price inflation. The story we told remains more or less the same whether labour is unionised or not. If there is an increase in the aggregate demand for goods and services, starting from a position of full employment unions will respond to the increase in prices. But so too will unorganised labour. In fact the evidence shows that union wages are less flexible than non-union wages so that in cyclical upswings the union mark-up declines. Thus unions may actually cause the rate of inflation to be lower than it otherwise would be in upswings (but also higher than it would be in recessions).

The counter view is that unions may, in certain circumstances, cause inflation, independently of the state of aggregate demand. We saw in the last chapter that there exists a union mark-up. As a matter of arithmetic, unions might then increase the rate of growth of money wages by increasing the union mark-up or by increasing the proportion of the labour force that is unionised, that is increase the proportion that receives the mark-up. They may also cause the growth of non-union wages to be more rapid than it otherwise would be, through union wage increases being generalised, through the system of awards, to non-union workers.

The arithmetic of the ways in which unions may influence the rate of growth of money wages is clear, but what is the actual mechanism? The basic idea is that the rate of wage inflation is strongly influenced by union militancy. Where wages are collectively bargained then militancy reflects the attitude of union bargainers and hence, unless offset by a corresponding change in employer attitudes, might be expected to influence the outcome of the bargain.

To investigate the proposition that wage inflation is determined by union militancy it is obviously necessary to devise a measure of the latter. There are several possibilities. One, proposed some thirty years ago in a celebrated article, is that militancy, or union pushfulness, could be measured by the rate of change of the proportion of the labour force that is unionised.[6] The rationalisation of this is that when unions are in a militant mood they simultaneously recruit members to increase bargaining power and push on wages. Hines showed that in the periods 1921–38 and 1949–61 this one variable was capable of explaining a high proportion of the variance in rate of change of wage rates in the United Kingdom, and further that the effect of pushfulness operated independently of the rate of unemployment.

In empirical work based on Australian data changes in union density, used on their own, do not explain variations in the rate of wage inflation. An alternative is to use strike activity as a proxy for militancy. Strike activity can be measured in various ways. Three possibilities are the number of disputes, the number of people involved in disputes, and the number of working days lost through strikes. As it is strike intensity that we are interested in, each of the three measures is expressed as a proportion of the labour force. Although strike activity is an intuitively appealing guide to militancy it is not ideal, as a strike is in a sense the outcome of the failure of militancy to achieve its aims. Thus a powerful militant union may win wage increases simply through the threat of a strike. Alternatively strikes may reflect employer militancy, or resistance to wage claims, and hence strike activity can be negatively related to wage inflation. There is also a problem that, while no single one of these measures of strike activity is obviously superior to the others, the statistical correlation between them is low.[7]

There are no recent estimates of the impact of union militancy on the rate of wage inflation because since 1983 the union movement has co-operated in the Accord (to be discussed in the final section of this chapter). For an earlier period, 1953–76, it was found that a large part of the annual variance in the rate of wage inflation could be explained by the number of working days lost through strikes per worker per year.[8] In turn the variations in strike activity were largely caused by the rate of unemployment, price expectations and changes in union density. Thus while union militancy seems to have played a part in the generation of wage inflation in Australia in the past its influence does not seem to be independent of the state of aggregate demand or of expectations of the rate of inflation.

11.4 Wages policy

By wages policy we mean a set of principles by which some authority determines the rate of growth of money wages. Because Australia has, in the form of the Industrial Relations Commission, an authority which could, or has to, fill the role specified in the definition, Australian economists have long been interested in wages policy. Australia has too, for many foreign observers, been seen to possess a set of institutions ready made for operating an incomes policy. We shall begin by looking at the case for using wages policy as a method of reducing the inflation rate. This will be followed by a discussion of the rules that might be used to guide wages policy.

Say the inflation rate is too high and we want to lower it. A case can be made out for control over wage growth as part of an anti-inflationary policy whether one adopts an explanation of inflation centred on an expectations-augmented Phillips curve or whether a cost-push explanation (based perhaps on militant trade unions pushing up wages) is accepted. In the former view, as we saw in Section 11.2, inflation is initiated by an expansion of aggregate monetary demand and the rate of inflation caused is then perpetuated by the incorporation of price expectations into the behaviour of transactors, particularly, in this context, the behaviour of firms and unions. To reduce inflation, it is argued that inflationary expectations must be lowered. A direct method of doing this is to impose constraints on the rate of growth of money wages. If labour market participants believed that such a policy would be successful then they would revise downwards their expectations of the future course of prices.

Now those who hold what may be termed free market views see no advantage (and in fact positive disadvantages) in imposed efforts to control wages. The argument is that in the same way that inflation was caused by a slack monetary policy in the past so a tight monetary policy must be used to reduce the rate of inflation. We saw that if, starting (say) from a position of price stability, an expansion of aggregate monetary demand occurred, there would follow, it is argued, a period of time in which output and employment increased. This would be the period of time during which the rate of inflation was incorrectly anticipated, or during which rigidities in the wage setting process prevented a complete adjustment. Once this period of time had passed, output and employment would return to their initial level but the rate of growth of money wages and prices would not. Subsequent increases in the rate of growth of monetary demand would ultimately lead to higher inflation rates. In Figure 11.2, this process was represented by a move from point A to point D, the move being made in two clockwise loops.

Having got to point D, if we want to return (say) to the lower rate of inflation represented by point A then the argument is that the move must be made in clockwise loops to the right of the non-accelerating inflation rate of unemployment (NAIRU) shifting the short-run Phillips curve downwards to the left. By reductions in the rate of growth of monetary demand, unemployment is generated and this, through its effects on wage bargains, tends to moderate wage inflation, inflationary expectations, and the rate of price inflation.

A wages policy may short-cut this process, which normally has to be lengthy if substantial reductions in the inflation rate are desired. Were a wages policy to be successful there would be a real gain to the economy, relative to the free market prescription, in that the need to hold unemployment above the NAIRU (probably for some years) is obviated. Monetarists would point to other costs of the wages policy method, such as resource misallocation, and we will return to this point shortly.

The case for a wages policy is more clear cut if one believes that the initial cause of inflation comes from autonomous pushes on money wages by unions. This may, as we have seen, take the form of militancy designed to influence the outcome of national wage cases, or, alternatively, wage increases won by one union may be generalised through coercive comparisons leading to what has been termed a wage-wage spiral. The process can be self-perpetuating if, once the initial set of relatives has been roughly restored, the group that initiated the process again attempts to improve its relative wage position. As changes in money wages are seen as the root cause of inflation it follows that adherents to this view generally place a wages policy in the centre of an anti-inflationary programme.

In principle then it seems that a wages policy may have a role to play in the reduction of the rate of inflation whether the initial cause of the inflation comes from demand or cost influences. Those who are opposed to the use of wages policy to control inflation stress two points. Wages policies do not seem to work in the long run; to the extent that they may be effective in the short run they impose resource costs on the economy through the distortions they create in labour markets. The first of these objections is based on actual experience in incomes policies. While the policy is in operation it often succeeds in reducing the rate of inflation (from what it would otherwise have been). Once it ceases there follows a period in which inflation is higher than it would have been. If the two periods are taken together any effect of the policy is usually hard to detect. It remains to be seen whether this will be the case when the Accord ends. The distortions that it is argued are created stem from the fact that incomes policies tend to prevent relative wage adjustments from occurring (as the same rate of increase tends to be applied to all wages) and thus prevent the market mechanism from functioning. Even if this were true, the cost of these distortions has to be set against the output losses caused by the alternative method, which is to reduce inflation through increased unemployment. In the Australian labour market it is not at all clear that this distorting effect would be large, the reason being that we have seen that the system operates in such a way that relative wage changes are limited by the widespread use of comparability in wage bargaining. Thus were a wages policy to be implemented in a labour market where relative wages were strongly influenced by supply and demand, the resource allocation costs might be significant. The Australian labour market is, however, some way removed from this and hence the additional distortions caused by wage restraint do not seem likely to be large.

What rules should be followed in determining the rate of growth of wages? Here circumstances alter cases. If it is desired to reduce the rate of inflation then, ignoring external factors and assuming profit margins to be constant, the rate of wage increase has to be less than the sum of the rate of price inflation and the rate of growth of labour productivity. In this context it is the rate of price inflation since the previous award that is relevant. If wages are constrained in this way then the rate of price inflation would decline year by year; the greater the difference between the two sides of the inequality the greater the reduction in any year.

Now take the case where the starting point is an inflation rate that is deemed to be desirable, or tolerable. One widely canvassed policy for determining the rate of growth of money wages in such circumstances was the 'average productivity rule.' This rule was first discussed in the 1960s and was often presented as a rule for obtaining price stability. Thus, if at the outset price inflation were zero then that rate could be secured if money wages rose in line with the average rate of productivity growth. Although this may not seem very realistic it is simplest to analyse this case (which carries over anyway, with minor modifications, to situations where constant rates of inflation are desired).

The rule as put above ignores external considerations and has to be amended accordingly. If export prices rose then, if wages were tied to average productivity growth, there would be an increase in the share of the national product accruing to exporting sectors in general and to the rural and primary sector in particular (and vice versa). To prevent the share of wages falling in this situation and to share across the economy the gains accruing to the export sector, wages should also be adjusted in line with export prices. Thus, if P_x is the rate of growth of export prices and is the rate of growth of average productivity,

$$\dot{W} = \dot{Q} + \dot{P}_x$$

Money wages, under this rule, are not adjusted in line with changes in import prices and hence, in effect, the rule states that real wages should be increased by the rate of growth of average productivity plus any improvement in the terms of trade (or minus any deterioration in the terms of trade). To see this point, say import prices rose in line with export prices, that is the terms of trade were unaltered. The increase in import prices would cause the domestic price level to rise; this decline in real wages would be offset by the adjustment of money wages to the rise in export prices. If the terms of trade improved, real wages would rise by more than the growth of domestic productivity, and vice versa.

Once these external effects are allowed for, the average productivity rule ceases to be a condition for price stability as changes in the foreign price level are reflected in the domestic price level. At least, however, it would avoid any domestically generated inflation. This problem led, however, to other variants of the rule in which, for example, temporary changes in the terms of trade were not taken into account.

It should be pointed out that, in the same vein as monetarists would argue that an appropriate monetary policy can reduce the rate of inflation, so, of course, is there a monetarist prescription for holding constant any desired rate of inflation. This is to increase the money stock in line with average productivity plus the desired rate of inflation—the so-called golden rule. Wages policy, they would argue, becomes redundant. This has to be amended slightly in an open economy and it also rests upon many other assumptions, for example, about the demand for money function and the ability of the authorities to control the growth of the stock of money. Nonetheless, this alternative view emphasises once again that the appropriate policy one suggests depends upon the view of the inflationary process, and of the way the economy operates, that one holds. We now turn to a discussion of a particular wages policy, the Accord.

11.5 The Accord

The history

The Prices and Incomes Accord was an agreement made in early 1983 between the Australian Labor Party and the Australian Council of Trade Unions (ACTU). Shortly afterwards the party was elected to government and the Accord became government policy. The principles underlying wage guidelines changed several times during the Accord and we can divide the agreement into six phases, as set out in Table 11.2.

To put the Accord into its historical context it is necessary to go back to 1981. In that year a wages policy that had been operated by the (then)

Table 11.2 Summary of the Accord, 1983–92

Mark I 1983–85	Full wage indexation	
Mark II 1985–87	Wage indexation discounted for currency depreciation	
	Tax cuts	
	Productivity award paid as employer contributions to superannuation schemes	
Mark III 1987–88	Two-tier system:	
	First tier:	flat rate payments to all workers
	Second tier:	percentage increase which had to be justified under the 'restructuring and efficiency' principle
Mark IV 1988–89	Percentage rise plus a flat rate payment under the 'structural efficiency principle'	
	Tax cuts	
Mark V 1989–91	Continuation of structural efficiency principle: two-stage wage increase	
Mark VI 1991–	Flat rate payment to all workers	
	Further wage rises through enterprise bargaining	

Arbitration Commission and which had since 1975 indexed wages to the rate of price inflation came to an end. This was followed by a wage explosion (see Table 1.1) and by a sharp rise in the rate of unemployment.

The partners to the Accord agreed to wage moderation and in 1983 a wage freeze that had been imposed by the outgoing government was extended. During the rest of phase I of the Accord award wages were fully indexed to prices. (There was one exception to full indexation. When Medicare was introduced in 1984 there was an artificial reduction in the Consumer Price Index. Thus although wages were in fact changed in line with the Index, the Index did not accurately reflect what was happening to the price level.) If wages rise in line with prices then any increase that occurs in labour productivity will decrease unit labour costs (see p. 227).

The phase II variant of the Accord contained three novel elements. First, wage rises were 'discounted' for the effects of the decline in the external value of the dollar. A depreciation of the dollar leads to increases in the dollar price of imports and hence increases the domestic price level. Were money wages to be raised in proportion to the increase in the price level the ultimate effect would be that the domestic price level would rise by the same proportion as the exchange rate had declined—thus negating any increase in competitiveness. Thus the Treasury was asked to estimate what proportion of the rate of inflation was due to the exchange rate changes and the wage rises were discounted by this proportion. Second, reductions in nominal income tax rates were negotiated between the government and the ACTU, as part of a tax-wage trade-off (see p. 228). Third, payments to workers were made in the form of employer contributions to superannuation schemes. Each employer had to create a new scheme for all workers covered by awards, and make contributions equal to 3 per cent of each worker's award wages.

In 1987 phase III involved a two-part wage increase. One was awarded automatically, but the second part had to be justified under the restructuring and efficiency principle. In each award negotiations took place to bring about improvements to work practices to raise productivity. These varied from innovative schemes to multi-skill workers and provide career paths where none previously existed, through curtailing tea breaks to agreements to discuss changes some time in the future.

Phase IV was similar in principle except that, under what was now termed the restructuring and efficiency principle, the aim was to remove obstacles to efficiency that were inherent in the structure of the awards themselves. A further tax-wage bargain was struck in this phase.

Phase V continued the emphasis on award restructuring but the commission required more substantive evidence that restructuring had occurred in an award before granting the second of the two stage increases.

Finally in 1991 the Accord moved into phase VI. A flat rate payment was made to all workers and an increase in employer contributions to superannuation schemes was legislated. Further wage increases could be negotiated through enterprise bargaining (see p. 193).

While the Accord was an evolving agreement between the government and the ACTU the increases to award wages were, of course, determined by the Industrial Relations Commission. In most cases the commission's decision both as to the extent of wage increases and to the wage fixing principles followed very closely the submissions made by the ACTU and the government. Thus although it is convenient to talk of the wages policy in terms of the Accord it could not have operated without the co-operation of the commission.

The economic effects

As it was a form of wages policy we would expect the Accord to have had a direct effect on the rate of growth of money wages and indirect effects on real wages and real unit costs and hence on employment and unemployment. Quite an amount of econometric work has been carried out on the economic effects of the Accord and there is considerable agreement as to the form of its impact although, as always, the magnitudes are in some dispute.

These differences arise in the following way. If we wish to estimate the effect of the Accord on the rate of wage inflation we have to first estimate what the course of wage inflation would have been in the absence of the Accord. We cannot assume that if, say, wages are indexed to prices and as a result money wages rise by 4 per cent in one year, the policy has reduced wage inflation. For in the absence of indexation wages might have risen by less than 4 per cent. To obtain the counter factual investigators have to estimate an equation to explain wage inflation in periods prior to the Accord. Thus take the equation of the expectations augmented Phillips curve.

$$\dot{W} = aU + b\dot{P}^e$$

where $\dot{W}$ is the rate of growth of money wages, U is the unemployment rate and $\dot{P}^e$ is the expected rate of inflation. If this equation is estimated for some period prior to 1983 the co-efficients a and b can be used to predict what wage inflation would have been in each year of the Accord given the actual levels of U and $\dot{P}^e$. Other researchers used alternative wage equations and hence produced different predictions. Further, to estimate the consequential effects, such as that on employment, one has to make assumptions about the elasticity of demand for labour whose precise magnitude is not known. The consensus results are as follows.

The effect of the Accord on the rate of growth of nominal wages in the period 1983-89 is estimated to have been a reduction of about 3 per cent per annum, that is if wage inflation were 7 per cent in any year it would have been 10 per cent in the absence of the Accord.[9] The cumulative result of wage moderation was such that by 1990 the real wage is estimated to have been about 10 per cent lower than it otherwise would have been.

There is no dispute that the reduction in the real wage stimulated employment although, again, there are different opinions as to the magnitude of this effect. A fairly central result would be that of Lewis and Kirby who estimated that over the period 1983-89 job growth was 8 per cent higher than it would have been, which translates into about 600 000 extra jobs.[10] Some of the growth in employment resulted in a decline in unemployment and some was reflected in increases in participation rates, particularly those of females.

Whether the Accord was successful in a broad sense is an issue which lies outside the scope of this book. There is convincing evidence as we have seen, however, that it reduced the rate of wage inflation, and the level of real wages, and that it increased employment.

Concepts for review

- Earnings drift
- Short-run Phillips curve
- Long-run Phillips curve
- Expectations-augmented Phillips curve
- Adaptive price expectations
- Rational price expectations

Questions

1. Outline and explain a possible set of macroeconomic relationships involving the interdependence between such factors as aggregate demand, output, employment, productivity, unemployment, the rate of wage and cost increase and inflation. Discuss the relevance of the wage determination component. (Macquarie University)
2. Outline ways in which the wage determination process might contribute to inflation. What are the implications, in the Australian context, for wages policy? (University of New England)
3. Briefly describe the Prices and Incomes Accord and explain how its effectiveness has been assessed. (Murdoch University)
4. 'Most would agree that moderation of wage rises is one of the key elements in the control of inflation, but there is considerable disagreement over the most appropriate way to achieve wage moderation. One way appears to place its faith in the level of unemployment reducing wage increases, while the other advocates incomes policies.' Outline and appraise these two alternative views. (Macquarie University)
5. What role should productivity play in Australian National Wage Cases? (La Trobe University)

References

1 A.W. Phillips, 'The relation between unemployment and the rate of change of money wage rates in the United Kingdom, 1861-1957', *Economica*, vol. 25, 1958, pp. 283-99.
2 R. Leeson, 'Reply: the validity of the expectations-augmented Phillips curve model', *Economic Papers*, vol. 10, no. 2, 1991, pp. 94-6.
3 M. Friedman, 'The role of monetary policy', *American Economic Reiew*, vol. 58, no. 1, 1968, pp. 1-17.
4 R.G. Gregory, 'Wages policy and unemployment in Australia', *Economica*, vol. 53, supplement, 1986, pp. 53-74.
5 P. Dawkins and M. Wooden, 'Labour utilisation and wage inflation in Australia: an empirical examination', *Economic Record*, vol. 61, no. 173, 1985, pp. 516-21.
6 A.G. Hines, 'Trade unions and wage inflation in the United Kingdom, 1893-1961', *Review of Economic Studies*, vol. 31, 1964, pp. 221-51.
7 P. Lewis, 'Measures of union militancy in Australia, 1949-77', *Journal of Industrial Relations*, vol. 22, no. 2, 1980, pp. 219-23.
8 L.J. Perry, 'Trade union activity and post war inflation in Australia', *Australian Economic Review*, 1978, no. 1, pp. 40-50.
9 B. Chapman, 'The labour market', *The Australian Macro-economy in the 1980's*, Reserve Bank of Australia, Sydney, 1990.
10 ibid.

Index